I SEE AMERICA DANCING

I SEE AMERICA DANCING

SELECTED READINGS, 1685–2000

Edited by Maureen Needham

UNIVERSITY OF ILLINOIS PRESS

Urbana and Chicago

Library of Congress Cataloging-in-Publication Data
I see America dancing: selected readings, 1685–2000 /
edited by Maureen Needham.
    p.   cm.
Includes bibliographical references (p.) and index.
ISBN 0-252-02693-4 (alk. paper)
ISBN 0-252-06999-4 (pbk. : alk. paper)
1. Dance—United States—History—Sources.
I. Needham, Maureen. II. Title.
GV1623.I22   2002
792.8'0973—dc21   2001002651

To my dearest husband Terry Charles Aldrich
with gratitude for his loving support
and
to Theresa, John, and Sarah Kate
as well as Mike, Kathy, Marianne, Lynn, and Amy

CONTENTS

ACKNOWLEDGMENTS

A book such as this is necessarily beholden to the kindnesses of various friends and strangers. I gratefully acknowledge the assistance of many people in this endeavor.

I wish to extend particular gratitude to those who went out of their way so generously to assist me in obtaining permissions and illustrations for this book: Penny Peirce and Jamie Adams, of the Learning Resource Center at Vanderbilt, who over the years have supported many of my educational endeavors; Ron Protas, who selected a most glamorous photograph of Martha Graham, and Jennifer Collandrea, also of the Martha Graham Trust, who went out of her way to assist me to meet deadlines; Martin O'Connor, who so loves to photograph the dance; Janelle Stovall of the Katherine Dunham foundation; Marice Wolfe, curator of Special Collections, Heard Library at Vanderbilt University; Charles Woodford, who donated a favorite picture of his mother, Doris Humphrey; and my good friends Pat and George Bullard for their helpful support and many kindnesses.

A special thanks to Dean Wait of Blair School of Music, Vanderbilt University, for his long-term support in this endeavor as well as to my research assistant, Colette Gagnon.

And, for their help and direction in this undertaking, I thank my editor at the University of Illinois Press, Judith McCulloh, her assistant, Margo Chaney, and Patricia Hollahan.

I am grateful to Lifeworks Foundation, as well as to Vanderbilt University, for a special grant to assist in underwriting costs for this publication. Many thanks are due to their generosity.

Most of all, to my dearest husband Terry Charles Aldrich, who stayed by my side, proofreading, photocopying, and supplying me with food and emotional sustenance—him I thank with unbounded love.

INTRODUCTION

Maureen Needham

> Why should our children bend the knee in that fastidious and servile dance, the Minuet, or twirl in the mazes of the false sentimentality of the Waltz? Rather let them come forth with great strides, leaps and bounds, with lifted forehead and far-spread arms, to dance the language of our Pioneers, the Fortitude of our heroes, the Justice, Kindness, Purity of our statesmen, and all the inspired love and tenderness of our Mothers. When the American children dance in this way, it will make of them beautiful beings, worthy of the name of the Greatest Democracy.
>
> That will be America Dancing.
>
> —Isadora Duncan, 1927

In her writings and by her personal example, Isadora Duncan trumpeted forth a clarion call to young Americans to create a new dance form that would reflect present-day political and social realities. Reject outdated forms inherited from decadent European aristocracies, she urged, and focus your dances on themes, settings, and emotions familiar from daily life experience. Then, and only then, she insisted, would the end result truly reflect "America dancing." She was joined in this inspiring vision by other modern dance pioneers who followed in her barefoot steps.

Duncan's message was revolutionary to its core, because the very concept of something called "American dance" is a relatively recent historical phenomenon. A construct of "*the* American dance," as it was often termed, appears to have been deliberately cultivated sometime in the late 1920s, when a swell of artists' voices was raised to refute the notion that dancing was mere recreation or entertainment imported, in whole, from Europe or perhaps Asia, as in the case of Ruth St. Denis and others inspired by her example. Conversely, prior to this time, African American, Asian American, Spanish American, and Native American dances were assumed to reflect character traits of "the other," which meant they did not follow the performance preferences or styles attributed to the dominant majority of the population.[1] Consequently their dances, as well as others that did not fit the stereotype, were excluded from the WASPian model used to define the so-called American national character. For example, in the excerpt from which the epigraph is taken, Isadora Duncan made it very clear that African American jazz dance was excluded from her vision of American dance, a judgment curiously inconsistent with her argument that the so-called Greek dancing was essentially American—as she interpreted it.

Dance in America, up through the nineteenth century and well beyond, was all too often viewed through the Eurocentric lens of the dominant majority. So it was that the majority population of English colonists, whether in ballrooms located throughout Canada or those of the United States, preferred English country dances, while citizens of French derivation, whether in Montreal or New Orleans, excelled in *contredanses*. Not surprisingly, in what was formerly Spanish territory, settlers favored the fandango and bolero. Sometimes the minority peoples from these areas had to fight to retain their cultural heritage, a most egregious example of which is seen in part 1 in the Indian Bureau regulations that forbad Native Americans to perform their religious dances, even during marriage ceremonies.

Similarly, art or theatrical dances reflected the ethnic origins of the urban population. For example, from the 1730s on, English dancing masters might occasionally perform comical harlequinades or hornpipes between acts at city theaters and taverns. During the 1790s, French émigrés fled the Haitian revolution for the safety of the United States. Professional dancers brought ballet with them, and such entertainments proved to be immensely popular attractions at theaters from New York to New Orleans. However, it did not take long for talented native-born dancers to become proficient in dancing ballet or in teaching the most fashionable French minuets. Titles of songs or costumes were often repackaged to accord with patriotic tastes, so that an English drinking song was turned into "The Star-Spangled Banner," and John Durang, America's first professional dancer, similarly combined two cultures when he specialized in the English hornpipe dressed "in the Character of an American Sailor." Ultimately, however, these dance and musical forms were but mere copies derived from Old World models. If members of diverse ethnic or racial groups were seen onstage, they were generally presented as exhibitions of the "other" (Native Americans doing "war" dances), local color atmospherics (Bayadere dancers at a Hindu temple), or comedy (demeaning caricatures of African Americans in minstrel shows).

This partiality for European-derived forms dominated life in North American parlors and theaters, particularly as the split widened between vernacular and elitist arts during the early nineteenth century.[2] The trend became even more noticeable as certain Americans lamented what they perceived to be a cultural gap between European cultivated taste and American boorishness. Europeans toured the lecture circuit and berated Americans' lack of culture, while overly sensitive Americans responded with stout denials or craven mea culpas.[3] When Fanny Elssler, the great Romantic ballerina, planned to visit the United States in 1840, one American correspondent warned that Europeans would judge the state of American culture by the public's reception of this icon of cultivated taste. Others were more concerned about the issue of American-born artists. "Where is our American Shakespeare?" lamented one writer. When a critic in the *Edinburgh Review* demanded, "Who, in the four quarters of the globe, reads an American book, or goes to an American play, or looks at an American painting or statue?"—the jibe must have stung.[4] Although commentators on occasion would call for a national theater and encourage the support of American poets, playwrights, composers, and so on, the concept of an American dance did not appear to fit into this agenda, if indeed it surfaced as a theme at all prior to the twentieth century.[5]

American dancers became more and more proficient in their technique and interpretive powers during the mid-nineteenth century, and some even toured internationally to Europe, Cuba, South America, Hawai'i, and Australia. Their names and accomplishments are often neglected today: the celebrated ballerina Augusta Maywood, the first professional dancer of African American origin William Henry Lane, the Ince sisters, la petite Celeste, la belle Oceana, Julia Turnbull, the four Vallee sisters, George Washington Smith, Harriet and Henry Wells, Loie Fuller, and Maude Allan. The great Isadora Duncan was in her person the culmination of this trend. Despite their fame, it was difficult for American dancers to be other than the last hired, and most American dancers were relegated to the back rows of the chorus, hidden behind the European stars and corps de ballet. Charles Durang observed with some asperity in his theatrical memoirs that talented (and underemployed) American dancers were consistently elbowed off the stage by glamorous overpaid European imports.

Ironically, while patriotic boosters fully anticipated "an American Shakespeare" to appear at any moment, the hold of European models in the New World was so powerful that truly original creations were all too often met with scorn.[6] Minstrel shows, which a few nineteenth-century writers touted as "the

American National Opera," "this, our only original American institution," and "the only true American drama," were generally denigrated as popular entertainment associated with lower socioeconomic classes.[7] Snob dynamics lay behind the early twentieth-century attempts to "clean up" and "make respectable" certain ballroom dances of African American origin, such as ragtime dances and cakewalks. Some reformers, notably Henry Ford, even attempted to replace the "vulgar" Charleston with the "refined" minuet. Needless to say, he and other elitists could not hold back the tide. No matter how much greatly respected elders lamented the fact, the younger generation of dancers who imitated the blacks were having too much fun to stop.

Tension between the vernacular or popular art adherents and the copycat mentality of those who touted elitist European forms only served to stoke the creative fires of American modern dance pioneers. Choreographers and writers of the 1930s rejected the past, and indeed went so far as to glory in the purported lack of *any* dance "tradition" whatsoever in America.[8] This artistic variant of social learning theorists' notion of the "blank slate" was used to free dancers from constraints inherent in academic dance, such as ballet. These modernists boasted that they owed no debts to the past, as is true with many another self-made man or woman. Their pride also translated into a somewhat grandiose denial that anything important in the way of theatrical dance had ever occurred before *their* arrival on the scene. Dance historians have converted this cherished myth into the current dogma that ballet did not become "established" in the United States until the 1930s. The extent to which this axiom has become the party line can be seen in the identical phrase eight contemporary studies of dance employ to describe the origins of ballet in America. These dance historians assert that ballet basically did not exist in the United States and had to be started "from scratch" after the Russians arrived en masse in the 1930s.[9] The historical issue is actually more complicated than they suggest, as is indicated by the essays in this collection, because a great deal of professional dance activity occurred on a consistent basis over the first fifty or more years of the Republic's existence from the 1790s through the 1840s. Almost without exception, on an annual basis in cities as far afield as Philadelphia and New Orleans, new dancers consistently made their debuts, young people were trained by professional dancers, and new ballets made their premieres.[10] Ballet continued to develop, with time out for the Civil War. By the early twentieth century, both Philadelphia and New Orleans still boasted their own ballet companies and ballet teachers right up to the moment of the Russian invasion.

But ballet was not the only game in town. The dance revolutionaries of the

1930s, who were mostly women, called for the creation of a new form of dance that would ultimately reflect the uniqueness of the American experience. As Doris Humphrey explained, the wellsprings of the new dance grew out of American geography and history. She, as well as many other American choreographers of that time, focused on the westward expansion as an unique facet of American character: "This new dance of action comes inevitably from the people who had to subdue a continent, to make a thousand paths through forest and plain, to conquer the mountains and eventually to raise up towers of steel and glass. The American dance is born of this new world, new life and new vigor."[11] This dance, other writers maintained, would spring forth from certain national character traits, which they variously defined as "streamlined," "vigorous," "young, crass, naive, but healthy," "free," "wholesome," "simple, direct, forthright," or illustrative of other American "virtues." However, no two dancers seemed to agree on which traits were distinctly American, a philosophical quandary exacerbated by the differing blends of ethnic and racial identities in a multicultural society. In the end, they agreed to disagree and settled for the simple proviso that this dance must be something "new." Doris Humphrey, for example, created her masterpiece *New Dance* as an expression of this aspiration. Years later, looking back over a career that began in the 1920s, modern dance pioneer Helen Tamiris insisted that "we [the modern dancers of the 1930s] have created a tradition" that translates into "a genuine expression of America."[12] She was not alone in her appraisal: contemporary historians concur with this view, as do present-day dancers. Within the lifetime of just one dance generation, a construct of the idea of "the American dance" has come to be accepted as a historical truth.

Today, American choreographers, dancers, and teachers circle the globe in jets as easily as Shakespeare's Puck could have skimmed the stage. American contemporary dance forms are applauded and studied as far afield as Japan, New Zealand, and France. Growing from thirty-five professional dance companies in 1973, regional companies number over seven hundred, and audiences for ballet reach into the millions.[13] As Agnes de Mille enthusiastically boasted about American dancers, "All this activity spells the most astonishing furor about dancing that the Western theater has ever known."[14] By the year 2000, ballet companies could be found in practically every midsize city throughout America, from Pasadena to Peoria to Sarasota.[15]

But with all these extraordinary successes, concerns loom on the horizon. The giants from the recent past—George Balanchine, Martha Graham, Doris Humphrey, Helen Tamiris, Hanya Holm, Charles Weidman, José Limón, Alvin Ailey, Pearl Primus, Alwin Nikolais, Jerome Robbins, Erick Hawkins—are all dead or, as in the case of Katherine Dunham, inactive. Then, too, AIDS has had a devastating effect on the dance world, as exemplified by the work of Bill T. Jones (set forth in the last piece printed in this volume). This plague has wiped out an entire generation of artists whose worth and contributions may never be recognized. The chain of tradition, by which dance is handed on, was snapped at its zenith. How will these artists, whether the famous or the forgotten, the young or the old, be replaced?

Creative movements—modern dance, the Judson movement, minimalism, not to speak of numerous trendy avant-gardisms—have come and gone during the twentieth century, with new spin-offs accelerating and fading all too soon. Often, unfortunately, the choreographer's creative vision would attract less notice than the star performer's thrilling leaps that were invariably followed by sucked-in gasps of astonishment from the audience. Technique for technique's sake, which may draw sold-out houses, is, however, no real substitute for artistic imagination. Spectacle alone does not stir the soul.

Dance in America, which began as an import, is now in the business of exporting dancers, teachers, and choreographers. At times, this may lead to odd juxtapositions of cultural expectations, as when, for example, the Paul Taylor Dance Company appeared in Beijing and depicted Popeye the Sailor Man dancing to the "Yellow Polka Dot Bikini" with Olive Oyl.[16] Even whole companies are forced to tour abroad in order to survive at home: studies suggest that fully 42 percent of American modern dance troupes' earned income may come from their foreign tours.[17] Frankly, many other countries have offered more favorable working conditions for an American artist during the 1980s and 1990s, while at the same time Russian superstars find ready welcome on our stages.[18] Consequently, some of our best artists, including John Neumeier, Glen Tetley, Don Redlich, William Forsythe, and Mark Morris, have at one time or another opted for exile. Others such as Trisha Brown, or even as far back as Alwin Nikolais, could find larger audiences at European or Asian dance festivals than at home. At one point, during the 1980s and 1990s, a thoughtful observer might have worried that this brain/body drain signified a grim future for dance in America.

However, going into the first decade of the new millennium, a number of prodigal sons and daughters have met up with the realities of a strong American economy and returned. Many of the expatriate choreographers have opted for the comforts of home (and the American dollar), while the American dance scene has also been enriched by immigration. For example, Sonjé Mayo's *Naked in America*, grew out of her own experiences of coming to the United States from South Africa, and of the eight dancers in her piece, three come from

Europe (Germany, Switzerland, and Albania). Economics also drives the emergence of regional ballet around the country. Impoverished Russian ballet dancers can be found in small towns all around America, and contemporary dancers wander far afield from their New York City origins. In fact, New York City can no longer claim a monopoly on creativity or quality, though inhabitants may brag that their company expenses are the highest in the nation. It should not be surprising that some of the most interesting experiments in the dance occur outside of the big established companies in New York, perhaps partially because of these high costs.

While the locus of creativity has been dispersed throughout the nation, the torch has been passed to those representatives of "the other" who formerly lacked or were denied a public voice in the dance, such as Asian Americans. The twenty-first century will no doubt see a rise in dance contributions from various groups of immigrants, their gift to their adopted country. The influence of black or Hispanic choreographers and dancers will likely continue to swell like a mighty stream, picking up force from the currents of creativity from their past. Isadora Duncan's vision of America dancing may truly come to pass, except that the voices will spring from many more sources than she ever imagined.

For those dance lovers who want to know more about contemporary dance in America but are concerned about the future, an examination of the past is a necessary concomitant. This volume of essays should prove useful in that endeavor. Dance changes much as society itself changes, and an analysis of the dynamics of the past assists us to examine present trends. As will be apparent in the readings that follow, human beings are remarkably creative when it comes to adapting dance to their needs, whether for theatrical, religious, or social reasons.

Dance in cultures around the world presents a dazzling variety of visions of the body in motion, and dance in America is no exception. Reading the pieces in this collection can be compared to viewing an American patchwork quilt. While each author's statement stands alone as an example of a particular point of view, it is from the holistic perspective that the book's impact can be fully appreciated. The function of each different item, then, is that it contributes to the whole, forming a kaleidoscopic impression of various dance themes crafted out of the living experiences of many different American dancers, past and present.

The essays and librettos in this book have all been chosen with an eye to presenting selected aspects of dance in America, from dances that function primarily in the religious sphere to those that are more social or theatrical in their orientation. Rejecting the 1930s' notion that a common American cultural identity has been forged out of diverse ethnic groups, I prefer to celebrate the unique contributions of different individuals and ethnic or racial groups. This has entailed some difficult choices. For example, part 5 has been limited to various choreographers writing about their vision of America—and one consequence of this decision is that a great choreographer such as Alvin Ailey has been omitted in favor of someone else who articulated certain themes in print. This section, therefore, should not be read as a survey of American theatrical dance in the twentieth century, which can best be found in other books published on the subject, but rather as a highly personal exploration of how certain artists interpreted their vision of America through their dance. Unfortunately, due to space limitations, musical theater and movies were not included in this volume, and, alas, many of my own personal favorites simply did not fit as exemplars of the five themes chosen for this volume. To compensate for the road not taken in terms of important writings that have not been included because they did not fit within the thematic purview of this collection or because they are widely available elsewhere, each section concludes with a brief list of suggested titles for further reading, as well as selected titles of video films of dance.

The first section, "Dances of the Native Americans," considers the first peoples known to dance within the confines of North America. Out of respect for the sensibilities of Native Americans and their understandable desire to keep their rituals private, this section focuses on attempts by nineteenth- and twentieth-century observers to interpret these activities through the prism of their own cultural experiences. The spectrum of attitudes ranges from highly romantic to excessively punitive. As will be seen, serious misunderstandings about the function of dance in Native American society led to great tragedy. Even though the prohibition of all dances by the Bureau of Indian Affairs from 1902 to the 1930s dealt a serious blow to the continuity of their traditions, these selections underscore reasons why modern Native Americans feel keenly the need to reinforce cultural identity through traditional dance and why, by the end of the twentieth century, the pow-wow dances had become one of the most popular Native American dance events available throughout the United States.

The second section, "Other Dance Traditions in America," is but a sampler of traditional dance in America. As is true for all the other sections, it would be impossible to attempt a survey of this huge field in anything less than a full-length book, so these essays reflect only the tip of the iceberg. Unlike the dances described in the first section, however, these dances cannot be designated primarily as expressions of religious worship. True enough, dances at Jewish weddings or the Japanese *bon* dances may have begun their existence as part of religious rituals, but today they tend to be highly social in nature. Other selections suggest how dance can be used by different ethnic or socioeconomic groups—whether aristocratic New Orleans Creoles or African American field hands—as a way to maintain their cultural identity. The first selection analyzes the popular appeal of English country dance, the longest-lived ballroom dancing form to survive in North America, while a later essay describes its survival under the guise of line dancing as seen in America's country music capital. The last selection explores the jitterbug revival as it has traveled from Harlem's Savoy Ballroom to southern California's swing dance palaces.

The next section, "The Anti-Dance Brigade," presents a contrary point of view concerning the delights of social dance, as articulated by a famous Puritan preacher and others. The anti-dance moralists represent a strain present since the early days of the Plymouth Plantation in Massachusetts when the maypole was ripped out of the ground and dancing was forbidden. These moralists have not lost their hold even today, according to a court case where high school students attacked a school board's prohibition of all prom dances. Other selections in this section include reflections of a former dancing master who, touched by repentance, argues that all dance is ipso facto wicked, and the arguments of a political reformer who counters with the claim that the environment itself is responsible for evils wrongfully ascribed to social dancing. Another writer recalls how the same evils ascribed to the Twist had earlier been laid at the door of the jitterbug, and of the Charleston before that.

The fourth section considers pioneers of theatrical dance in America, all of whom predate the twentieth century. Because so little has been published on this subject, even though recent research has expanded our knowledge, this section represents an effort to redress historical neglect of these early American artists. Three representative performers and their contributions to stage dancing are described: John Durang, America's first native-born professional dancer; Jean Baptiste Francisqui, an eighteenth-century French choreographer and ballet dancer; and Fanny Elssler, the greatest international exponent of ballet in the Romantic period who toured North America from 1840 to 1842. Other selections recount audience reaction to the most famous of all nineteenth-century musical extravaganzas, *The Black Crook,* and include the text for a minstrel show parody of this same show. Taken together, these selections give an abbreviated but balanced flavor of theatrical dancing up to the turn of the twentieth century.

The fifth section, entitled "The Creators: Visions of America," is the longest in the book. Here the dancers and choreographers speak for themselves. Rather than attempt to recount the history of ballet, jazz, tap, modern dance, and so forth in the twentieth century—an impossible task in this space and one better suited to a variety of books on these subjects (see the suggested list of readings)—this section sets forth selected artists' attitudes about America as expressed in their creative works. Arranged primarily in chronological order, these highly personalized visions of America dancing are taken from different literary forms that deal exclusively with theatrical dance: librettos, critical reviews, and choreographers' writings about specific works on an American theme or about dance in America. Assumptions about America have obviously changed over the centuries, much as they differ from person to person. What all these artists have in common is a unique vision of America conveyed through the medium of theatrical dance.

The section opens with an excerpt from a French ballet performed by the Placides, members of the first ballet troupe to tour and settle in America during the 1790s. Catering to American prejudices against the British, the libretto extols the virtues of a Native American heroine who rescues and falls in love with an ungrateful English sailor. The second selection is excerpted from another libretto, this one taken from a mammoth production given at the 1893 Chicago World's Fair. The production was intended to represent the entire scope of American history, but only positive aspects of America's "Progress" were stressed while recent events, including the Civil War, were glossed over.

Views of twentieth-century choreographers make up the bulk of this section, and these artists tended to be far more critical than their predecessors. Martha Graham's *American Document,* for example, explores tarnished aspects of American democracy using the minstrel show format, and Katherine Dunham's *Southland* graphically portrays a racial lynching. A more recent trend is illustrated by choreographers who engage in political activism through the dance, as in Yvonne Rainer's *Flag Dance,* an anti–Vietnam War protest. Many of these works have been greeted with critical disapproval for political as much as aesthetic reasons, from both ends of the spectrum: George Balanchine's *Stars and Stripes,* an almost xenophobic celebration of the American flag, inspired political controversy at its premiere. Bill T. Jones and Sonjé Mayo are the latest in a long line of critics of the American way of life. Mayo captures the immigrant experience in her *Naked in America,* while Bill T. Jones, in his excerpt *Last Supper at Uncle Tom's Cabin/The Promised Land,* raises a host of significant social issues that range from AIDS to gay rights to racism in America to nudity as well as existential issues of good and evil.

This section also includes essays by choreographers who describe their vision of the role for dance in America. It proved a difficult task to winnow out essays for this purpose, because so many artists had so much to say about this particular subject. Isadora Duncan, in her autobiography, exhorts her follow-ers to express the spirit of America in their dance and to dance "the language of our pioneers," while Ted Shawn foresees a new role for American men. Martha Graham, in her "Platform for the American Dance," asserts that America artists should create a dance form typically American. Doris Hum-phrey is equally adamant that this "new dance" should be an expression of contemporary American life. What these and other women revolutionaries of the 1930s stated as their goals has essentially come to pass.

The Native Americans and the Native Hawaiians who express the love of their land or honor the ancient gods through their dance, the different national and racial groups who continue their dance traditions even on shores far dis-tant from their ancestors' homes, Isadora Duncan and all who followed in her footsteps to carry their dance visions around the world—to all of them is this book dedicated, for without the American dancer, there would be no dance in America. As William Butler Yeats poses the ultimate question in his poem "Among School Children," "How can you tell the dancer from the dance?"

NOTES

Many of the pieces in this book have been abridged, either by the authors or by me. A footnote at the beginning of each selection will alert the reader to changes that have been made, as well as to minimal stylistic alterations (such as modern punctuation) that were considered necessary. In essays which have not been revised by the authors for this collection, ellipses are used to signal places where I have dropped text; in the few cases where there are ellipses in the original articles, their presence is noted. In a few cases, I have added notes to an essay, but such changes are prominently labeled. Original spelling, however idiosyncratic, has been retained.

1. The concept of "the other," defined in opposition to a noninclusive model, is ex-plored in Simone de Beauvoir's *The Second Sex,* trans. with introduction by H. M. Parshley (New York: Alfred A. Knopf, 1953).

2. See John Kouwenhoven, *Made in America: The Arts in Modern Civilization* (Gar-den City, N.Y.: Doubleday & Company, 1948); also see part 2 of H. Wiley Hitchcock, *Music in the United States: A Historical Introduction,* 2d ed. (Englewood Cliffs, N.J.: Prentice-Hall, 1974); Lawrence Levine, *Highbrow/Lowbrow: The Emergence of Cultural Hierarchy in America* (Cambridge, Mass.: Harvard University Press, 1988).

3. See, for example, the *New Orleans Bee*'s response (Nov. 21, 1832) to Frances Trol-lope's scathing *Domestic Manners of the Americans* (London, 1832).

4. Sydney Smith, quoted by Hitchcock, *Music in the United States,* p. 55. The *New Orleans Bee* expanded on this theme, "But, as for America, what national music has

she—when even her 'Yankee Doodle' and 'Star-spangled Banner' are transplanted from England?" (Oct. 13, 1835).

5. [Philadelphia] *United States Gazette,* Mar. 27, 1815. See also Barbara Tischler, *An American Music: The Search for an American Musical Identity* (New York: Oxford University Press, 1986), chap. 5.

6. *New Orleans Bee,* Oct. 13, 1835. See also Harold Nicholas, "The Prejudice against Native American Drama from 1778 to 1830," *Quarterly Journal of Speech* 60, no. 3 (1974): 288.

7. Quotations are taken from Robert Toll, *Blacking Up: The Minstrel Show in Nineteenth Century America* (New York: Oxford University Press, 1974), p. v.

8. Ted Shawn, *The American Ballet* (New York: H. Holt and Company, 1926), p. 27; Betty Carue, "New Dance Style to Develop in America," *American Dancer,* July, 1929, p. 10; Estelle Reed, "The American Dance and Internationalism," *American Dancer,* May, 1929, p. 13. See also Ruth Eleanor Howard, "Interview with Ruth St. Denis," *American Dancer,* Feb., 1929, p. 30.

9. Anatole Chujoy, *The New York City Ballet* (New York: Alfred A. Knopf, 1953), p. 34; Walter Terry, *Dance in America* (New York: Harper & Row, 1956), p. 9; John Percival, *Modern Ballet,* rev. ed. (London: Herbert Press, 1980), p. 8; Jack Anderson, *Dance* (New York: Newsweek Books, 1974); Alexander Bland, *History of Ballet and Dance in the Western World* (New York: Praeger Publishers, 1976), p. 93; Clive Barnes, *Inside American Ballet Theater,* foreword by Justin Colin (New York: Hawthorn Books, 1977), p. 3; Mary Clark and Clement Crisp, *History of Dance* (New York: Crown Publishers, 1981), p. 107; Jennifer Dunning, *But First a School: The First Fifty Years of the School of American Ballet* (New York: Viking, 1985), p. 17.

10. See Maureen Needham [Costonis], "Ballet Comes to America: 1792–1842, French Contributions to the Establishment of Theatrical Dance in New Orleans and Philadelphia" (Ph.D. diss., New York University, 1989). The next fifty-year period, from 1843 to 1893, has not been studied in any published accounts, but it likely would reflect similar trends up to the time that New Orleans was subjugated to military rule. The Philadelphia theater had been toppled from its preeminent position by that of New York City during that period.

11. Doris Humphrey, *The Art of Making Dances,* ed. Barbara Pollack (New York: Rinehart & Company, 1959), p. 18.

12. Helen Tamiris, "Dance: A Need—Choreographer Urges Formation of a Modern Dance Repertory Company," *Dance Observer,* May, 1960.

13. Paul Gray, "U.S. Ballet Soars," *Time Magazine* 111, no. 18 (May 1, 1978): 88; Jan Ellen Spiegel, "Where the Dance Boom Continues," *Dance Magazine,* Feb. 1998, p. 4.

14. Agnes de Mille, *America Dances* (New York: Macmillan Publishing Company, 1980), p. 176.

15. John Munger, in an extensive study drawn from Dance/USA's census data of dance organizations, has written a detailed essay on economic trends as they impact

U.S. dance companies. See "Dancing with Dollars in the Millennium (Dance Companies in the 1990's)," *Dance Magazine,* Apr. 2001.

16. Elizabeth Rosenthal, "Paul Taylor Dance Company: Bikini Song and Popeye Please China," *New York Times,* June 20, 2001.

17. Don Moore, "The Perilous '80s," in *On the Edge: Challenges to American Dance,* proceedings of the 1989 Dance Critics Association, comp. Janice Ross and Stephen Cobbett Steinberg ([New York]: Dance Critics Association, 1990), p. 92.

18. Ibid. See also Sali Ann Kriegsman, "New Opening for American Dance," pp. 96–97; and Brenda Way, "The Obsession with the Future," pp. 90–91; both in *On the Edge.*

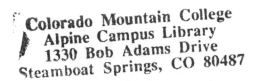

PART 1

DANCES OF THE NATIVE AMERICANS

INTRODUCTION

Ancient Native American dances were fully integrated, communal ceremonies that combined chants, prayers, and music, as well as ritualistic movement, and this traditional blend continues today. As soon as Europeans arrived in the New World, however, they classified these activities as distinguishable art forms even though, as will be apparent from the following selections, it is difficult to separate the dance from the totality of the event. While the attempt to distinguish audience from performer is valid for most Western theatrical productions, the elaborate religious processions and dances of the Native Americans do not exclude spectators from being participants. In fact, present-day Tewa Indians consider attendance at dance ceremonies to be a form of communal prayer: "You go there [to the dance] like to go to church," one man explained.[1]

From the very first moment of contact, Europeans and Native Americans found it difficult to understand each other's worldview, since they examined one another through the prism of their own past cultural experiences; for one thing, dance for Europeans was often associated with mating or courtship dances whereas Native Americans used dances to honor and worship the spirits. Christopher Columbus requested that his sailors dance a hornpipe in honor of the Native Americans who came to visit his ship. Alarmed, the latter responded by hiding behind their shields and letting arrows fly. Captain Cook witnessed Native American dancers who performed rhythmic, expressive gestures while seated in a canoe, but did not recognize their movements as dance. English settlers commonly regarded the Indian dances as a form of devil worship, preparations for war, or, worse yet, both at the same time. Eighteenth-century French observers tended to be somewhat more objective; a number of them studied and categorized dances according to function or compared regional variations of similar dances.[2] By the early nineteenth century, many Americans took up the romantic cause of the "vanishing Indians" and resolved to record them for posterity. Even with all the goodwill possible, these early ethnologists remained highly ethnocentric in their outlook. Present-day researchers can take advantage of systematic training in scientific methodology that is available at universities and the consequent development of modern fieldwork techniques. In particular, researchers owe a great debt to the vision of the well-known dance ethnologist Gertrude Prokosch Kurath.[3]

George Catlin (1796–1872), author of the first selection in part 1, was an extraordinarily talented man, both as an artist and as a pioneer ethnologist. Armed with his paintbrushes and canvases, he set off on a series of explorations from 1830 to 1836 with the goal of "describing the living manners, customs, and character of a people who were rapidly passing away from the face of the earth—a dying nation who had no historians or biographers of their own."[4] Such an apocalyptic vision of extinction was hardly exaggerated: only a few years after Catlin was the first European American to see the great Buffalo Dance and other ceremonies of the Mandan Indians of North Dakota (described below), the *New Orleans Times Picayune* reported on January 23, 1838, that the entire tribe of thousands, with the exception of fifteen persons, had died from smallpox. The portraits that Catlin painted and the notes that he took were intended, as he said, to rescue the Native Americans "for the use and instruction of future ages."[5] Today his pictures—some eight hundred of them in all—hang in the Smithsonian Institution in Washington, D.C., and 180 objects that he collected are also on exhibit.

In his travels, Catlin came to enjoy the Native Americans' sense of humor as expressed in their great variety of dances, and, most especially, he admired their "highly moral and religious" sensibility.[6] Catlin noted that "every dance has its peculiar step, and every step has its meaning."[7] The dance, he explained, was "much more frequently practiced by them than by any civilized society; inasmuch as it enters into their forms of worship, and is often their mode of appealing to the Great Spirit—of paying their usual devotions to their *medicine*—and of honouring and entertaining strangers of distinction in their country."[8]

James A. Mooney (1861–1921), in the second selection, represents an example of the new breed of researcher who applied the scientific method to the study of social phenomena. A self-trained ethnologist, his orientation was strictly empirical. His information came, not only from observing the Indian dances, but also by participating in them himself. Thus he was close enough to notice the use of hypnosis in the Ghost Dances, which began as a nativistic revival that blended elements of Native American spiritual lore with Christian resurrection theology. The Bureau of American Ethnology sent Mooney to investigate the Ghost Dances among the Sioux after newspapers and Indian agents fanned fears of a Native American uprising. His field research lasted more than three years, from 1890 to 1893; he traveled more than thirty-two thousand miles and visited twenty tribes where he observed the tragic outcome of this clash of cultures at first hand.[9]

Mooney ascribed the origins of the Ghost Dance to the influence of a Native American prophet, Jack Wilson, also called Wo'Voka, who preached that the Indians, all Indians, must dance and continue to dance until the Great Spirit would come again. The dance swept unimpeded across the plains, with the insatiable appetite of a prairie fire.

Alarmed government authorities attempted to stop its rapid spread. The 1890 massacre at Wounded Knee, in which troops slaughtered more than three hundred women, children, and old men, was directly attributable to government officials' panic about the large numbers of Native Americans who gathered to dance. From this time on, frightened agents of the Bureau of Indian Affairs forcibly prevented all Ghost Dances, and later Sun Dances were also prohibited

By 1902, the Bureau of Indian Affairs commissioner, W. A. Jones, prohibited *all* Native American dances on the grounds that the government's mission of "civilizing" the "savages" was made more difficult if any native culture were left intact. In that observation, he relied on precedent of long standing. Henry Schoolcraft, for example, had noted in 1848 the significance of dance retention as an index of the civilizing process. Schoolcraft, a former bureau agent, commented that dance "is observed to be almost the last thing abandoned by bands and individuals, in their progress to civilization and Christianity. So true is this, that it may be regarded as one of the best practical proofs of their advance, to find the native instruments and music thrown by, and the custom abandoned."[10] Because dance was interwoven throughout the entire texture of Indian life, Schoolcraft and others remarked its presence as a useful marker in judging a tribe's movement toward what they considered to be "progress."

Progress, nineteenth-century-American style, was bound to bury the Native American, according to Schoolcraft, because "civilization had more of the principles of endurance and progress than barbarism; because Christianity was superior to paganism; industry to idleness; agriculture to hunting; letters to hieroglyphics; truth to error." Herein, he insisted, lay "the true secrets of the Red Man's decline," although he neglected to mention the demoralizing toll taken by disease and whiskey, both imported from European Americans.[11] Schoolcraft was one of many who subscribed to the view that white America's mission was to haul the reluctant "savages" into the mainstream of "civilization," while, incidentally, stealing away the land that was theirs by treaty.

When Commissioner Jones decided in 1902 to forbid any dancing or feasts, presumably including marriage rites, he had previously threatened Native Americans with loss of jobs, food rations, and even "confinement in the guardhouse at hard labor" if they did not cut their braids. In the selection reprinted here, dancers were similarly threatened. The resulting public protest forced Jones to "clarify" his orders on hair length; however, dances were still forbidden or forcibly discouraged for decades to come. In 1923, yet another bureau commissioner appealed to Native Americans to forgo "evil or foolish things," meaning the dances that he insisted "should be stopped."[12] A great public controversy arose when John Collier and the American Indian Defense Association blocked proposals to mandate federal penalties to be levied on any dances held for whatever purpose, including marriage feasts.[13] Public recognition that religious and political liberties had been denied was the signal for the demise of forcible assimilation as a matter of public policy, and today Native Americans are at last free to dance.

In short, the so-called vanishing Indians have refused to cooperate with the dominant majority culture and conveniently fade into the sunset of history. The modern Tewa Indians of New Mexico, as described by Jill Sweet in the fourth selection, devised ways over the centuries to keep Tewa rituals alive despite persecution. She found the dance rituals to be crucial to the community, because they are "perhaps the single most important expression of Tewa cultural continuity" in the face of intense pressure to conform to majority cultural practices.

So far, each selection has been drawn from other Americans' writings about a people who, up until recently, have preferred their oral tradition and have written comparatively little about their own dance forms, perhaps out of a need to preserve them from prying eyes and persecution. It seems only fitting, then, that a Native American should have the last word: in the next essay, Tara Browner, an exponent of both Women's Jingle and Southern Cloth styles of dance, writes of the phenomenal resurgence of the pow-wow, with new and evolving practices accommodating to modern needs. The pow-wow's appeal reaches out to all tribes, all social classes, all ages, all races. It provides a medium of expression for both men and women "fancy" dancers, a term originally applied to early nineteenth-century American theatrical dancers who used fancy footwork in their performing efforts, which has come to categorize certain kinds of exhibition dancing seen in contemporary pow-wows. The final selection is an excerpt of a prayer used as the recurrent theme in the Navajo

Night Chant ceremony, one of the most popular as well as important of all Navajo religious events. The ceremony is intended to heal in both the spiritual and the physical sense of the word. At the end of the nine-day ceremony that brings together dance, song, ritualistic practices, poetry, and healing practices, the patient is exhorted to "walk in beauty." During this chant, here translated by Washington Matthews, the Dance of the Thunderbirds is continuously performed from dark until sunrise.

NOTES

1. Jill D. Sweet, *Dances of the Tewa Pueblo Indians: Expressions of New Life* (Santa Fe: School of American Research Press, 1985), p. 81.

2. See, for example, Charles Compan, *Dictionnaire de danse* (1787; reprint, New York: Broude Brothers, 1974), pp. 148–56, 160–62, 194–95.

3. See Gertrude Prokosch Kurath's views on training, found in "Panorama of Dance Ethnology," *Current Anthropology* 1, no. 3 (1960): 247–49. Kurath's work presents a model for its thoroughness and depth of research; see, for example, her collaboration with Antonio Garcia, *Music and Dance of the Tewa Pueblos* (Santa Fe: Museum of New Mexico Press, 1970).

4. George Catlin, *Letters and Notes on the Manners, Customs, and Condition of the North American Indians*, ed. Michael Mooney (New York: Clarkson N. Potter, 1975), p. 89.

5. Ibid.

6. George Catlin, *Illustrations of the Manners, Customs, and Condition of the North American Indians* (London: Chatto & Windus, 1876), vol. 1, p. 243.

7. Ibid., vol. 2, p. 126.

8. Ibid., vol. 1, p. 244.

9. James A. Mooney, *The Ghost-Dance Religion and the Sioux Outbreak of 1890*, 14th Annual Report of the Bureau of Ethnology to the Secretary of the Smithsonian Institution (1896; reprint, Chicago: University of Chicago Press, 1965), pp. xi–xii.

10. Henry Rowe Schoolcraft, *The Indian in his Wigwam* (New York: W. H. Graham, 1848), p. 222.

11. Ibid., p. 369.

12. Francis Paul Pruncha, *The Great Father* (Omaha: University of Nebraska Press, 1984), vol. 2, p. 802.

13. Ibid., p. 806; see also Sweet, *Dances of the Tewa Pueblo Indians*, p. 76.

CHAPTER 1

The Manners, Customs, and Condition of the North American Indians (1836)

George Catlin

Dancing is one of the principal and most frequent amusements of all the tribes of Indians in America; and, in all of these, both vocal and instrumental music are introduced. These dances consist in about four different steps, which constitute all the different varieties: but the figures and forms of these scenes are very numerous, and produced by the most violent jumps and contortions, accompanied with the song and beats of the drum, which are given in exact time with their motions. It has been said by some travellers, that the Indian has neither harmony or melody in his music, but I am unwilling to subscribe to such an assertion; although I grant, that for the most part of their vocal exercises, there is a total absence of what the musical world would call melody; their songs being made up chiefly of a sort of violent chaunt of harsh and jarring gutturals, of yelps and barks, and screams, which are given out in perfect time, not only with "method (but with harmony) in their madness." There are times too, as every traveller of the Indian country will attest, if he will recall them to his recollection, when the Indian lays down by his fire-side with his drum in his hand, which he lightly and almost imperceptibly touches over, as he accompanies it with his stifled voice of dulcet sounds that might come from the most tender and delicate female.

These quiet and tender songs are very different from those which are sung at their dances, in full chorus and violent gesticulation; and many of them seem to be quite rich in plaintive expression and melody, though barren of change and variety.

Dancing, I have before said, is one of the principal and most valued amusements of the Indians, and much more frequently practiced by them than by any civilized society; inasmuch as it enters into their forms of worship, and is often their mode of appealing to the Great Spirit—of paying their usual de-

Selected excerpts from George Catlin, *Illustrations of the Manners, Customs, and Condition of the North American Indians* (London: Chatto & Windus, 1876), vol. 1, pp. 243–44; vol. 2, pp. 126–28.

Buffalo dance in Mandan village, 1830s, by George Catlin. Originally published in George Catlin's *North American Indians* (Philadelphia: Leary, Stuart and Company, 1913), plate 67, facing p. 184.

votions to their *medicine*—and of honouring and entertaining strangers of distinction in their country.

Instead of the "giddy maze" of the quadrille or the country dance, enlivened by the cheering smiles and graces of silkened beauty, the Indian performs his rounds with jumps, and starts, and yells, much to the satisfaction of his own exclusive self, and infinite amusement of the gentler sex, who are always lookers on, but seldom allowed so great a pleasure, or so signal an honour, as that of joining with their lords in this or any other entertainment. Whilst staying with these people on my way up the river, I was repeatedly honoured with the dance, and I as often hired them to give them, or went to overlook where they were performing them at their own pleasure, in pursuance of their peculiar customs, or for their own amusement, that I might study and correctly herald them to future ages. I saw so many of their different varieties of dances amongst the Sioux, that I should almost be disposed to denominate them the "*dancing Indians.*" It would actually seem as if they had dances for every thing. And in so large a village, there was scarcely an hour in any day or night, but what the beat of the drum could somewhere be heard. These dances are almost as various and different in their character as they are numerous—some of them so exceedingly grotesque and laughable, as to keep the bystanders in an irresistible roar of laughter—others are calculated to excite his pity, and forcibly appeal to his sympathies, whilst others disgust, and yet others terrify and alarm him with their frightful threats and contortions. . . .

The Mandans, like all other tribes, lead lives of idleness and leisure; and of course devote a great deal of time to their sports and amusements, of which they have a great variety. Of these, dancing is one of the principal, and may be seen in a variety of forms: such as the buffalo dance, the boasting dance, the begging dance, the scalp dance, and a dozen other kinds of dances, all of which have their peculiar characters and meanings or objects.

These exercises are exceedingly grotesque in their appearance, and to the eye of a traveller who knows not their meaning or importance, they are an uncouth and frightful display of starts, and jumps, and yelps, and jarring gutturals, which are sometimes truly terrifying. But when one gives them a little attention, and has been lucky enough to be initiated into their mysterious meaning, they become a subject of the most intense and exciting interest. Every dance has its peculiar step, and every step has its meaning; every dance also has its peculiar song, and that is so intricate and mysterious oftentimes, that not one in ten of the young men who are dancing and singing in it, know the meaning of the song which they are chanting over. None but the medicine-men are allowed to understand them; and even they are generally only initiated into these secret arcana, on the payment of a liberal stipend for their tuition, which requires much application and study. There is evidently a set song and sentiment for every dance, for the songs are perfectly measured, and sung in exact time with the beat of the drum; and always with an uniform and invariable set of sounds and expressions, which clearly indicate certain sentiments, which are expressed by the voice, though sometimes not given in any known language whatever.

They have other dances and songs which are not so mystified, but which are sung and understood by every person in the tribe, being sung in their own language, with much poetry in them, and perfectly metered, but without rhyme. On these subjects I shall take another occasion to say more; and will for the present turn your attention to the style and modes in which some of these curious transactions are conducted.

My ears have been almost continually ringing since I came here [Mandan Village, Upper Missouri], with the din of yelping and beating of the drums;

but I have for several days past been peculiarly engrossed, and my senses almost confounded with the stamping, and grunting, and bellowing of the *buffalo dance*, which closed a few days since at sunrise (thank Heaven), and which I must needs describe to you.

Buffaloes, it is known, are a sort of roaming creatures, congregating occasionally in huge masses, and strolling away about the country from east to west, or from north to south, or just where their whims or strange fancies may lead them; and the Mandans are sometimes, by this means, most unceremoniously left without any thing to eat; and being a small tribe, and unwilling to risk their lives by going far from home in the face of their more powerful enemies, are oftentimes left almost in a state of starvation. In any emergency of this kind, every man musters and brings out of his lodge his mask (the skin of a buffalo's head with the horns on), which he is obliged to keep in readiness for this occasion; and then commences the buffalo dance, of which I have above spoken, which is held for the purpose of making "buffalo come" (as they term it), of inducing the buffalo herds to change the direction of their wanderings, and bend their course towards the Mandan village, and graze about on the beautiful hills and bluffs in its vicinity, where the Mandans can shoot them down and cook them as they want them for food.

For the most part of the year, the young warriors and hunters, by riding out a mile or two from the village, can kill meat in abundance; and sometimes large herds of these animals may be seen grazing in full view of the village. There are other seasons also when the young men have ranged about the country as far as they are willing to risk their lives, on account of their enemies, without finding meat. This sad intelligence is brought back to the chiefs and doctors, who sit in solemn council, and consult on the most expedient measures to be taken, until they are sure to decide upon the old and only expedient which "never has failed."

The chief issues his order to his runners or criers, who proclaim it through the village—and in a few minutes the dance begins. The place where this strange operation is carried on is in the public area in the centre of the village, and in front of the great medicine or mystery lodge. About ten or fifteen Mandans at a time join in the dance, each one with the skin of the buffalo's head (or mask) with the horns on, placed over his head, and in his hand his favorite bow or lance, with which he is used to slay the buffalo.

I mentioned that this dance always had the desired effect, that it never fails, nor can it, for it cannot be stopped (but is going incessantly day and night) until "buffalo come." Drums are beating and rattles are shaken, and songs and yells incessantly are shouted, and lookers-on stand ready with masks on their heads, and weapons in hand, to take the place of each one as he becomes fatigued, and jumps out of the ring.

During this time of general excitement, spiers or "lookers" are kept on the hills in the neighbourhood of the village, who, when they discover buffaloes in sight, give the appropriate signal, by "throwing their robes," which is instantly seen in the village, and understood by the whole tribe. At this joyful intelligence there is a shout of thanks to the Great Spirit, and more especially to the mystery-man, and the dancers, who *have been the immediate cause of their success!* There is then a brisk preparation for the chase—a grand hunt takes place. The choicest pieces of the victims are sacrificed to the Great Spirit, and then a surfeit and a carouse.

These dances have sometimes been continued in this village two and three weeks without stopping an instant, until the joyful moment when buffaloes made their appearance. So they *never fail;* and they think they have been the means of bringing them in.

Every man in the Mandan village (as I have before said) is obliged by a village regulation, to keep the mask of the buffalo, hanging on a post at the head of his bed, which he can use on his head whenever he is called upon by the chiefs, to dance for the coming of the buffaloes. The mask is put over the head, and generally has a strip of skin hanging to it, of the whole length of the animal, with the tail attached to it, which, passing down over the back of the dancer, is dragging on the ground. When one becomes fatigued of the exercise, he signifies it by bending quite forward, and sinking his body towards the ground; when another draws a bow upon him and hits him with a blunt arrow, and he falls like a buffalo—is seized by the bye-standers, who drag him out of the ring by the heels, brandishing their knives about him; and having gone through the motions of skinning and cutting him up, they let him off, and his place is at once supplied by another, who dances into the ring with his mask on; and by this taking of places, the scene is easily kept up night and day, until the desired effect has been produced, that of "making buffalo come."

CHAPTER 2

The Ghost Dance (1890)

James A. Mooney

The ceremony of "giving the feather" . . . was an official ordination of the priests in the dance, conferred on them by the apostle who first brought the ceremony to the tribe. Among the Arapaho, Caddo, Kiowa, and adjoining tribes in the south, the feather was conferred by Sitting Bull himself. The feather was thus given to seven leaders, or sometimes to fourteen, that is, seven men and seven women, the number seven being sacred with most tribes and more particularly in the Ghost dance. The feather, which was worn upon the head of the dancers, was either that of the crow, the sacred bird of the Ghost dance, or of the eagle, sacred in all Indian religions. If from the crow, two feathers were used, being attached at a slight angle to a small stick which was thrust into the hair. The feathers were previously consecrated by the priest with prayer and ceremony. The chosen ones usually reciprocated with presents of ponies, blankets, or other property. After having thus received the feather the tribe began to make songs of its own, having previously used those taught them by the apostle from his own language.

Besides the seven leaders who wear the sacred crow feathers as emblems of their leadership, nearly all the dancers wear feathers variously painted and ornamented, and the preparation of these is a matter of much concern. The dancer who desires instructions on this point usually takes with him six friends, so as to make up the sacred number of seven, and goes with them to one who has been in a trance and has thus learned the exact method in vogue in the spirit world. At their request this man prepares for each other a feather, according to what he has seen in some trance vision, for which they return thanks, usually with a small present. The feathers are painted in several colors, each larger feather usually being tipped with a small down feather painted a different color. On certain occasions a special day is set apart for publicly

Selected excerpts from James A. Mooney, *The Ghost-Dance Religion and the Sioux Outbreak of 1890,* 14th Annual Report of the Bureau of Ethnology to the Secretary of the Smithsonian Institution (1896; reprint, Chicago: University of Chicago Press, 1965), pp. 184–200.

painting and preparing the feathers for all the dancers, the work being done by the appointed leaders of the ceremony.

The painting of the dancers is done with the same ceremonial exactness of detail, each design being an inspiration from a trance vision. Usually the dancer adopts the particular style of painting which, while in the trance, he has seen worn by some departed relative. If he has not yet been in a trance, the design is suggested by a vision of one who does the painting. In making the request the dancer lays his hands upon the head of the leader and says, "My father, I have come to be painted, so that I may see my friends; have pity on me and paint me," the sacred paint being held to sharpen the spiritual vision as well as to be conducive to physical health. The painting consists of elaborate designs in red, yellow, green, and blue upon the face, with a red or yellow line along the parting of the hair. Suns, crescents, stars, crosses, and birds (crows) are the designs in most common use.

The dance commonly begins about the middle of the afternoon or later, after sundown. When it begins in the afternoon there is always an intermission of an hour or two for supper. The announcement is made by the criers, old men who assume this office apparently by tacit understanding, who go about the camp shouting in a loud voice to the people to prepare for the dance. The preliminary painting and dressing is usually a work of about two hours. When all is ready, the leaders walk out to the dance place, and facing inward, join hands so as to form a small circle. Then, without moving from their places they sing the opening song, according to previous agreement, in a soft undertone. Having sung it through once they raise their voices to their full strength and repeat it, this time slowly circling around in the dance. The step is different from that of most other Indian dances, but very simple, the dancers moving from right to left, following the course of the sun, advancing the left foot and following it with the right, hardly lifting the feet from the ground. For this reason it is called by the Shoshoni the "dragging dance." All the songs are adapted to the simple measure of the dance step. As the song rises and swells the people come singly and in groups from the several tipis, and one after another joins the circle until any number from fifty to five hundred men, women, and children are in the dance. When the circle is small each song is repeated through a number of circuits. If large, it is repeated only through one circuit, measured by the return of the leaders to the starting point. Each song is started in the same manner, first in an undertone while the singers stand still in their places, and then with full voice as they begin to circle around. At intervals between the songs, more especially after the trances have begun, the dancers unclasp hands and sit down to smoke or talk for a few minutes. At such times the leaders sometimes deliver short addresses or sermons, or relate the recent trance experience of the dancer. In holding each other's hands the dancers usually intertwine the fingers instead of grasping the hand as with us. Only an Indian could keep the blanket in place as they do under such circumstances. Old people hobbling along with sticks, and little children hardly past the toddling period sometimes form a part of the circle, the more vigorous dancers accommodating the movement to their weakness. Frequently a woman will be seen to join the circle with an infant upon her back and dance with the others, but should she show the least sign of approaching excitement watchful friends lead her away that no harm may come to the child. Dogs are driven off from the neighborhood of the circle lest they should run against any of those who have fallen into a trance and thus awaken them. The dancers themselves are careful not to disturb the trance subjects while their souls are in the spirit world. Full Indian dress is worn, with buckskin, paint, and feathers, but among the Sioux the women discarded the belts ornamented with disks of German silver, because the metal had come from the white man. Among the southern tribes, on the contrary, hats were sometimes worn in the dance, although this was not considered in strict accordance with the doctrine.

No drum, rattle, or other musical instrument is used in the dance, excepting sometimes by an individual dancer in imitation of a trance vision. In this respect particularly the Ghost dance differs from every other Indian dance. Neither are any fires built within the circle, so far as known, with any tribe excepting the Walapai. The northern Cheyenne, however, built four fires in a peculiar fashion outside of the circle, as already described. With most tribes the dance was performed around a tree or pole planted in the center and variously decorated. In the southern plains, however, only the Kiowa seem ever to have followed this method, they sometimes dancing around a cedar tree. On breaking the circle at the end of the dance the performers shook their blankets or shawls in the air, with the idea of driving away all evil influences. On later instructions from the messiah all then went down to bathe in the stream, the men in one place and the women in another, before going to their tipis. The idea of washing away evil things, spiritual as well as earthly, by bathing in running water is too natural and universal to need comment.

The peculiar ceremonies of prayer and invocation, with the laying on of hands and the stroking of the face and body, have several times been described and need only be mentioned here. As trance visions became frequent the subjects strove to imitate what they had seen in the spirit world, especially where they had taken part with their departed friends in some of the old-time games. In this way gaming wheels, shinny sticks, hummers, and other toys or implements would be made and carried in future dances, accompanied with appropriate songs, until the dance sometimes took on the appearance of an exhibition of Indian curios on a small scale. . . .

The most important feature of the Ghost dance, and the secret of the trances, is hypnotism. It has been hastily assumed that hypnotic knowledge and ability belong only to an overripe civilization, such as that of India and ancient Egypt, or to the most modern period of scientific investigation. The fact is, however, that practical knowledge, if not understanding, of such things belongs to people who live near to nature, and many of the stories told by reliable travelers of the strange performances of savage shamans can be explained only on this theory. Numerous references in the works of the early Jesuit missionaries, of the Puritan writers of New England and of English explorers farther to the south, would indicate that hypnotic ability no less than sleight-of-hand dexterity formed part of the medicine-man's equipment from the Saint Lawrence to the Gulf. Enough has been said in the chapters on Smoholla and the Shakers to show that hypnotism exists among the tribes of the Columbia, and the author has had frequent opportunity to observe and study it in the Ghost dance on the plains. It can not be said that the Indian priests understand the phenomenon, for they ascribe it to a supernatural cause, but they know how to produce the effect, as I have witnessed hundreds of times. In treating of the subject in connection with the Ghost dance the author must be understood as speaking from the point of view of an observer and not as a psychologic expert.

Immediately on coming among the Arapaho and Cheyenne in 1890, I heard numerous stories of wonderful things that occurred in the Ghost dance—how people died, went to heaven and came back again, and how they talked with dead friends and brought back messages from the other world. Quite a number who had thus "died" were mentioned and their adventures in the spirit land were related with great particularity of detail, but as most of the testimony came from white men, none of whom had seen the dance for themselves, I preserved the scientific attitude of skepticism. So far as could be ascertained, none of the intelligent people of the agency had thought the subject sufficiently worthy of serious consideration to learn whether the reports were true or false. On talking with the Indians I found them unanimous in their statements as to the visions, until I began to think there might be something in it.

The first clew to the explanation came from the statement of his own experience in the trance, given by Paul Boynton, a particularly bright Carlisle student, who acted as my interpreter. His brother had died some time before, and as Paul was anxious to see and talk with him, which the new doctrine taught was possible, he attended the next Ghost dance, and putting his hands upon the head of Sitting Bull, according to the regular formula, asked him to help him see his dead brother. Paul is of an inquiring disposition, and, besides his natural longing to meet his brother again, was actuated, as he himself said, by a desire to try "every Indian trick." He then told how Sitting Bull had hypnotized him with the eagle feather and the motion of his hands, until he fell unconscious and did really see his brother, but awoke just as he was about to speak to him, probably because one of the dancers had accidentally brushed against him as he lay on the ground. He embodied his experience in a song which was afterward sung in the dance. From his account it seemed almost certain that the secret was hypnotism. The explanation might have occurred to me sooner but for the fact that my previous Indian informants, after the manner of some other witnesses, had told only about their trance visions, forgetting to state how the visions were brought about.

This was in winter and the ground was covered deeply with snow, which stopped the dancing for several weeks. In the meantime I improved the opportunity by visiting the tipis every night to learn the songs and talk about the new religion. When the snow melted, the dances were renewed, and as by this time I had gained the confidence of the Indians I was invited to be present and thereafter on numerous occasions was able to watch the whole process by which the trances were produced. From the outside hardly anything can be seen of what goes on within the circle, but being a part of the circle myself I was able to see all that occurred inside, and by fixing attention on one subject at a time I was able to note all the stages of the phenomenon from the time the subject first attracted the notice of the medicine-man, through the staggering, the rigidity, the unconsciousness, and back again to wakefulness. On two occasions my partner in the dance, each time a woman, came under the influence and I was thus enabled to note the very first nervous tremor of her hand and mark it as it increased in violence until she broke away and staggered toward the medicine-man within the circle.

Young women are usually the first to be affected, then older women, and lastly men. Sometimes, however, a man proves as sensitive as the average woman. In particular I have seen one young Arapaho become rigid in the trance night after night. He was a Carlisle student, speaking good English and employed as clerk in a store. He afterward took part in the sun dance, dancing three days and nights without food, drink, or sleep. He is of a quiet, religious disposition and if of white parentage would perhaps have become a minister, but being an Indian, the same tendency leads him into the Ghost dance and the sun dance. The fact that he could endure the terrible ordeal of the sun dance would go to show that his physical organization is not frail, as is frequently the case with hypnotic or trance subjects. So far as personal observation goes, the hypnotic subjects are usually as strong and healthy as the average of their tribe. It seems to be a question more of temperament than of bodily condition or physique. After having observed the Ghost dance among the southern tribes at intervals during a period of about four years, it is apparent that the hypnotic tendency is growing, although the original religious excitement is dying out. The trances are now more numerous among the same number of dancers. Some begin to tremble and stagger almost at the beginning of the dance, without any effort on the part of the medicine-man, while formerly it was usually late in the night before the trances began, although the medicine-men were constantly at work to produce such result. In many if not in most cases the medicine-men themselves have been in trances produced in the same fashion, and must thus be considered sensitives as well as those hypnotized by them.

Not every leader in the Ghost dance is able to bring about the hypnotic sleep, but anyone may try who feels so inspired. Excepting the seven chosen ones who start the songs there is no priesthood in the dance, the authority of such men as Sitting Bull and Black Coyote being due to the voluntary recognition of their superior ability or interest in the matter. Any man or woman who has been in a trance, and has thus derived inspiration from the other world, is at liberty to go within the circle and endeavor to bring others to the trance. Even when the result is unsatisfactory there is no interference with the performer, it being held that he is but the passive instrument of a higher power and therefore in no way responsible. A marked instance of this is the case of Cedar Tree, an Arapaho policeman, who took much interest in the dance, attending nearly every performance in his neighborhood, consecrating the ground and working within the circle to hypnotize the dancers. He was in an advanced stage of consumption, nervous, and excitable to an extreme degree, and perhaps it was for this reason that those who came under his influence in the trance constantly complained that he led them on the "devil's road" instead of the "straight road;" that he made them see monstrous and horrible shapes, but never the friends whom they wished to see. On this account they all dreaded to see him at work within the circle, but no one commanded him to desist as it was held that he was controlled by a stronger power and was to be pitied rather than blamed for his ill success. A similar idea exists in Europe in connection with persons reputed to possess the evil eye. Cedar Tree himself deplored the result of his efforts and expressed the hope that by earnest prayer he might finally be able to overcome the evil influence.

We shall now describe the hypnotic process as used by the operators, with the various stages of the trance. The hypnotist, usually a man, stands within the ring, holding in his hand an eagle feather or a scarf or handkerchief, white, black, or of any other color. Sometimes he holds the feather in one hand and the scarf in the other. As the dancers circle around singing the songs in time with the dance step the excitement increases until the more sensitive ones are visibly affected. In order to hasten the result certain songs are sung to quicker time, notably the Arapaho song beginning *Nû'nanû'naatani'na Hu'hu.* We shall assume that the subject is a woman. The first indication that she is becoming affected is a slight muscular tremor, distinctly felt by her two partners who hold her hands on either side. The medicine-man is on the watch, and as soon as he notices the woman's condition he comes over and stands immediately in front of her, looking intently into her face and whirling the feather or the handkerchief, or both, rapidly in front of her eyes, moving slowly around with the dancers at the same time, but constantly facing the woman. All this time he keeps up a series of sharp exclamations, Hu! Hu! Hu! like the rapid breathing of an exhausted runner. From time to time he changes the motion of the feather or handkerchief from a whirling to a rapid up-and-down movement in front of her eyes. For a while the woman continues to move around with the circle of dancers, singing the song with the others, but usually before the circuit is completed she loses control of herself entirely, and, breaking away from the partners who have hold of her hands on either side, she staggers into the ring, while the circle at once closes up again behind her. She is now standing before the medicine-man, who gives his whole attention to her, whirling the feather swiftly in front of her eyes, waving his hands before her face as though fanning her, and drawing his hand slowly from the level of her eyes away to one side or upward into the air, while her gaze follows it with a fixed stare. All the time he keeps up the Hu! Hu! Hu! while the song and the dance go on around them without a pause. For a few minutes she continues to repeat the words of the song and keep time with the step, but in a staggering, drunken fashion. Then the words become unintelligible sounds, and her movements violently spasmodic, until at last she becomes rigid, with her eyes shut or fixed and staring, and stands thus uttering low pitiful moans. If this is in the daytime, the operator tries to stand with his back to the sun, so that the full sunlight shines in the woman's face. The subject may retain this fixed, immovable posture for an indefinite time, but at last falls heavily to the ground, unconscious and motionless. The dance and the song never stop, but as soon as the woman falls the medicine-man gives his attention to another subject among the dancers. The first one may lie unconscious for ten or twenty minutes or sometimes for hours, but no one goes near to disturb her, as her soul is now communing with the spirit world. At last consciousness gradually returns. A violent tremor seizes her body as in the beginning of the fit. A low moan comes from her lips, and she sits up and looks about her like one awaking from sleep. Her whole form trembles violently, but at last she rises to her feet and staggers away from the dancers, who open the circle to let her pass. All the phenomena of recovery, except rigidity, occur in direct reverse of those which precede unconsciousness.

Sometimes before falling the hypnotized subject runs wildly around the circle or out over the prairie, or goes through various crazy evolutions like those of a lunatic. On one occasion—but only once—I have seen the medicine-man point his finger almost in the face of the hypnotized subject, and then withdrawing his finger describe with it a large circle about the tipis. The subject followed the direction indicated, sometimes being hidden from view by the crowd, and finally returned, with his eyes still fixed and staring, to the place where the medicine-man was standing. There is frequently a good deal of humbug mixed with these performances, some evidently pretending to be hypnotized in order to attract notice or to bring about such a condition from force of imitation, but the greater portion is unquestionably genuine and beyond the control of the subjects. In many instances the hypnotized person spins around for minutes at a time like a dervish, or whirls the arms with apparently impossible speed, or assumes and retains until the final fall most uncomfortable positions which it would be impossible to keep for any length of time under normal conditions. Frequently a number of persons are within the ring at once, in all the various stages of hypnotism. The proportion of women thus affected is about three times that of men.

It is impossible to give more than an approximate statement as to the area of the Ghost dance and the messiah doctrine and the number of Indians involved. According to the latest official report, there are about 146,000 Indians west of Missouri river, exclusive of the five civilized nations in Indian Territory. Probably all these tribes heard of the new doctrine, but only a part took any active interest in it. Generally speaking, it was never taken up by the great tribe of the Navajo, by any of the Pueblos except the Taos, or by any of the numerous tribes of the Columbia region. The thirty or thirty-five tribes more or less concerned with the dance have an aggregate population of about 60,000 souls. A number of these were practically unanimous in their acceptance of the new doctrine, notably the Paiute, Shoshoni, Arapaho, Cheyenne, Caddo, and Pawnee, while of others, as the Comanche, only a small minority ever engaged in it. Only about one-half of the 26,000 Sioux took an active part in it. It may safely be said, however, that the doctrine and ceremony of the Ghost dance found more adherents among our tribes than any similar Indian religious movement within the historic period, with the single possible exception of the crusade inaugurated by Tenskwatawa, the Shawano prophet, in 1805.

Among most of these tribes the movement is already extinct, having died a natural death, excepting in the case of the Sioux. The Shoshoni and some others lost faith in it after the failure of the first predictions. The Sioux probably discontinued the dance before the final surrender, as the battle of Wounded Knee and the subsequent events convinced even the most fanatic believers that their expectations of invulnerability and supernatural assistance were deceptive. The Paiute were yet dancing a year ago, and as their dream has received no such rude awakening as among the Sioux, they are probably still patiently awaiting the great deliverance, in spite of repeated postponements, although the frenzied earnestness of the early period has long ago abated. The Kiowa, who discarded the doctrine on the adverse report of the Ä'piatañ, have recently taken up the dance again and are now dancing as religiously as ever under the leadership of the old men, although the progressive element in the tribe is strongly opposed to it. Among the other tribes in Oklahoma—especially the Arapaho, Cheyenne, Caddo, Wichita, Pawnee, and Oto—the Ghost dance has become a part of the tribal life and is still performed at frequent intervals, although the feverish expectation of a few years ago has now settled down into something closely approaching the Christian hope of a reunion with departed friends in a happier world at some time in the unknown future.

CHAPTER 3

Indian Bureau Regulations (1902)

W. A. Jones, Commissioner

DEPARTMENT OF THE INTERIOR,
OFFICE OF INDIAN AFFAIRS,
WASHINGTON, February 19, 1902

MR. SECRETARY:

Some references of yours in a recent conversation affords me an opportunity, of which I avail myself, to offer some expressions upon a matter which has occupied the public mind for some little time past. Although comparatively trivial in my estimation it seems the entire press of the country considered it otherwise, for it has thought it important enough to give it extended notice and make it the subject of unfavorable comment on the one hand, and some wit and much good-natured badinage on the other; the latter, according to my observation, largely predominating. Indeed, the principal object of the papers seems to have been to get out of it all the fun they could. And it must be admitted they have succeeded very well. With all of this I find not the least fault. But now that the excitement has subsided and we have had our laugh, let us put on a sober face and indulge in a reflection or two on the serious side.

The innocent cause of all this agitation was a letter written by this office in the usual course of business to agents having charge of Indian tribes, in the latter part of December last and the early part of January.
Here it is:

SIR: This office desires to call your attention to a few customs among the Indians which it is believed should be modified or discontinued.

The wearing of long hair by the male population of your agency is not in keeping with the advancement they are making, or will soon be expected to make, in civilization. The wearing of short hair by the males will be a great step in advance, and will certainly hasten their progress toward civilization. The returned male

Directive issued by W. A. Jones, commissioner, on October 16, 1902. Reprinted in Wilcomb E. Washburn, *The American Indian and the United States: A Documentary History* (New York: Random House, 1973), vol. 2, pp. 724–27.

student far too frequently goes back to the reservation and falls into the old custom of letting his hair grow long. He also paints profusely and adopts all the old
habits and customs which his education in our industrial schools has tried to
eradicate. The fault does not lie so much with the schools as with the conditions
found on the reservations. These conditions are very often due to the policy of
the Government toward the Indian, and are often perpetuated by the agent's not
caring to take the initiative in fastening any new policy on his administration of
the affairs of the agency.

On many of the reservations the Indians of both sexes paint, claiming that it
keeps the skin warm in winter and cool in summer, but instead this paint melts
when the Indian perspires and runs down into the eyes. The use of this paint leads
to many diseases of the eyes among those Indians who paint. Persons who have
given considerable thought and investigation to the subject are satisfied that this
custom causes the majority of the cases of blindness among the Indians of the
United States.

You are therefore directed to induce your male Indians to cut their hair, and
both sexes to stop painting. With some of the Indians this will be an easy matter;
with others it will require considerable tact and perseverance on the part of yourself and your employees to successfully carry out these instructions. With your
Indian employees and those Indians who draw rations and supplies, it should be
an easy matter, as a noncompliance with this order may be made a reason for
discharge or for withholding rations and supplies. Many may be induced to comply with the order voluntarily, especially the returned student. The returned students who do not comply voluntarily should be dealt with summarily. Employment, supplies, etc., should be withheld until they do comply and if they become
obstreperous about the matter a short confinement in the guardhouse at hard
labor with shorn locks, should furnish a cure. Certainly all the younger men
should wear short hair, and it is believed by tact, perseverance, firmness, and withdrawal of supplies the agent can induce *all* to comply with this order.

The wearing of citizens' clothing, instead of the Indian costume and blanket,
should be encouraged.

Indian dances and so-called Indian feasts should be prohibited. In many cases
these dances and feasts are simply subterfuges to cover degrading acts and to disguise immoral purposes. You are directed to use your best efforts in the suppression of these evils.

On or before June 30, 1902, you will report to this office the progress you have
made in carrying out the above orders and instructions.

To my surprise this letter created considerable excitement, outside of the
service at least, and the impression seemed to prevail that the Government
intended to accomplish its desires by main strength and awkwardness, and

there was some silly talk about "revolt" and "uprising." To counteract any mistaken impression, the following was written on January 21 to those to whom the former letter was addressed:

SIR: From criticisms that have appeared in the newspapers and from information that has reached this office from other quarters it appears that the recent circular letter issued, directing the modification or discontinuance of certain savage customs prevailing among Indian tribes, has been misunderstood. This letter is therefore written to remove any doubt on the subject.

The circular letter referred to was simply a declaration of the policy of this office and indicated what should be carried out by those having charge of the Indians, using tact, judgment, and perseverance. It was not expected or intended that they should be so precipitate as to give the Indians any cause for revolt, but that they should begin gradually and work steadily and tactfully till the end in view should be accomplished. Let it be distinctly understood that this is not a withdrawal or revocation of the circular letter referred to, but an authoritative interpretation of its meaning.

This is what is known as the "short-hair" order and this is all there is of it. From beginning to end there is not a single suggestion of force as applied to the untutored Indian, but, on the contrary, patience, tact, perseverance. With the case of employees and returned students the case is different. The former is a salaried servant of the Government, employed because he is an Indian, while the latter has been the recipient of bounteous favors. In both cases the Government has a right to expect a proper observance of rules established for their good. The letter, it will be observed, deals with several objectionable and immoral practices, long hair, painting, dancing, feasts, etc., but curiously enough the press has noticed only that part which advocates the cutting of the hair. In it there is nothing new, nothing but what has been according to the precept and practice of twenty years and more. In 1882 Senator Teller, then Secretary of the Interior, who perhaps was, and is, as well equipped, both by observation and experience, as any other person to speak intelligently on the Indian question, addressed a letter to the Commissioner of Indian Affairs which I would like to quote as extremely pertinent to the subject under discussion, but refrain on account of its length. He presented in vigorous language what he regarded as hindrances to civilization; he named the continuance of the old heathenish dances with their degrading influences; he spoke of the laxity of the marriage relation; he included the medicine men and their practices in his category of obstacles; he urged the inculcation of the value of property as an agent of civilization, and concluded by saying:

It will be extremely difficult to accomplish much toward the civilization of the Indians while these adverse influences are allowed to exist.

The Government having attempted to support the Indians until such time as they shall become self-supporting, the interest of the Government as well as that of the Indians demands that every possible effort should be made to induce them to become self-supporting at as early a day as possible. I, therefore, suggest whether it is not practicable to formulate certain rules for the government of the Indians on the reservations that shall restrict and ultimately abolish the practices I have mentioned. I am not ignorant of the difficulties that will be encountered in this effort, yet I believe in all the tribes there will be found many Indians who will aid the Government in its efforts to abolish rites and customs so injurious to the Indians and so contrary to the civilization that they earnestly desire.

Upon this the office, with the approval of the Department, organized the court of Indian offenses, with a code of regulations the purpose of which was to suppress the practices the indulgence in which was fatal to Indian progress. The judges of these courts (always Indians) are appropriated for by Congress. The rules governing their courts will be found in the regulations of the Indian Department. It is true long hair and painting may not be specifically mentioned, but it is not necessary, as they are merely concomitants of the demoralizing practices proscribed. It may be interesting to note that although these rules are stringent to a degree beyond anything suggested in the recent letter which has created so much excitement, and have been enforced all these years, yet they have not received, so far as I can learn, any adverse notice from the press, if they have been noticed at all.

But, whether there be a precedent for the late letter or not, I have no apology to make. I still think, with all due deference to the opinions of others, that it is not only in the line of sound public policy, but it is in the interests of decency and justified by practices which are still too prevalent—practices which are too often encouraged by white spectators, sometimes, I regret to say, in the name of science, who are either actuated by a morbid curiosity or impelled by a desire to gratify the longings of a depraved taste.

It was only a few years ago that issue day at some of the ration agencies partook somewhat of the character of a levee. Visitors would come from a distance to see the animals, wild by nature and frenzied by their surroundings, turned loose to be hunted down over the prairie by the whooping and yelling Indians in imitation of the savage methods of buffalo days. This has been done away. But other and worse things remain. Dances that are degrading and so-called religious rites that are immoral, though gradually disappearing, still prevail. It is these and similar practices, and the customs that are incident to them, that the Indian must relinquish if he is to succeed, and it is against the encouragement of these that the letter was aimed.

It is a familiar saying that error lies at two extremes and truth in the middle, and a striking illustration of the truth of this is found in the Indian question. At one extreme there is a cold brutality which recognizes the dead Indian as the only good Indian, and at the other a sickly sentimentalism that crowns the Indian with a halo and looks up to him as a persecuted saint. Between the two will be found the true friends of the Indian, who, looking upon him as he really is and recognizing his inevitable absorption by a stronger race, are endeavoring in a practical way to fit him under new conditions for the struggle of life. With these I desire to be numbered.

A year ago and again recently, in the annual reports I had the honor to make to you, I took occasion to make some observations upon the obstacles in the way of the Indian's progress and to offer some suggestions looking to their removal and his becoming an independent factor in our civilization. It is not necessary to repeat them here. It is enough to say that the central idea was that the Indian must work out his own salvation. To do that he must learn to labor. He must put aside all savage ways that are inimical to that. He must adapt himself to the ways of the civilization around him and cease to be a mere curiosity and a show. It was ideas like these that led to the writing of the letter under discussion and others in the same direction. There was no idea of interfering with the Indian's personal liberty any more than civilized society interferes with the personal liberty of its citizens. It was not that long hair, paint, blankets, etc., are objectionable in themselves—that is largely a question of taste—but that they are a badge of servitude to savage ways and traditions which are effectual barriers to the uplifting of the race.

Let me say in conclusion that I have no objection whatever to any legitimate criticism of any action taken by this office. In fact it is invited. In the multitude of councillors there is wisdom, and I can not help feeling that if the Indian question were more closely studied and better understood any honest effort to elevate the race would meet with better entertainment than a sneer.

W. A. JONES,
Commissioner.

Hon. E. A. Hitchcock,
Secretary of the Interior.

This incident is now almost forgotten, and may be closed with the statement that the reports of agents on the subject are now all in, and the consensus of their opinion, as expressed by one of them, is that "the order while it has been bitterly denounced in the press, appealed to me as a step forward and in the right direction."

CHAPTER 4

Keeping the Rituals Alive (1985)

Jill D. Sweet

Village ritual performance is perhaps the single most important expression of Tewa cultural continuity. While their material culture and economic activities have become increasingly "Americanized," the Tewas' commitment to traditional village performances has remained unshaken by years of involvement in theatrical shows for tourists. Even Pojoaque and Nambe, the villages that have suffered the greatest cultural disruption, are reviving some of their ritual performances with the help of Tewa elders from neighboring pueblos. Such conviction surprises many outsiders. Why are the Tewas so dedicated to their ritual calendar of village performances? How have they kept their village rituals vital in the face of pressures to conform to the larger Hispanic and Anglo societies? Moreover, how do they perceive the differences between theatrical and ritual performance? And what is the future of Tewa performance?

The Tewas' commitment to their religious rituals became most violently apparent in the Pueblo Revolt of 1680, for which Spanish interference in village rituals was among the primary causes. The Spaniards had punished the Tewas for participating in native rituals, raiding their kivas and destroying their ritual objects. They forced the Indians to attend mass and work for the missionaries. During the revolt, the Pueblo Indians killed twenty-one out of thirty-three Spanish missionaries and successfully, if temporarily, drove the Spaniards

Jill D. Sweet, *Dances of the Tewa Pueblo Indians: Expressions of New Life* (Santa Fe: School of American Research Press, 1985), pp. 75–81.

from the area. After the reconquest, missionaries were never again so intolerant of the native ritual performances.

A more recent example dates to the 1920s, when John Collier took his delegations of Tewa and other Pueblo Indians to lobby in Washington, D.C. Among their primary concerns were several circulars sent by Charles H. Burke, commissioner of Indian affairs, to all superintendents of Indian reservations throughout the United States, suggesting that most forms of Indian ritual dance be discouraged or banned. Although his recommendations never became government policy, Burke caused a great furor among the Pueblo Indians. Some encouraged their Anglo friends to write letters and articles in defense of the Indian's right to dance. One of the most insightful of these appeared in *The New Republic,* in which Elizabeth Sergeant wrote: "the reason why certain powers, deeply influential in Indian life, are out to 'get' Indian dances is not that they are harmful, but that so long as they continue, the Indian cannot be transformed into a white man. . . . with the dances, will die Indian costume and handicraft and decorative symbolism, Indian rhythm and music and song, Indian worship and communal consciousness. Then will every Indian surely prefer the Y.M.C.A. to the kiva, the cornet to the tombe, and the movies to the Deer Dance."[1]

Opposition to Indian dance is no longer a political issue, yet these earlier conflicts taught the Tewas not to take for granted the right to perform their ritual dances. They learned that commitment to their village ritual performances is simultaneously a commitment to religious freedom. The ritual performance as a whole, with its multitude of related meanings and messages, is the most potent symbol or public expression of the people's refusal to become anything other than Tewa. Other aspects of their lives have changed and will continue to do so, but so long as the people hold their village performances, they remain Tewa and are not swept into the mainstream of contemporary American life. Simply put, the Tewas are committed to their village performances because they are committed to the survival of their culture and society.

Over the years of contact with successive waves of non-Pueblo peoples, the Tewa Indians have developed innovative yet conservative techniques for keeping their ritual performance cycle intact. In the early years of coexistence with the Spaniards, the Tewas and other Pueblo Indians practiced what some anthropologists call "compartmentalization."[2] By adopting but deliberately practicing separately (that is, keeping in separate "compartments") certain aspects of Spanish culture, the Pueblos managed to keep the borrowed traits as additions to, rather than replacements for, their native customs. An example is the separate practice of Catholic and kiva rituals. With the relaxation of Spanish policies, the Tewas began more freely to combine, recombine, and juxtapose the foreign with the native. Yet they continued to practice a cognitive form of compartmentalization by remaining aware of the origins of most borrowed elements. They are masters at discriminately selecting foreign objects and practices with existing Tewa traditions, all the while maintaining a clear distinction between what came from "us" and what came from "them." The ability to selectively integrate aspects of other cultures into their own has served the Tewas well in creating their own ceremonials by combining Anglo theatrical practices with Tewa notions of ritual performance.

The results of this selective interlacing of cultural features can also be seen in many village performances. The Comanche dance, for example, compares with other Tewa dances in having a formation of two long parallel lines. The women wear typical Tewa costumes, carry ears of corn and sprigs of evergreens, and contain their movements in Tewa style. The music resembles that of the Tewa buffalo dance, and the whole performance is a gesture of thanksgiving, a celebration of life, and a prayer for community health and prosperity. At the same time, the male dancers and singers wear costumes knowingly adopted from the Plains Indians. Some of the song texts include Comanche words. Since the Comanche dance is frequently performed at patron saint's day celebrations, a Catholic element also appears; at least some of the performance is done before a statue of the village's patron saint. The people remain well aware of the Tewa, Comanche, and Spanish Catholic sources of the dance's symbols.

A Catholic mass at a Tewa village church may show the interlacing of a few Tewa elements into a "foreign" event. The altar is often decorated with traditional Tewa rain or cloud symbols. The chalice may be made of pottery painted with Tewa designs, and some of the priest's robes may be embroidered with native symbols. During the 1970s, the priest at San Juan began saying parts of the mass in Tewa and printing Tewa translations of prayers for the congregation. During a patron saint's day celebration or on Christmas Eve, Tewa dancers sometimes perform in the village church.

The conscious borrowing and combining of foreign practices and symbols most easily occurs when a group has a strong sense of its own culture, and cultural self-consciousness is only intensified by contact with foreigners. Perhaps because the Tewas have for so long dealt with so many outsiders who did things differently and held different values, they have been challenged and forced to sharpen their definition of themselves and their world. Interaction with tourists can especially stimulate cultural self-consciousness because the tourist's inquisitiveness demands that the host group examine and be able to articulate its beliefs and practices. Much of what was taken for granted must be systematically rationalized. Even the brief explanations prepared for theatrical performances outside the villages force the Tewas to think about and explain some of the meanings behind their traditions and beliefs.

A traditional principle of secrecy is another Tewa device for keeping the village performances vital and meaningful. The Tewas believe there is power in the esoteric, and sacred information that becomes public may lose its power. Members of the village religious societies never discuss their activities with nonmembers, and in some cases, if a nonmember villager inadvertently witnesses a society's private rituals, he or she will be obliged to join the group. Thus the esoteric knowledge stays within the religious society and retains its power. Tewa youths occasionally complain that their elders are unwilling to tell them about religious practices and beliefs. This intergenerational secrecy stems from the idea that young people must demonstrate maturity and responsibility before learning about such matters.

Because the Tewas already valued secrecy, they found it a ready tool to use against outsiders. While the Catholic priests said mass, the Tewas secretly kept their native religion alive. Later, anthropologists who came to study that religion met with frustration upon finding the Tewas extremely close-mouthed. Tourists also face silence when they question Tewas about private religious matters.

Peer pressure helps sustain the secrecy principle. Tewas sometimes gossip about people who talk too much with outsiders about religious matters. Gossip also keeps Tewas from behaving disrespectfully during village rituals. For example, people will talk about someone who is obviously intoxicated during a village performance, and the clowns may publicly ridicule the individual.

The selective interlacing of native and foreign traits reflects the Tewas' innovations in making room for new patterns and symbols, while secrecy and social control represent the conservative side of Tewa response to culture contact. The combination of these mechanisms enables the Tewas to keep their village rituals vital.

At first glance, one might assume that the Tewas' participation in theatrical productions is a sign that they are abandoning their religious foundations and becoming a more secular society. Quite the opposite is true. When Tewas compare theatrical shows with village rituals, they often insist that both kinds of performances contain the same fundamental meanings. Performing in a theatrical event can promote growth, fertility, rainfall, and life and can bring blessing to the people and the village, if only the Tewas dance and sing "from the heart." So long as the performers are sincerely committed to the gestures and words of the songs, the meanings remain intact. As one Tewa man expressed it, "You've still got to dance with your whole heart because the songs and dance still are sacred and bring beauty, no matter if you dance here or out there."

The Tewas do not segregate that which a Western thinker might consider to be sacred from that which would be considered secular. They have long celebrated both in ritual performance, juxtaposing the solemn and the humorous, the serious and the absurd, the mystical and the mundane, the ancient and the contemporary. For them, there is no contradiction in adapting segments of their ritual dances for secular, commercial theatrical events.

From the Tewa perspective, the theatrical differs from the ritual not in meaning but in form. Theatrical productions are kept separate in space and time: they are not held in the sacred village plazas and kivas, and they are not part of the native ritual calendar. Their form is distinct in that only segments of songs and dances are performed, and the audience is primarily non-Tewa. These changes in form not only are necessary adjustments made for theatrical productions, but they also stand as markers that commercial tourist shows are different from village ritual events, despite their shared higher-order meanings. The separateness of the theatrical performances, both cognitively and in practice, prevents them from influencing or altering the ritual performances.

In short, the Tewa Pueblo Indians can take part in theatrical productions without destroying their ancient ritual cycle because they maintain a strong commitment to their rituals as indicators of cultural survival; because they respond to other cultures creatively, selectively, and conservatively; and because they perceive the two types of performances as differing in form but not in meaning. The Tewa Indians are neither great resistors of change nor victims of secularization. Rather, they respond to contact situations with their own form of creative ingenuity.

Throughout the first quarter of the twentieth century, Anglo writers predicted that it was only a matter of time before the Pueblo Indians' elaborate ritual performances would cease to exist. Some cited Nambe and Pojoaque, whose performance cycles had virtually died out, as examples of what was bound to happen to other villages. These dire predictions proved wrong. The other Tewa villages have a vigorous ritual performance system in the 1980s, and even Nambe and Pojoaque have shown dramatic signs of recovery during the last twenty years. I would predict that, since village ritual performances are such central and important symbols of Tewa culture, they will thrive rather than diminish as the world around the Tewas continues to change. The future of southwestern theatrical productions is less clear, but at least two trends will probably continue: the rise of semiprofessional dance troupes, and a movement toward greater Indian control of theatrical shows.

As commercial productions became common in the Southwest, Tewa participants began forming semiprofessional dance troupes, the leadership of which generally fell on the oldest male, who took the role of singer and drummer while the younger members danced. Today, about eight Tewa dance troupes perform regularly for theatrical productions, their membership changing from time to time. Some groups consist of children, others of adults; a few travel considerable distances to perform outside the Southwest. The most widely traveled Tewa troupe in recent years is a group of teenagers who call themselves the San Juan Indian Youth Dancers. Beginning as an Ala-teen organization, part of a national program designed to help children of alcoholics cope with their social, emotional, and substance abuse problems, the group decided in 1975 to form a dance troupe and perform at schools, hospitals, and centers for recovering alcoholics. They have also presented segments of Tewa dances and songs at ceremonials, arts and crafts fairs, and festivals as far away as Toronto, Mexico City, and Washington, D.C. Their performing not only promotes cultural pride and helps ensure the preservation of Tewa dance, but it also helps prevent substance abuse among the members. The San Juan Indian Youth Dancers are successfully using tradition to cope with a contemporary social problem.

Semiprofessional dance troupes will probably increase among the Tewas, primarily because many people enjoy performing and traveling and welcome the opportunity to earn extra money. Although members of these groups complain that some people resent the attention they receive from outsiders, they also describe southwestern theatrical productions as exciting events where they enjoy socializing with other Indians. I believe, however, that these groups are unlikely to be composed of full-time professional entertainers since there are no models for such a role in traditional Tewa culture and there are a limited number of events for them to participate in.

As ceremonials wane and arts and crafts fairs wax profitable, we can see a corresponding movement away from Anglo-inspired events to those conceived, organized, and run by Tewas themselves. If Tewa-organized ceremonials were a first step toward the creation of tourist events more acceptable to the Tewas, arts and crafts fairs such as the ENIPC Artist and Craftsman Show are another step in that direction. The future of southwestern theatrical productions involving Tewa performance is increasingly in the hands of the Tewas themselves, as they exercise greater control over what tourists may see of their performance traditions.

Though Tewa-organized theatrical productions may flourish, village rituals will remain the more important kind of performance. Through them the

Tewa people can fully express their perceptions of the world and its beauty, humor, and vitality. The gentle, subtle movements, elaborate costumes, and strong voices singing poetically create a magical experience dedicated to the search for and renewal of life. "Our ancestors used to tell us . . . Go there to the dance and ask the gods there to give good life—regain your life and make your life a longer life . . . You go there like to go to church . . . To ask the spirits to give us better life—a longer life—regain life [Sweet's ellipses]."

NOTES

1. Elizabeth Sergeant, "Death to a Golden Age," *New Republic* 33 (1923): 357. Sweet's ellipsis.

2. Edward Spicer, "Spanish-Indian Acculturation in the Southwest," *American Anthropologist* 56 (1954): 665–70. Edward Dozier, "Rio Grande Pueblos," in *Perspectives in American Indian Culture Change,* ed. Edward Spicer (Chicago: University of Chicago Press, 1961), p. 94.

CHAPTER 5

Contemporary Native American Pow-wow Dancing (2000)

Tara Browner

North America's indigenous peoples—Indian, Aleut, and Inuit—have been creating and performing dances for thousands of years, since their earliest times on the continent. Contacts with non-Native settlers were devastating in their impact on traditional Indian lifeways, yet music and dance endured. In today's Indian communities, age-old religious ceremonies exist side by side with Christian and Native American (Peyote Way) church gatherings, thriving in cultures where tradition, adaptation, and innovation have always been central elements of life.

Thanks to Tara Browner (Choctaw) who wrote this essay specifically for this volume.

Across North America, attendance at pan-Indian pow-wows—including singing, dancing, trading, and watching from the audience—is arguably the most popular participatory form of entertainment in Indian country. Pow-wows have a multiplicity of meanings for devoted "pow-wow'ers," from a place to rendezvous with friends and family to a profound spiritual experience. A few participants may even regard pow-wows as a form of ceremony. This view, however, is not the norm. Pow-wows are generally considered to be events of spiritual significance and value, but not truly ceremonial in nature.

A "pow-wow," to put it simply, is an event where Native North Americans come together to celebrate their cultures through the medium of music and dance. As opposed to a War Dance, Gourd Dance, or "49" (a dance that happens after a pow-wow, and accompanied by "49"—war journey—songs), pow-wows are inclusive, and the term specifically designates an event that is "pan-Indian," meaning that all tribal (and nontribal) people are invited to participate. In the times before pow-wows, various nations had (and continue to have) their own tribal-specific dance events, and occasionally invited members of other nations to their "Dance." But open-invitation dancing to traditional music while wearing old-fashioned regalia was not widespread until about 1920, when intertribal pow-wows began in rural Oklahoma as a way to honor returning World War I veterans.

The word "pow-wow" is probably derived from the words *pau wow,* a Narragansett term glossed as "he/she dreams" that was used to denote a specific type of doctoring used by traditional healers in those northeastern Native societies. Early European settlers of Germanic origin picked up the word while traveling through Massachusetts on their way to Pennsylvania, and practitioners of Pennsylvania German folk medicine—known as "Powwow doctors"—coined the term "powwowing" to describe their use of herbal medicines. Traveling from place to place, these "powwow doctors" styled themselves as "Indian Healers" and sold cure-alls in bottles. According to Virgil Vogel, in the two decades following the Civil War, "[t]he most dramatic promotional stunt in the vending of alleged Indian remedies was the medicine show, which once ranked with the circus and chautauqua as a seasonal relief to the monotony of small-town existence. From the post Civil War era until the beginning of World War I, these spectacles toured the country with bands of 'real live Indians,' pitching their tents in some mud flat and advertising their presence with a noisy and colorful parade down Main Street. Audiences were treated to an exhibition of 'war dances' and other sights of the 'wild west.'"[1] These "medicine shows" predated by twenty years the famous "Wild West Shows" of Buffalo Bill and Pawnee Bill, popular from the early 1880s until the onset of World War I. Although

Indian dances had served the purpose of entertaining non-Indian spectators prior to this time, the use of dancing in tandem with "powwow" doctors resulted in the term "pow-wow" being associated with the concept of "Indians dancing" by largely White audiences. Soon after the end of World War I, Indians themselves began to refer to their secular dance celebrations as pow-wows, having picked up the term from the dominant society. Although indigenous terms such as "wacipi" (Lakota) are still in use, "pow-wow" is by far the most common for dance-only events. "Fairs," such as Navajo Fair or Crow Fair, denote a pow-wow combined with a rodeo and carnival.

Pow-wows are first classified as "Northern" (Northern Plains and Great Lakes) or "Southern" (Oklahoma), and then as "competition" (for prize money) or "traditional." Dance categories are as follows: Men's and Women's Traditional, Men's Straight, Women's Southern Cloth, Men's Grass, Women's Jingle Dress, and Men's and Women's Fancy. All of these dance categories are of an individual free-form style, where dancers are free to improvise their movements within established limits.

In precontact North America, women and men did not dance as couples holding hands, and some dances were single-gender, such as Plains war dances (male only). Although dances associated with war were a male domain, women did participate along the sidelines, dancing around the edges of the arena. Most forms of dance, however, included both men and women of all ages in some capacity, although women's movements were usually more restricted than men's. Since women were considered to be spiritual conduits to Mother Earth, their ceremonial role often included keeping part of one foot in contact with the ground (and the Mother Earth), thus limiting their movements during dances.

The origins of dances within Indian communities are similar to the origins of songs: dreams or visions, imitations of animal movements, and the exchange of dance styles and regalia with neighboring tribes, usually done in a formal ceremony of transmission. Some dances are "owned," and as individual or communal property are not to be used without their owner's permission. Most dance forms have a specific body of songs that accompany them, and these were traded in conjunction with the dance from group to group through a process known as diffusion. As time passes, new footwork, regalia, and songs are layered onto the original dance, and tribal distinctions develop among what had once been similar types. Through this mechanism, continuity and change occur side by side, with older forms retained while new ones evolve. Pow-wows are a good example of this phenomenon, with older dances (pre-nineteenth century) performed in the same arena with twentieth-century forms.

The central "Traditional" dances associated with pan-Indian pow-wows are derived from old-style war dances and warrior societies, as is the music. Until the twentieth century, these dances were done by men in preparation for war or by men and women in celebration of a war's successful conclusion. Today's male dancers orient themselves more toward dramatization of a story, while women's footwork and carriage symbolize their connection with the Earth. One difference between Northern and Southern Traditional (and Cloth) dancers is that Southern women's footwork is a slow, stylized walk, while Northern women (in competition), stand in one place, shifting their heels to face in different directions. Southern Straight dancing is seen primarily in Oklahoma, and features male dancers following a "trail" with their dance sticks, circling at certain points in the music.

Grass Dancing is also an outgrowth of an older warrior society and is Lakota in origin. In this form the dancers wear outfits lined with yarn of chainette fringe to symbolize grass and dance with a swaying motion, metaphorically flattening the grass of the dance arena with their feet. Women's Jingle Dress was a gift to the pow-wow community from the Ojibwe (Chippewa) Nation; it is danced as a form of healing in a dress covered with cones made of snuff-can lids. Oftentimes audience members will approach Jingle Dancers with tobacco (a traditional gift) and request that the dancer pray for a sick relative during the next performance.

The most recent dances in the pow-wow repertoire are the Fancy styles, which came about as a result of Traditional dancers performing at various Wild West shows. In order to better entertain the audience, dancers were asked to "fancy it up," meaning to speed up their footwork and add spins not found in the traditional forms. The dancers complied, and then took the new style back to their communities upon leaving the show.

Fancy Dance as seen at pow-wows today was codified in Oklahoma and spread outward from there during the 1920s and 1930s. Women's styles—also called Fancy Shawl or Butterfly Dance—came about as a direct result of the men's dance, when young women, tired of seeing men have all the fun, created their own style and began to dance it. The likely origin point of Women's Fancy styles is on the Lakota reservations of South Dakota during the 1940s.

Musical style has a central role in how dancers execute their footwork. Songs have a large variety of steady beat patterns and tempos, with distinctive footwork and movement styles for each dance category matching up to each song type. For example, a Jingle Dress dancer performs one kind of step for a standard war dance song (a moderate tempo, duple-beat style), and an entirely different step for a round or shuffle dance. Understanding how to dance with different song types is essential to any pow-wow dancer's repertory, and this often takes years to master. The best dancers must also learn a variety of tribal and regional styles of music, as tempos, accent patterns (key to upper-body movement), and differing musical forms (primarily Northern vs. Southern) can be heard at any large event. Among dancers, it is commonly said that the "trick" to being a successful pow-wow dancer is stopping on time, and in order to accomplish this feat, dancers *must* know song styles.

Contemporary pan-Indian pow-wow has become a major force for music and dance innovation among today's Indian populations, especially those with far-flung tribal memberships. Pow-wows not only provide a gathering place for Indian dancers and musicians, they are fertile ground for change, as members of diverse tribal groups interact and share music, the latest footwork "moves," and dance regalia. Cassettes, compact discs, and video tapes featuring the newest songs and dance footwork are sold at such gatherings, resulting in stylistic mixtures impossible only a few decades ago.

Consequently, a new pan-Indian culture, with regional music and dance layered upon a Plains Indian framework, is shaping much of contemporary urban "Indian" identity. Pow-wow dance styles in urban areas now tend toward the generic, with widely varying personal interpretations in regalia and footwork of the various categories (although Southern Straight dancing seems immune to change). Adding to the mixture is the prevalence of competition pow-wows offering large monetary prizes, where "different" is frequently equated with "better." In this climate, the rate of change in dance and regalia styles at urban events escalates ever more rapidly. Community elders, however, take upon themselves the responsibility to preserve older forms for younger generations, and in doing so, continually revitalize the pow-wow with tradition.

As a dancer myself (Women's Jingle Dress and Southern Cloth), I have found over the years that pow-wows provide a sense of community and pride, bringing together a far-flung population of people in a wonderful fellowship. When I first began dancing, a number of women approached me after my "giveaway" (a giving of gifts in celebration of a specific life-changing event) and said "Welcome to our circle." This "Circle," symbolic of the cultural ties and history that all Indians share, is the living body of the pow-wow, with the beating drum at its heart. *Ihokeh.*

NOTE

1. Virgil J. Vogel, *American Indian Medicine* (Norman: University of Oklahoma Press, 1970), p. 141.

CHAPTER 6

Navajo Night Chant for the Dance of the Thunderbirds

Translated by Washington Matthews

Happily I recover.
Happily for me the spell is taken off.
In beauty happily I walk.
With beauty before me, I walk.
With beauty behind me, I walk.
With beauty below me, I walk.
With beauty above me, I walk.
With beauty all around me, I walk.
It is finished again in beauty.
It is finished in beauty.
It is finished in beauty.
It is finished in beauty.

Washington Matthews, *The Night Chant, a Navaho Ceremony* (New York: Memoirs of the American Museum of Natural History, 1902), vol. 6, pp. 144–45.

SUGGESTED BOOKS AND FILMS

Axtell, James. *The European and the Indian: Essays in the Ethnohistory of Colonial North America.* New York: Oxford University Press, 1981.

Bierhorst, John. *Four Masterworks of American Indian Literature.* New York: Farrar, Straus & Giroux, [1974].

Champe, Flavia Waters. *The Matachines Dance of the Upper Rio Grande.* Lincoln: University of Nebraska Press, 1983.

Ellis, Clyde. "'We Don't Want Your Rations, We Want This Dance': The Changing Use of Song and Dance on the Southern Plains." *Western Historical Quarterly* 30 (Summer, 1999): 133–54.

Frisbie, Charlotte. *Southwestern Indian Ritual Drama.* Albuquerque: University of New Mexico Press, 1980.

Heth, Charlotte, ed. *Native American Dance: Ceremonies and Social Traditions.* Washington, D.C.: Museum of the American Indian, Smithsonian Institution, with Starwood Pub., 1992.

Highwater, Jamake. *Ritual of the Wind: North American Indian Ceremonies, Music and Dance.* Toronto: Methuen Publications, 1984.

Hittman, Michael. *Wovoka and the Ghost Dance.* Edited by Don Lynch. Lincoln: University of Nebraska Press, 1997.

Horse Capture, George. *Powwow.* Cody, Wyo: Buffalo Bill Historical Center, 1989.

Kurath, Gertrude Prokosch. *Half a Century of Dance Research: Essays by Gertrude Prokosch Kurath.* Flagstaff, Ariz.: Cross-Cultural Dance Resources, 1986.

Kurath, Gertrude Prokosch, and Antonio Garcia. *Music and Dance of the Tewa Pueblos.* Santa Fe: Museum of New Mexico Press, 1970.

Laubin, Gladys, and Reginald Laubin. *Indian Dances of North America: Their Importance to Indian Life.* Norman: University of Oklahoma Press, 1976.

Lomax, Alan, Irmgard Bartenieff, and Forrestine Paulay. "Choreometrics: A Method for the Study of Cross-Cultural Pattern in Film." 3d Conference on Research in Dance, Tucson, Ariz., 1972. *New Dimensions in Dance Research.* [New York, c. 1974.] Pp. 193–212.

Martí, Samuel, and Gertrude Prokosch Kurath. *Dances of Anáhuac: The Choreography and Music of Precortesian Dances.* [New York]: Wenner-Gren Foundation for Anthropological Research, 1964.

Philip, Kenneth R. *John Collier's Crusade for Indian Reform, 1920–1954.* Tucson: University of Arizona Press, 1977.

Powers, William K. *War Dance: Plains Indian Musical Performance.* Tucson: University of Arizona Press, 1990.

Royce, Anya Peterson. *The Anthropology of Dance.* Bloomington: Indiana University Press, 1980.

Rust, Ezra Gardner. *The Music and Dance of the World's Religions: A Comprehensive, Annotated Bibliography of Materials in the English Language.* Westport, Conn.: Greenwood Press, 1996.

Speck, Frank G., and Leonard Broom. *Cherokee Dance and Drama.* Berkeley: University of California Press, 1951.

Twofeathers, Manny. *The Road to the Sundance: My Journey into Native Spirituality.* New York: Hyperion, 1996.

Wilder, Carleton. *The Yaqui Deer Dance: A Study in Cultural Change.* [Washington, D.C.: U.S. Government Publications Office], 1963.

There are many sources that distribute movies on dance, so check with your local distributor, regional colleges, and state archives for listings. Videos available for purchase or rental are expanding constantly, so this list represents a bare minimum of relevant titles. Dance Films Association's *Dance Film and Video Guide* (see Selected General Readings and References on Theatrical Dance) lists the addresses for the distributors named in this selected bibliography.

American Indian Dance Theater: Finding the Circle. 58 minutes, color. Intermedia Arts, c. 1987. Intersperses cuts of intertribal pow-wow dances and Pueblo dance rituals with artistic performances by the American Indian Dance Theater company. Offers a varied program from Plains, Pueblo, and other populations.

Ballet Folklórico Nacional de México. 110 minutes, color. Gessler Productions. Performances by Mexico's premier folkloric troupe of Native American dances, including the Yaqui or deer dance.

Erick Hawkins' America. 58 minutes, color. Dance Horizons Video, 1988. The Hawkins Company performs his *Plains Daybreak,* a modern dance piece inspired by traditional Indian stories of creation.

JVC Video Anthology of World Music and Dance, vol. 27: "The Americas—I; Native American Indians." 60 minutes, color. Rounder Records, 1998. North American Indians, includes dances of the Inuit and Nez Percé. Several versions of the eagle, war, hoop, and other fancy dances for men and women.

Live and Remember. 29 minutes, color. Solaris, c. 1987. Directed by Henry Smith. Discussion by Lakota elders, tribespeople, and dancers on difficulties of maintaining Native American traditions. Includes performances of eagle and hoop dances, sneak-up and fancy dancing.

Vision Dance. 58 minutes, color. Solaris, Lakota Project, c. 1982. Prize-winning film of imaginative dance created by Henry Smith and Lloyd One Star, performed in the Black Hills of South Dakota by Lakota Sioux in conjunction with the Solaris Dance Theatre.

In addition, videos of various Native American dances are now available for sale at various pow-wows. Since most of them are distributed locally, they have been omitted from this list.

PART 2

OTHER DANCE TRADITIONS IN AMERICA

INTRODUCTION

"Tradition! Tra-di-tion!" was the refrain of a song that Zero Mostel, in the role of Tevye, sang lustily in the 1964 Broadway show, *Fiddler on the Roof.* The chorus words are easier to sing than it would be to describe how this complex process actually works. Since dance is basically an ephemeral art, it must be personally handed on by those well versed in its customs rather than exclusively by literary means. In the case of many dance traditions in America, some of which have been preserved for hundreds of years, dancers seem to have imbibed their knowledge of dance forms at their mothers' knees, rather than to have learned them in schools. For example, generations of Kentuckians and French Canadians alike have been known to study traditional dances as wide-eyed babes in their cradles, watching their parents promenade about the barn on Saturday nights. This custom, too, dates back many years: one European described his astonishment at seeing five generations of the same family dancing in Tyler County, Virginia, in 1829: "the father, the grandfather, and the great grandfather; the daughter, mother, and grandmother; the son, and great grandson, all in a dance on the same floor at the same time." The intergenerational mode of passing down traditional dances is a highly effective method to insure their survival, particularly against inroads made by popular social dances that tend to change from season to season.

Fads may come and go with rapidity: the exotic Brazilian *lambada,* one of the latest of a long line of Latin American dances that periodically hit North America, made a splash for less than a season in 1989. Traditional dances, on the other hand, have remarkable staying power. Some, as we will see in the first selection that deals with English country dances brought to North America, have been around for hundreds of years and, thanks to a revival in the early twentieth century, bode well to continue for many more. Kate Van Winkle

Keller discovered a cache of notated dances that dated back to early eighteenth-century New York and traced these dances back to Playford's *English Dancing Master: Or Plaine and Easie Rules for the Dancing of Country Dances, with the Tune to Each Dance,* the first English-language dancing manual. John Playford, an English music publisher, collected over one hundred different English country dances, notated their tunes, and published a manual in 1651 that swelled, some seventeen versions later in 1728, to 918 dances in three volumes.

Today these dances have been reconstructed for our pleasure and are staples of various "Playford Balls" presented by regional country dance societies in the United States and Canada. Nashville offers such an annual event, complete with five-piece orchestra to play the original tunes and several hundred dancers in period costume who perform dances arranged by Cecil Sharp. Sharp, an English collector of English folk music and dance, spurred a revival of interest in these and other so-called folk dances in late nineteenth-century England and North America. While rivalry exists between the "traditionalists" who perform idiosyncratic regional versions of traditional dances and the "revivalists" who adhere strictly to Sharp's written instructions for these dances, both would seem to be valid ways of maintaining traditions.

The English tradition of country dance is one of the longest-lived and most widely popular on these shores (in the eighteenth century, over 2,738 different country dances were recorded).[1] However, other European immigrants took their dancing even more seriously, as shown by the second selection, "The War of the Quadrilles." My account of dance in old New Orleans shows how conflict between two cultures can be acted out on the ballroom floor. The French Creoles of 1804 resented the Americans who had recently arrived in Louisiana, and the resultant "War of the Quadrilles," as I facetiously term it, led to the first (and probably only) American legislation to set out equal opportunity for dances associated with different ethnic and political groups: a ratio of two contredanses and quadrilles for the Creoles, two reels and jigs for the Americans, to one waltz as a compromise for those of Spanish ancestry.

"Sunday Afternoon Dances in Congo Square," taken from a New Orleans visitor's diary dated 1819, presents a different perspective on the same city. Benjamin Henry Latrobe's descriptions appear to be the most detailed eyewitness reports published about early dance in Congo Square, an open field located outside the New Orleans city limits. Congo Square's importance for the history of American dance lies partly in the tales spread about it as the supposed place of origin for jazz music and partly in its actual use as a gathering place for slaves to participate in traditional tribal music and dance activities on Sunday afternoons. Latrobe sketched the musical instruments and recorded the dancers' movements, which he considered too African to suit his English tastes. Small groups formed into circles while musicians played in the center. One dance that he described, that of two women dancing in place with their handkerchiefs held outstretched, sounds remarkably similar to the Haitian Chica described by Moreau de Saint-Méry in 1796.[2]

Soon after his visit, Congo Square gained the reputation of being a "lurid" tourist attraction. The 1822 edition of *Paxton's Directory* claimed that the square was notable "on account of its being the place where the Congo, and other negroes dance, carouse, and debauch on the Sabbath, to the great injury of the morals of the rising generation."[3] The writer added that citizens did not approve of this practice, but hesitated to prohibit it. At least, he commented huffily, it could be moved out of sight. The dances appear to have ended by 1835, although sporadic efforts were made to restore the slaves' "ancient privilege" in 1845.[4] In this case once again, as in the Ghost Dances, a dominant majority culture may label dance as subversive political activity and seek to control it.

In a very different kind of ghost dance from that of the Native Americans described by James Mooney in the previous section, this time in contemporary Hawai'i rather than on the North American plains, the dominant majority culture seeks to join the dance that comes out of an ethnic subgroup. Judy Van Zile, in "Japanese *Bon* Dance Survivals in Hawai'i," describes how dances originally central to Buddhist ceremonies designed to honor the dead have adapted themselves to life in modern Oahu. Within less than a hundred years of official sponsorship by Buddhist temples, an observer notes that the *bon* dance "is no longer a Buddhist Japanese festival only, but a many-sided religious, secular, American Hawaiian island, Buddhist, and Japanese occasion for expressing ethnic distinctiveness while sharing and modifying it at the same time."[5] In 1959, Hawaiian statehood celebrations featured a performance of the *bon* dance, thus demonstrating the incorporation of this famous dance of death into American political culture. Song texts praised the famous 442d Battalion, Japanese American soldiers who fought with such extraordinary bravery during World War II. Van Zile notes that *bon* dancers today are attracted by the emphasis on community participation, and may even be unaware of the ceremony's religious underpinnings.[6]

Several examples in this section illustrate how original purposes may be forgotten or perhaps even subverted. Unquestionably, a valid way to adapt to new conditions may be to expand roles for older dances. All of the dances described in these first two sections, and indeed this may be true for practically all traditional dances to some extent, function as pleasurable ways to maintain ethnic identity and social bonding within a group. The American dance heritage, it should be no surprise to learn, is composed of dances drawn from radically diverse national sources. Whether in the temple or the private home, dancing to a fiddle or a brass band, barefooted or high-heeled, these dancers share a true delight in traditional dances as a healthy way to have good times in company with friends and strangers. Such bonds can deepen over the years; as one lighthearted writer in the *New Orleans Daily Picayune* put it: "A good *pastorale* has often procured an *acred* wife; the *ballancez* has influenced the *scale* of many fortunes; and the *chaine anglaise* has been exchanged for the *chaine du dame*, and that not infrequently for the *fetters* of Hymen" (Jan. 5, 1839).

Dances are born, mature, and die over the years. Some that seem moribund come back from the dead and transform themselves to fit new social mores and customs. The Playford dance "longways for as many as will" takes on a new spin under the modern name of "country line dancing." This time around the dance steps are much easier to perform and the formations of geometrical shapes are much less complicated than was popular in the seventeenth century, but, as can be seen in my "All Lined Up at the Wildhorse Saloon," the dance retains its democratic appeal after all these years.

After Woodstock, the tradition of couple dancing was nearly destroyed. Dancers dropped hands and began looking inwards to "do their own thing." The 1990s saw a revival of a 1930s dance known as the "lindy hop" (allegedly named after Charles Lindbergh's "hop" or trans-Atlantic flight). Today the dance is renamed "swing dance," but its afficionados study old movies to reconstruct their moves and haunt vintage clothing stores for zoot suits or other fetishistic paraphernalia from the World War II years when the same dance was called "jitterbug." In "Swingin' Out: Southern California's Lindy Revival," Juliet McMains and Danielle Robinson take a lively look at the revival of swing dance, which began in California and has swept across the nation. The two graduate students of dance visit the Satin Ballroom and discover that they are not alone in their research studies: it seems that swing dancers are so obsessed with "authentic" re-creations of the lindy hop that they virtually moonlight as dance historians.

Americans, no doubt about it, love to dance: what one commentator noted about the New Orleanians, that "on aime passionnément la danse" ("they passionately love the dance") could apply equally to the masses of whirling, twirling figures who continue throughout American history to sashay through the complex mazes of the dance floor. Debutantes at Charleston's eighteenth-century St. Cecilia Society who complain of pinched toes from too-tight high heels, slaves who once raised clouds of dust as they shuffled barefoot on the Mississippi River levees, or hula dancers whose long black hair blows in the wind as they perch on the rocky shores of Kona—people find that anywhere at all will do for a dance. Long before the avant-garde performance artists took dance into New York's Grand Central Terminal, skinny little kids tapped for pennies tossed by departing trans-Atlantic passengers from the wharfs, and so-called solid citizens would strut the streets during Mardi Gras in New Orleans or the annual Mummer's Day Parade in Philadelphia. College students might barricade the streets on fraternity row and dance all night to white-hot blasting music; some of their grandparents, that very night, might opt for a rather staid jitterbug to the smooth sounds of a retrograde big-band orchestra at the local country club, while other students' parents would prefer to dance the *merengue* at their neighborhood salsa club.

NOTES

1. See Robert Keller's compilation, *Dance Figures Index, American Country Dances 1730–1810* (Darnestown, Md.: Hendrickson Group, n.d.).

2. M. L. E. Moreau de Saint-Méry, *Dance: An Article Drawn from the Work by M. L. E. Moreau de St.-Méry,* trans. with introduction by Lily Hastings and Baird Hastings (Brooklyn: Dance Horizons, 1976), p. 61; originally published as *Danse: Notice Extrait d'un Ouvrage de M. L. E. Moreau de St-Méry* (Philadelphia: author, 1796.) I personally viewed a similar dance in 1947 in Port-au-Prince, Haiti.

3. *Paxton's Directory of 1822* (New Orleans: printed by John A. Paxton, 1822), p. 40.

4. Henry A. Kmen, "Roots of Jazz and the Dance in Place Congo: A Reappraisal," Inter-American Musical Research, *1972 Anuario Yearbook,* p. 11.

5. Van Zile notes that the earliest reference to Hawaiian *bon* dances occurred in a 1905 newspaper article. See Judy Van Zile, *The Japanese Bon Dance in Hawaii* (Kailua: Press Pacifica, 1982), p. 4. The quotation is taken from Lawrence Fuchs as cited on p. 12.

6. Suggestions for where and when to observe these dances can be found in Susan Yim, "Festival of Dancing and Light," *New York Times,* May 26, 1996.

CHAPTER 7

Playford's "English Dancing Master" (1651) and Country Dancing in America

Kate Van Winkle Keller and Genevieve Shimer

Country dancing was first mentioned as a specific type of social dance in England in the middle of the sixteenth century when Elizabeth I was queen. She enjoyed watching the ladies of her court dancing "country dances," although she herself preferred the [Italian] galliard, volta, and other more demanding couple dances. Although none of the country dance choreographies from this early period have survived, a few dances in the first edition of [John] Playford's collection of seventy-five years later have forms and movements which may be similar to those danced in Elizabeth's court and are, in turn, strongly derivative of earlier Italian *balli*. [In 1651, the English music publisher John Playford (1623–1686) published *The English Dancing Master*, a collection of 105 country dances with their tunes and dance directions.][1]

Unlike the couple dances, in which the steps are most important, country dances are created from a vocabulary of often symmetrical floor tracks along which the dancers move with or around one another. While a galliard or a volta is best viewed from ground level, the country dance is most dramatic from above. The weavings and turnings create a kaleidoscopic effect on the floor, and the steps used are secondary to the figures and vary with changing fashion.

Country dances appear to have always been regarded as a pleasing alternative to the formal dances which required great skill in performance. Two distinguishing characteristics are that the country dance is a group dance in which there is interaction between two or more couples, and it is a democratic dance in that the couples often change positions in the set and take turns leading the figures. Only in a culture in which the absolute power of the king had been

This selection has been shortened and edited, due to the considerable length of the original. Material in brackets reflects a condensation of or addition to the authors' wording.

Kate Van Winkle Keller and Genevieve Shimer, *The Playford Ball: 103 Early Country Dances, 1651–1820: As Interpreted by Cecil Sharp and His Followers*, published simultaneously by the Society of Dance History Scholars in *Studies in Dance History* 1, no. 2 (Spring/Summer, 1990): viii–x, 110–11, and by A Cappella Books and the Country Dance and Song Society (Chicago: A Cappella Books, 1990).

tempered by the demands of democracy could such a dance form flourish. And flourish it did! From 1650 to 1850 it was a significant medium of social expression for rising bourgeois society. The English country dance was eventually exported to most of the countries of Europe and to America.

Both forms of social dance continued to exist side by side. Voltas and galliards were replaced by minuets and allemandes, which in turn gave way to waltzes and polkas, while the country dances themselves went through a gradual evolution. The earliest country dances were dances for sets of two, three, or four couples in round, square, or longways formations, a few of the latter for "as many as will" [as directed by Playford in *The English Dancing Master*]. By the mid-eighteenth century, most of the set dances had vanished from the ballroom, and only longways dances for an indefinite number of couples were danced. By 1800, square set cotillions were in the ascendancy, and soon the longways country dances were but a lingering memory. Near the end of the nineteenth century, "a nostalgic public began to look with favor on things 'old-world,' and various efforts were made to revive the 'old country dances,' . . . attempts more romantic than truly historic."[2] The time was ripe for serious musicologists and dance historians to study the early country dance, [including Cecil Sharp (1859–1924), whose interest and reconstructions would spark a revival that continues today].

The earliest source on English country dance, and therefore the most interesting to Cecil Sharp, had been compiled in 1651 by John Playford, music publisher, bookseller, clerk to the Temple Church, and vicar-choral of St. Paul's Cathedral in seventeenth-century London. Born in Norwich in 1623, he came to London in 1639 and served a seven-year apprentice to John Benson. He then became a member of the Yeomanry of the Stationer's Company in 1647 and opened his own shop in the porch of the Temple Church.

The times were tumultuous in the London of his day: King Charles I was under arrest and soon to be beheaded; the dissenters held power; the populace was scattered and confused. Although they were still wealthier and more powerful, the upper classes had lost forever their unquestioned hold over society. Political unrest and periodic outbreaks of plague and fire encouraged many to seek refuge, education, and leisure within their homes or away from the city. . . . Never was a time more ripe for a do-it-yourself book on social dancing. . . .

On November 7, 1650, [John Playford] registered with the authorities that he intended to publish the *English Dancing Master*. He produced his groundbreaking volume the following year, tactfully dedicating it to the young heirs of the upper middle class and nobility who attended the several law schools in London. His book contained the music and verbal instructions for 105 country dances. Its acceptance was immediate, a second edition appeared the next year and a third in 1665, the year of the great plague! Fire struck London in 1666, yet [despite these calamities] by 1670 Playford published a fourth edition. . . .

[The ailing John Playford turned business affairs over to his son Henry in 1684; by then a seventh edition, doubled in size, was in publication.] Edition followed edition, dances were dropped and new ones added as fads and fashion changed. John Young took over the series in 1706, and in 1710 compiled a second volume that reached four editions, first with 200 dances, later expanded to 360. He issued a third volume shortly afterward, adding another 200 dances to the canon. He continued to release editions of the first volume, which peaked at 358 dances in its final edition published around 1728. . . .

John Playford died in 1686, but the legacy of *The Dancing Master* lived on. So great was his contribution that his name is now synonymous with social dancing of his time, particularly as it was interpreted by Cecil Sharp [in the twentieth century].

But it is a misunderstanding to think that "Playford" dances are the only true English country dances. While John Playford was musically sophisticated and published and sold music and dance books, he was not a dancing master. In addition, although *The English Dancing Master* was unique in its time, it opened the door for many similar publications that contained similar dances. . . .

[Today, the term "Playford" dances most often describes the English country dances as they were revived under Sharp's directions. He encountered certain difficulties when he began to study the Playford editions around the turn of this century.] He was a musician, not a dancer, and had no training in dance research. . . . The directions for performing the dances were terse and frequently obscure. Much of the early music was unbarred. Since [the books] were intended purely as reminders to dancers who were already familiar with steps and figures, no mention was made of the steps or the style in which dances were to be performed. . . .

[Sharp persevered in his endeavor.] With "Jenny Pluck Pears" in *The Country Dance Book, Part 2* (1911), he began a tradition that continues today, an ambitious attempt to take the abbreviated verbal descriptions of complex historical dance choreographies and make them understandable and enjoyable for a new generation of dancers. He knew [how important it was] that they be fun to dance, or they would be relegated to the library shelf once again. . . . Sharp did not try to interpret them for historical purposes. He saw them as lost folk dances which, with some modification for modern dress and deportment, could be enjoyed just as much as they had been many years before. . . .

MODERN COUNTRY DANCE TECHNIQUE

Over the years, modifications have altered some of Cecil Sharp's dicta on how to perform certain steps and figures. Yet his fundamental philosophy is still valid. He was committed to making the dances appropriate for an informal setting: not for display, but for recreation. He chose a style adapted to suit the average man in the street rather than the dance expert primarily interested in the authenticity of interpretation and steps. Sharp repeatedly spoke of the "gay simplicity" of the country dance, a term he found in an early nineteenth-century dancing manual. "Every movement should . . . be executed quietly, easily, and with an economy of motion, and in a simple unaffected manner . . . The spirit of merriment, however, although never wholly absent from the dance, is not always equally obvious."[3]

This restrained, almost inhibiting description does not really fit today's dancers. Perhaps the most marked change since 1915 is in the social aspect of the dance. Here in the United States particularly, dancers now enjoy the interplay between partners to the full. Their eye-contact is sometimes carried to extremes, and the physical pleasure found in hand-turns or swings is open and unfettered. Energy and exuberance are more obvious than in the early days, and there may well be less elegance and refinement. Today's dancers let their enthusiasm and enjoyment create a wonderful community spirit, [which may help to explain why the establishment of annual "Playford Balls" has been growing in popularity around the country].

The way in which a country dancer moves and uses the body has also undergone some modification over the years. Changing footwear has had the biggest impact. Until World War II, dancers wore sneakers or gym shoes. The rubber soles gripped the dance floor and permitted the dancer[s] to lean, indeed to swoop into figures [of the dance]. . . . In the late 1940s, . . . May Gadd [the director of the English Country Dance Society in America urged dancers to wear "dancing shoes" and to maintain erect balance]. . . . The whole look of the dancing changed.

But still, by contrast with the robust, driving energy of the average American square or contra dance, English country dance as Sharp constructed and his followers have promoted it has very special qualities, hard to define or put into words. There is more lightness to it, the feeling of moving above the floor rather than sliding over it. There is a lilting to the step, never a march, dancing on the ball of the foot rather than coming down on the heels, though never dancing on the toes. The poise of the body is vitally important, relaxed yet standing tall. . . . [In short], there is a buoyant quality to English country dancing which comes from the ability to prepare oneself ahead of time and to appreciate the all-essential up-beat that launches the dancer from inaction into movement. . . .

[Maud Karpeles, one of Sharp's assistants and his disciple,] spoke with deep appreciation of his work: "Sharp made no attempt to give an exact reproduction of the style of dancing that may have been current in the seventeenth century, but allowed the style to be gradually evolved. The re-creation which was thus effected was a thing of great beauty: lovely to behold and completely satisfying to the dancers."[4]

NOTES

1. John Playford, *The English Dancing Master: Or Plaine and Easie Rules for Dancing of Country Dances, with the Tune to Each Dance* (London: John Playford, 1651).

2. Margaret Dean-Smith, *Playford's English Dancing Master, 1651* (London: Schott & Company, 1957), p. xix. A facsimile edition of the 1651 edition. Keller and Shimer's ellipsis.

3. Cecil Sharp, *English Country Dance, Graded Series,* vol. 3 (1911; reprint, London: Novello and Company, 1951), p. 10. Keller and Shimer's ellipses.

4. Maud Karpeles, *Cecil Sharp: His Life and Work* (London: Routledge and K. Paul, 1967), p. 104.

CHAPTER 8

The War of the Quadrilles: Creoles vs. Americans (1804)

Maureen Needham

On December 20, 1803, the United States flag was raised in New Orleans, officially transferring the Louisiana Territory to the United States. By January the New Orleans Creoles, French-speaking, Louisiana-born descendants of the Spanish and French settlers, constituting some 90 percent of the population of the city, were spoiling for a fight with the English-speaking newcomers. And fight they did, not on the battlefields but in the dance halls.

Participants at the public balls engaged in combat to assert their right to take the floor for the next dance. Whether it was to be a French quadrille or a Virginia reel became a matter to be settled under the dueling oaks in the early dawn. The disorder grew serious enough to engender prolonged correspondence between Secretary of State James Madison and the American governor, W. C. Claiborne, on the subject. The War of the Quadrilles, as it might aptly be termed, was even reported in newspaper headlines up and down the East Coast of the United States. An editor in the *New-York Herald,* on March 10, 1804, raised the specter of Napoleon's having perpetrated some kind of elaborate swindle in the Louisiana Purchase, and hinted that the Americans had been left to deal with the possibility of insurrection instigated by Creole Bonapartist sympathizers: "What the national consequences of this quarrel will be, God only knows. It is very apparent from the whole, taken together that it is the only breaking out of long smothered animosities of which we fear we have not heard the last. Bonaparte has got his millions of our money." Eventually the cultural clash between Creoles and Americans resulted in the first legislation enacted in the United States that ordered public ballrooms to maintain a set proportion of French quadrilles to English country dances, an eccentric anticipation of modern-day "equal opportunity" quota systems.

The citizens of New Orleans felt abandoned. Less than a month after the

Edited and abridged by the author, Maureen Needham [Costonis], "The War of the Quadrilles: Creoles vs. Americans, 1804," New York Public Library *Bulletin of the Humanities* 1 (1986–87): 63–81.

Spanish had originally ceded the Louisiana Territory to the new French governor, Pierre Clement de Laussat, the whole town turned out to watch the ceremonies marking Louisiana's transfer to the Americans on December 20, 1803. The (New Orleans) *Moniteur de la Louisiane* of January 2, 1804, reported that Creoles sobbed openly in frustration and despair while the French flag was lowered for the last time on the Place d'Armes, the square that today is located between the St. Louis Cathedral and the Mississippi River. The Creoles bitterly resented that the uncouth "Kaintucks" were now their masters. These emotions—resentment, fear, helplessness, and scorn—had simmered throughout 1803 in the cultural melting pot that New Orleans represented. The resultant volatile brew engendered the War of the Quadrilles, which ignited during January of 1804, that first month of American occupation.

In hindsight it seems predictable that the dance floor would become the nexus for this curious war between the Creole natives and American interlopers, because the New Orleanian had long been reputed to be extravagantly devoted to the dance. Berquin-Duvallon marveled in 1802 that the women were content to remain uneducated but were so "passionately fond of dancing [that they would] pass whole nights in succession at this exercise."[1] A French visitor to the city the next year was equally impressed. Even compared to the luxurious resources of Saint Dominigue, he claimed, "it's the land where they dance more than any other."[2] The New Orleans *Abeille* reporter on April 2, 1829, summarized the views of nearly all observers with his boast, "On aime passionnément la danse à la Nouvelle-Orléans" (they passionately love the dance in New Orleans).

The Creoles devoted long hours to the dance, and were repaid by the expertise that they gained in the art. An English writer, Thomas Ashe, was lavish in his praises of the women: "Their persons are eminently lovely, and their movements indescribably graceful, far superior to any thing I ever witnessed in Europe . . . various charms of grace and symetry [sic] are heightened by the most enchanting expressions of joy and ilegance [sic] of motion."[3] Another writer was amazed at the children's proficiency: "The carriage of the infantile gentlemen was graceful and easy; and they wound through the mazes of the dance with an air of manliness and elegance truly French. But the tiny demoiselles moved with the lightness and grace of the fairies."[4] The famous architect Benjamin Henry Latrobe admitted, "the dancing of the ladies was what is to be expected of French women," but added with English disdain, "that of the Gentlemen, what Lord Chesterfield would have called too good for Gentlemen."[5]

By 1805 New Orleanians could attend balls every night of the week with their choice of fifteen different ballrooms in which to dance. Within the next ten years, thirty public ballrooms and innumerable private homes were available for their pleasure.[6] Balls would begin at eight o'clock or else directly after the opera performances at the opera house itself. They continued throughout the night, halted at three o'clock for a hearty breakfast (such as gumbo and venison) and would shut down operations when dawn interrupted to spoil the fun. In this respect the dances were similar to contemporary Mardi Gras balls.

It goes without saying that the ceremonies attendant upon the transfer of Louisiana from Spain to France to the United States provided many an occasion for sumptuous balls. When the Spanish returned the Louisiana Territory to the French government on December 4, 1803, the new French governor Pierre de Laussat celebrated the resumption of French rule after a forty-year hiatus. He threw an elaborate ball and described his invitation list as consisting of "one hundred women, for the most part beautiful or pretty, all well built, elegant, brilliantly attired and from one hundred and fifty to two hundred men."[7] The thoughtful custom to invite twice as many men as women was designed to keep the ladies dancing all evening long, and many Creoles continue this practice today. Banquet tables were lavishly set with fresh oysters and game. Laussat went so far as to arrange for toasts in several different colors of champagne to be drunk successively in honor of Spain, France, and the United States.

The ball's festivities commenced with a formal minuet danced by the marquis de Casa-Calvo, the senile Spanish commissioner, in which he was accompanied by Madame Almonaster, an enormously wealthy widow. General dancing continued scarcely without interruption for the next twelve hours. Even older women, whom Laussat mentioned in his diary as having "renounced participating in dances for many years before, developed a renewed taste for dancing."[8]

Out of sensitivity to American tastes, English country dance alternated one out of three rounds with French contredanses or quadrilles. Country dancers lined up in long rows and performed complicated formations in which the head couple "progressed" down to the end of the line. Quadrilles, in contrast, were performed by four or eight persons in a square formation. They were more lively than the minuets, which generally were used at the formal openings of a ball. These dances were danced to popular tunes executed with such rapidity that the dancers were often left breathless.[9]

At the French governor's ball ethnic divisions were clearly defined in the dance. The Creoles of French or mixed French-Spanish ancestry preferred the French quadrilles, whereas the Americans wanted to dance English country dances. However, the participants agreed to compromise. Waltzes, the favorite of the minority population who had been born in Spain, were deemed the most popular by the evening's end. At five in the morning, according to Laussat's diary, "The quadrilles were still going strong. At seven the boat dance, and the gallopades still survived and it was eight o'clock when the last of the gamesters left the tables and called it a day."[10]

Some three weeks later, on December 20, 1803, the French flag was officially lowered for the last time on Louisiana soil. Rumors flew about the city that all public balls were to be prohibited by the new American regime. The alarmed populace besieged the Americans for permission to continue their dances, and Governor William C. Claiborne reassured them by making a number of personal appearances at the public balls.

Both he and the former French governor attended the same ball on January 8, 1804, when a fierce quarrel erupted between the French and the Americans. Claiborne termed it a mere "fracas" and naively commented that it was quickly resolved. Laussat's account is more detailed:

> Two quadrilles, one French, the other English, were formed at once. An American, taking exception, brandished his stick over a fiddler, and there was at once, great turmoil. Claiborne . . . , finally, used more persuasion than rigor to prevail upon the American, who was but a surgeon attached to the detachment of soldiers who had come here. The French quadrille was allowed to go on, but the American interrupted it on its second time around with an English quadrille, taking his position on the floor; some one cried out: "If the women have a drop of French blood in their veins, they will not give in!"[11]

The ladies vanished from the ballroom in a scene worthy of Aristophanes, and Laussat noted that the former Spanish emissary, the marquis de Casa-Calvo, was laughing and remained later at the ball primarily to relish the Americans' embarrassment.

The Creoles and Americans geared up for more serious hostilities in time for the next ball on January 22. It may well have been this dance that the wealthy Creole Bernard de Marigny had in mind when he recalled that a certain ball was "selected to test which would carry it over the other, the waltz, or the reel."[12]

Claiborne was fair-minded enough to concede that some "warm and impudent young Men" of American extraction took the opportunity to make a "Theatre of all this Disorder."[13] Laussat simply blamed Claiborne, although he did agree that, from the very beginning of the ball, "the spirit being seen [was] generally inclined to show an ugly disposition."[14]

According to Laussat, the crowd grew unruly when rumors spread that a young Frenchman was under arrest for an unknown cause. General Wilkinson, the military governor, leaped upon a bench to address the crowd, but his

French was too poor to be understood. An impatient Creole interrupted with a call to resume the next quadrille. He was escorted from the room by armed guard. One insult led to another, and in an instant some thirty hot-headed Americans and Frenchmen had grabbed each other by the collars. The ladies hastily withdrew to safety. Armed partisans attacked and wounded the major participants, while others issued challenges to meet under the ancient dueling oaks early in the morning.

A squad of militia arrived. General Wilkinson broke into a loud patriotic rendition of "Hail, Columbia!" The Creoles countered with the "Marseillaise." Shouts of "Vive le République!" drowned out the ignominious retreat of Governor Claiborne and General Wilkinson. Most important of all, the musicians, too, made ready to depart. The ball was over, and it was not yet dawn.

Equal time should be offered to the American version at this point. The War of the Quadrilles offered choice morsels to U.S. news editors, and the story was reported from Washington to New York. The *New-York Herald,* March 10, 1804, printed a long dispatch, which excused the brouhaha on the grounds that it simply reflected cultural misunderstandings. When a French officer replied to General Wilkinson that "We want the Walse," his reply was in the French language, which "not being understood by the Americans, but on the contrary, being interpreted into a menace, increased the disorder."

U.S. Secretary of State James Madison grew alarmed at various reports of the growing polarization of the two cultures as seen at the dances. Claiborne admitted his embarrassment, and wisely proceeded to extricate himself from future responsibility. He "cheerfully" surrendered his authority in "this gallant duty" to the City Council, which stepped into the breech with a full set of regulations. This "Projet d'Arrête," signed January 25, 1804, contained eight articles designed to counter the types of disorders "which troubled the public balls last Sunday, the 22nd of this month." Citizens were prohibited from carrying arms into the ballroom and were required to leave them at the entrance checkroom. Governor Claiborne provided good example and voluntarily surrendered his sword at the door. Two city policemen were added to supervise guards, and the governor sent fifteen soldiers to assist. Arrest was sanctioned for any person who dared "interrupt any dance or tune." Furthermore, the City Council set the order of dances so as to prevent further quarrels over precedence. The new regulations specified that dances of English and French origin were to be rotated according to schedule: 2 French contredanses, 1 English contredanse (or country dance) performed by two sets of twelve couples, and 1 waltz. Thus the French, American, and Spanish dancing preferences were each represented.

The regulations, while born of good intentions, met with hostility. One witty mademoiselle of a prominent family harangued a group of malcontented dancers, "We have been Spaniards thirty years and the Spaniards have never forced us to dance the Fandango. We do not wish to dance either the reel or the jig." General Wilkinson translated her appeal into English, commanded the musicians to play the waltz, and, to the great astonishment of the entire gathering, began to waltz himself. The crowd huzzaed his gallantry and the "Anglo-Saxons, vanquished by beauty, commenced to waltz also."[15]

Peace overtures were subsequently extended. The Americans invited the Creoles to a "banquet of reconciliation." After a great deal of coaxing, the Creoles agreed. Presumably everyone was anxious for the balls to continue because the Mardi Gras season would soon draw near. It would have been characteristic of the Creoles that they preferred to forego their brawls in order to continue the balls. By year's end, Claiborne boasted of the "good order" in the city, where "two descriptions of Citizens meet frequently at the Theatre, Balls, and other places of Amusement, and pass their time in perfect Harmony."[16] He still did not feel comfortable enough to permit masked balls during the Mardi Gras season, for years to come.

Dance preferences are no longer the occasion for bloodshed in modern-day New Orleans. However, divisions on the dance floor do endure. Private Mardi Gras balls remain separated into those dominated by descendants of the old Creole families (as in the Krewe of Proteus) and those with Anglo-Saxon surnames (in the Krewe of Comus). African Americans have their own social organizations. One of the functions of the Mardi Gras balls is to introduce young debutantes of marriageable age to young men of acceptable lineage, so it would seem that the New Orleans ballroom continues to reinforce the ethnic and racial divisions in the city.

The 1804 War of the Quadrilles may have resulted in a mutually agreed upon cessation of hostilities at the public balls; but it could not be expected to resolve the issues of cultural or social precedence in this society, the first to be incorporated into the United States in which the Anglo-Saxon minority highhandedly refused to permit political power to be exercised by other European settlers who preceded them. The first skirmish between the two cultures took place on the dance floor; after that, the Creoles turned to the political process in order to agitate for their rights as United States citizens. Although the Creoles—and not the Americans who wished to continue in power—circulated petitions to Jefferson requesting statehood as early as the fall of 1804, it was not until April 8, 1812, that Louisiana was finally admitted.

NOTES

1. Berquin-Duvallon, *Travels in Louisiana and the Floridas in the Year 1802, Giving the Correct Picture of Those Countries,* trans. John Davis (New York: I. Riley & Company, 1806), p. 42.

2. Louis Baudry des Lozières, *Second Voyage à la Louisiane* (Paris: Chez Charles, 1803), vol. 1, p. 333.

3. Thomas Ashe, *Travels in America, Performed in 1806* (London: William Sawyer & Company, 1808), p. 343.

4. Joseph Holt Ingraham, *The South-West by a Yankee* (New York: Harper, 1835), p. 120.

5. Benjamin Henry Latrobe, *Impressions Respecting New Orleans,* ed. Samuel Wilson, Jr. (New York: Columbia University Press, 1951), p. 34.

6. Henry Kmen, *Music in New Orleans: The Formative Years, 1791–1841* (Baton Rouge: Louisiana State University Press, 1966), pp. 6–7.

7. Pierre Clement de Laussat, *Memoirs and Correspondence of Pierre Clement de Laussat,* trans. Henri Delville de Sinclair, typescript sponsored by WPA of Louisiana, 1940, p. 137, in author's collection.

8. Ibid., pp. 137–38.

9. Charles Compan, *Dictionnaire de danse* (1787; reprint, New York: Broude Brothers, 1974), pp. 101, 327–28.

10. Laussat, *Memoirs and Correspondence,* p. 138.

11. Ibid., pp. 156–57.

12. Bernard de Marigny, *Reflections on the Campaign of General Andrew Jackson* (New Orleans: J. L. Solee, 1848), trans. Grace King in *Louisiana Historical Quarterly* 6 (Jan., 1923): 78.

13. William Claiborne, *Official Letter Books of W. C. C. Claiborne,* ed. Dunbar Rowland (Jackson, Miss.: State Department of Archives and History, 1917), vol. 1, p. 354.

14. Laussat, *Memoirs and Correspondence,* p. 162.

15. Marigny, *Reflections on the Campaign,* p. 78.

16. Claiborne, *Official Letter Books,* vol. 3, p. 35.

CHAPTER 9

Sunday Afternoon Dances in Congo Square (1819)

Benjamin Henry Latrobe

[One day in February 1819, I accidentally stumbled] upon an assembly of negroes, which, I am told, every Sunday afternoon meets on the Common in the rear of the city. My object was to take a walk on the bank of the Canal Carondelet as far as the Bayou St. John. In going up St. Peter's Street and approaching the Common, I heard a most extraordinary noise, which I supposed to proceed from some horse-mill—the horses trampling on a wooden floor. I found, however, on emerging from the house to the Common that it proceeded from a crowd of five or six hundred persons assembled, in an open space or public square.[1] I went to the spot and crowded near enough to see the performance. All those who were engaged in the business seemed to be blacks. I did not observe a dozen yellow faces. They were formed into circular groups, in the midst of four of which that I examined (but there were more of them) was a ring, the largest not ten feet in diameter. In the first were two women dancing. They held each a coarse handkerchief, extended by the corners, in their hands, and set to each other in a miserably dull and slow figure, hardly moving their feet or bodies.

The music consisted of two drums and a stringed instrument. An old man sat astride of a cylindrical drum, about a foot in diameter, and beat it with incredible quickness with the edge of his hand and fingers. The other drum was an open-staved thing held between the knees and beaten in the same manner. They made an incredible noise. The most curious instrument, however, was a stringed instrument, which no doubt was imported from Africa. On the top of the finger board was the rude figure of a man in a sitting posture, and two pegs behind him to which the strings were fastened. The body was a calabash. It was played upon by a very little old man, apparently eighty or ninety years old.

Excerpt from Benjamin Henry Latrobe, *The Journal of Latrobe* (1905; reprint, New York: Burt Franklin, 1971), pp. 179–82. Paragraph divisions have been added by the editor of this anthology.

The women squalled out a burden to the playing, at intervals, consisting of two notes, as the negroes working in our cities respond to the song of their leader. Most of the circles contained the same sort of dancers. One was larger, in which a ring of a dozen women walked, by way of dancing, round the music in the center. But the instruments were of different construction. One which from the color of the wood seemed new, consisted of a block cut into something of the form of a cricket bat, with a long and deep mortise down the center. This thing made a considerable noise, being beaten lustily on the side by a short stick. In the same orchestra was a square drum, looking like a stool, which made an abominable, loud noise; also a calabash with a round hole in it, the hole studded with brass nails, which was beaten by a woman with two short sticks.

A man sung an uncouth song to the dancing, which I suppose was in some African language, for it was not French, and the women screamed a detestable burden on one single note. The allowed amusements of Sunday have, it seems, perpetuated here those of Africa among its inhabitants. I have never seen anything more brutally savage and at the same time dull and stupid, than this whole exhibition.

Continuing my walk about a mile along the canal, and returning after sunset near the same spot, the noise was still heard. There was not the least disorder among the crowd, nor do I learn, on inquiry, that these weekly meetings of the negroes have ever produced any mischief.

NOTE

1. Editor's note: Known in those days as Congo Square, and later mythologized as the location of jazz's birthplace, Beauregard Square now fronts the New Orleans Municipal Auditorium on Rampart Street.

CHAPTER 10

Japanese *Bon* Dance Survivals in Hawai'i (1982)

Judy Van Zile

The *O-Bon* festival and New Year are the two most important occasions in the Japanese Buddhist calendar. With origins traced to Sanskrit India, the *O-Bon* celebration gradually worked its way through Asia until it reached Japan. When Japanese emigrants left their homeland, starting in 1868, to work on Hawai'i's sugar plantations, they brought these and many other traditional celebrations with them. The *O-Bon* festival, and the dancing that is one component, gradually became a regular part of life in the islands. At the same time it continued to be integral to Japanese celebrations, it became accessible to people of all ethnicities.

Sanskrit religious texts relate that *bon* dancing originated with a dance performed by Mauggallena (which became Mokuren in Japanese), one of the disciples of the Buddha. Because of meritorious actions, he was granted the power to see beyond the surface reality of the world. Through this power he saw that his mother had been condemned to a world of suffering and hunger because of ill deeds she performed during her lifetime.

Mauggallena tried to aid his mother by sending her a bowl of rice. Each time she tried to eat it, however, it burst into flames. Mauggallena turned to his teacher for advice on how to help his mother. The priest told him to feed the priestly spirits on the fifteenth day of the seventh month. Mauggallena did so and then saw that his mother had been freed from her suffering. He saw her carrying a tray of food and dancing. Mauggallena was so happy that he, too, danced for joy. People around him became greatly excited and joined in his dancing.

Buddha's disciples in India continued to celebrate this event, and as Buddhism spread to China and Japan, so did the festival. When it reached Japan,

This essay has been adapted by the author, Judy Van Zile, from her book *The Japanese Bon Dance in Hawaii* (Kailua: Press Pacifica, 1982).

it merged with indigenous celebrations and became a dance to honor the dead performed for three days in mid-July as a part of *O-Bon.*

Traditional belief maintains that the souls of the departed return to earth to be with the living during *O-Bon.* Thus, although the occasion honors the dead, it is a joyous event celebrating the temporary return of the souls and expressing happiness at their achieving a higher state of being. The activities of the observance occur between the thirteenth and seventeenth days of the seventh month, traditionally according to the solar calendar. Celebrations include the cleaning of graves of ancestors and friends; the placing of food offerings on graves; devotions at the family altar in the home and at grave sites; recitation of scriptural verses; participation in a special temple service; lighting of welcome and farewell fires; the use of lanterns, and, in some places, floating lanterns to guide the souls on their return to earth and then back to the spirit world; and dancing.

While the original festival lasted only three days, the "*Bon* dance season" in Hawai'i extends from the end of June to early September. Extending the dates occurred as early as 1938, and most likely began because temples chose to celebrate according to either the solar or lunar calendar (there being approximately a month's difference in time between them); priests from neighboring temples were invited as guest speakers for services; and weekends relatively free of *O-Bon* celebrations in neighboring communities were sought in order to foster the success of their own events.[1]

Over time, another consideration for some temples became the availability of dance and music clubs, whose participation was deemed important to the success of celebrations. Because there are so many Japanese temples in Hawai'i and only a limited number of *bon* dance clubs, a schedule is established whereby club members participate at one temple usually for two consecutive nights and proceed to different temples each weekend. Thus, during any summer weekend a *bon* dance may be observed at one, and often several, temples.

Each *bon* dance club, with the exception of one, specializes in the music and/ or dance of one of the prefectures of Hawai'i's early immigrants. The tradition highlighted at a particular temple depends on the place of origin of the ancestors of temple members, personal preferences of temple members, and availability of the clubs. Some clubs provide musicians and a group of dancers to lead the dancing, as well as several rehearsal sessions at the host temple prior to the dance so that temple members may refresh their memories of old dances and learn new ones. Other clubs provide only live music, and one provides only dancers.

Temples that do not rely on the formal *bon* dance clubs enlist the services of temple members, teachers from nearby Japanese dance studios, or visiting teachers from other islands or from Japan. They, too, provide for several nights of rehearsal prior to the actual *bon* dance. At these temples music is provided by commercially recorded discs, tape recordings, or a few individuals who can sing some of the songs or play the drums.

Bon dancing in Hawai‘i is as much an occasion for socializing as it is a religious event. Young and old gather to participate as well as to chat and observe the dancing. Concessionaires set up booths to sell such Japanese snacks as *saimin* (noodles in a soup broth), thin slices of barbecued beef on sticks, and such American favorites as hot dogs and soft drinks. Temple donations are always accepted, and the amount and donor's name are often written on white strips of paper and displayed where all may see. Formerly donations were frequently material goods such as sacks of rice and kegs of fish.

Tenugui (small towels approximately the size of hand towels), with a special design for each temple or Buddhist sect, are given to members of the participating clubs. At some temples they are given to all participants, and at others to anyone who wishes to make a donation to the temple. At some temples, for an additional donation one can have his or her name written on the towel in Japanese lettering.

Many people of non-Japanese ancestry participate in *bon* dancing. Attendance ranges from one hundred to two hundred in rural communities to as many as one thousand at some of the larger temples in Honolulu. Each dance is led by members of a *bon* dance club or temple members who know the dances. However, anyone may participate and people of non-Japanese origin are genuinely encouraged to do so.

The *bon* dance is performed out-of-doors, usually in the evening, and generally follows the *segaki*, a religious ceremony to honor deceased ancestors. The considerably larger number of people participating in the dancing as compared with the numbers attending the service undoubtedly reflects the change in focus from religious to secular and social. Dancing begins at 7:30 or 8:00 P.M. and continues until between 10:30 and 11:30. In some rural areas where the *bon* dance stands out as a major event, the dancing may continue until midnight. With increasing enforcement of noise codes, however, temples in residential areas frequently shorten their celebrations.

The dance formation is typically a circle or several concentric circles, depending on the number of participants. Musicians are usually in the center, in a *yagura* (a tower approximately ten feet square and fifteen to twenty feet high, from which paper lanterns may be strung) assembled for the occasion. Recorded music for modern dances is amplified through speakers.

In addition to the instrumental music and the sung text, one may also hear *hayashi*. These are mnemonic syllables or phrases interspersed between verses of the sung text. They may be called out by anyone, whether dancer or spectator. When live music is used, a designated club member tries to lead the dancers in calling out the *hayashi*.

Standard attire for *bon* dancing is a *yukata* (lightweight cotton summer *kimono*), *obi* (sash), *tabi* (white bifurcated socks), and *zori* (straw or rubber slippers). Occasionally *geta* (wooden slippers) are worn, and *tasuki* (long cloth sashes) are used to tie back the *yukata* sleeves. The *tasuki* are tucked into the *obi* when not in use, as are other implements used in some of the dances, such as fans and sticks with small paper flags on them. The *tasuki* are most often used in dances where such properties are manipulated, to keep the sleeves out of the way.

Those who are not *bon* dance club members may join in the dancing, but most temples request that they wear a *yukata* or *happi* coat (a short jacket-type top resembling the top portion of a *yukata*). Men often wear *happi* coats sporting the insignia of a *bon* dance club, temple, or other organization on the back and dark-colored trousers. Over the years the younger generation, both male and female, began wearing *happi* coats of brightly colored Hawaiian floral print fabrics. And in 1979 one club adopted *yukata* of a Hawaiian-style fern print in shades of blue and white.

Some temples inform those in attendance (through the public address system used for announcements or for singers) that they may not participate unless appropriately attired. But a few temples are no longer concerned with what dancers wear, and female dancers may be seen wearing pants and *happi* coats and dancers of either sex may be seen in almost any attire. At temples where specific attire is requested, however, during the last dance of the evening everyone may join in, regardless of what they are wearing.

Some *O-Bon* celebrations include the presence of one or more individuals wearing humorous or grotesque masks. These individuals are usually extrovert men who may be imitating a family member in whose memory they are dancing, may simply be providing a humorous touch,[2] or may be attempting to disguise themselves.[3]

Some temples occasionally invite a folk dance group from Japan or students from a local Japanese dance studio to participate in their celebration. Toward the middle of the evening local participants withdraw from the performing area to observe a special presentation staged by the visiting group. The evening then concludes with some of the typical dances in which all may participate. These appearances by visiting performers tend to attract large crowds.

Each *O-Bon* celebration has its own distinctive quality, and some include practices not found at other temples. One of the most well known is held at the Haleiwa Jodo Mission, next to a beach on Oʻahu's north shore. The celebration occurs early in August, and begins in the same manner as other dances. About 10:00 P.M. on the second evening, dancers and spectators (of which there are usually a great number) begin to wander down to the edge of the water, where a brief religious service is held. Then, one by one, celebrants wade a short distance into the water to set adrift *toronagashi,* small paper boats with candles on them, to guide the souls of the ancestors on their return to the spirit world. Several hundred boats are set afloat, and the gently bouncing light of the candles harkens back to practices originating in celebrations in Japan in towns located on rivers or the ocean.

Some people attend one *bon* dance during the summer—that of the temple to which they belong or that of a temple close to where they live. But some people attend many *bon* dances. There is a relatively large group of people, particularly on the island of Oʻahu, who participate in *bon* dances every weekend throughout the summer months. While many of these regular participants are senior citizens and/or members of *bon* dance clubs, some are younger people who simply go from temple to temple on their own.

What draws people to participate in such an activity so often during the summer months? While motivations are as varied as the number of participants, some are fulfilling a religious obligation. Others are simply enjoying a family activity. Members of one non-Japanese Christian family belong to a *bon* dance club and feel that this allows their family to do something together. "It's the night set aside for family fun," they say, but also point out that the children understand the religious overtones, which allows them to experience other cultures and appreciate that all are equal.[4]

A middle-aged woman of pure Hawaiian ancestry was an active participant for many years in one of the *bon* dance clubs. In addition to dancing, she sang and played an instrument with the club's musical ensemble. She felt a sense of responsibility to show active participation by members of non-Japanese ethnic groups.

The most frequently stated reasons for participating in *bon* dances are simply to have a good time, get together with old friends, and make new friends. Equally alluring, however, are the balmy summer Hawaiian nights, the aroma of freshly cooked snacks, and the comfortably paced rhythmic music with easy, repetitive movement patterns that do not have to be rigidly followed.

Hawaiʻi's *bon* dance clubs developed for two primary reasons. First, it is considered important to have live music and dancers who know traditional dances at *O-Bon* celebrations. Second, the overall social nature of *bon* dancing and *O-Bon* celebrations is fostered by assuring the participation of a significant number of club members.

One of the oldest clubs is the Ewa Bon Odori Club (*odori* simply means "dance"). The group takes its name from the Ewa area of Oʻahu, an old plantation region west of Honolulu. As original members of the club passed away, those remaining became worried that eventually no one would carry on the tradition. They turned to a local high school to seek out students taking flute lessons, as the flute is an important part of their musical ensemble. Several students began to play with the club, and eventually learned to drum as well.

One of the largest groups is the Fukushima Bon Dance Club. Originally comprised primarily of individuals who traced their ancestry to Fukushima prefecture in Japan, the club was formally incorporated in 1964. The club has its own musicians, and dancers and musicians number approximately one hundred. The group meets periodically during the year on special occasions, such as the New Year, an important birthday of a member, or the visit of people from Japan. Dancing, including *bon* dancing, is usually a part of these occasions.

Just prior to the summer months the group meets more frequently. Several times a week they gather to review old dances and learn new ones that will be performed during the coming months. The oldest dances they perform are *Fukushima Ondo* and *Yagi Bushi.* The sources of these dances are unknown, but they have been performed in Hawaiʻi as long as most dancers can remember, and are believed to have originally been performed in Japan. Other dances are learned at *kokan,* or exchange parties. When dancers from Japan come to Hawaiʻi there is usually a social gathering, and in this setting those in attendance often teach each other new dances.

Another major source of dances for many of the clubs is the Hawaiʻi Minyo Kai (Hawaiʻi Folk Dance Association). In 1961 and 1962 the United Japanese Society and the Japanese Chamber of Commerce brought folk dance groups and teachers from Japan to Hawaiʻi. Dances taught by the visiting teachers, either in their original or an adapted form, began to be used at *O-Bon* celebrations. In 1963 these gatherings of dance enthusiasts led to the establishment of the Hawaiʻi Minyo Kai. In subsequent years teachers from Japan have been invited to teach workshops, and many members of different *bon* dance clubs have joined. Many of the dances taught, or adaptations of them, are included in *O-Bon* celebrations.

The existence of formal *bon* dance and *bon* dance music clubs is most extensive on the island of Oʻahu. On the other islands dance leadership typically comes from members of temple women's clubs or wives of ministers. These people learn new dances from visiting dance teachers or at workshops sponsored by headquarters of various Buddhist sects. Many temples maintain a close relationship with other temples on their islands, and members who know dances share their knowledge and happily participate in more than one *O-Bon* celebration.

In continuing the *bon* dance tradition, the Japanese, like many ethnic groups in Hawai'i, maintain traditional practices, foster an understanding of such practices among members of the younger generation, and mark their distinctive identity in a multicultural community.

NOTES

1. Katsumi Onishi, "'*Bon*' and '*Bon-Odori*' in Hawaii," *Social Process in Hawaii* 4 (1938): 50.
2. Barbara B. Smith, personal communication, 1978, Honolulu, Hawai'i.
3. Onishi, "'*Bon*' in Hawaii," p. 56.
4. Joe Paganiban, "The *Bon* Dance—It's a Family Affair for Christians, Too," *Sunday Star Bulletin and Advertiser,* June 25, 1987, sec. A, p. 8.

CHAPTER 11

All Lined Up at the Wildhorse Saloon (1997)

Maureen Needham

Perhaps you've come across the country line-dancers on TNN while you were idly gunning the channels on your television set. It's really rather picturesque to watch the clouds of cowboy hats drift from left to right as the dancers spin across the tube. Although you'd never admit to it, perhaps you've managed to stagger up from the couch and tried a move or two when nobody

Maureen Needham, originally published as "Everybody Move!" in *The Nashville Scene,* Sept. 18, 1997. This version has been edited and abridged by the author.

was looking. If you cared to, you could even go one step further and visit the scene in person—the show is taped at the Wildhorse Saloon, deep in the heart of tourist tinsel-town on Second Avenue in Nashville, Tennessee.

If you have yet to attain the fabled 15 minutes of fame that Andy Warhol touted as the birthright of every American, this is your chance. What an opportunity—to be on national television every night of the week! Regular dancers on The Nashville Network's *Live at the Wildhorse Saloon* often find themselves approached by strangers seeking autographs.

Best of all, you don't even need to know how to dance; the club offers free lessons to all newcomers. A lithe young dancing instructor, dressed in cowboy boots and hat, lackadaisically goes through the motions while an earnest crew of youngsters and oldsters follows her every move. More or less.

The instructor's voice crackles into the portable microphone: "Put your right foot out." Most people can manage that. "Together! Left foot stamp!" OK so far. Grins of relief all around. "Whirl halfway about and step forward three counts, end on the right!" Whoopsadaisy! Lost her there.

By the time the thirty-minute lesson is done, however, there is a palpable semblance of confidence on the floor. The motley crew has changed into a purposeful covey of dancers moving in step. A trio of teen-aged girls occasionally heads in the wrong direction, collapsing in loud giggles exquisitely calculated to attract everyone's attention. A little girl skips about in lively insouciance, her long hair flowing behind her. Mom and Dad attempt the choreography while their daughter plays London Bridge and cuts between them. A couple, dressed in sneakers and shorts, solemnly passes them by, their faces furrowed with concentration as they privately intone the rhythmic count.

The music revs up even more. Breathing hard from the exertion, the dancers eventually take a well-deserved break. An exuberant spirit of accomplishment and self-congratulation fills the air as people smile broadly, hug or slap each other on the back, and stroll off for a drink. A few remain on the floor to practice the hard bits while the leader intones with forced cheerfulness, "Don't go away! We'll be right back for more at 5 o'clock!"

Twice per week, the television crews invade, and the atmosphere is charged with electricity. In all, five tapings are filmed from 7 to 10 o'clock, but the TNN film editors parcel them out over the length of a week. There is time out for promotions (euphemistically called interviews) of young hopeful country music stars and, of course, for commercial breaks courtesy of the sponsors. Some of the regular dancers also use the occasion to change their costumes so that—heaven forbid!—they won't be seen on national television in the same outfits three days running.

These regulars have a culture of their own. They pretend not to notice any-thing other than the dance itself, whereas tourists tend to stop all dancing and grin directly at the camera if it happens to pan their direction. On occasion the better dancers might perform a special spin or a personalized, highly in-dividualistic combination of steps. Before you can say "Jack Robinson," the red light of the camera eye swoops in for a close-up. The cameraman dances about the couple for a minute or two and then moves on.

The majority of the dancers come as couples. Most of the regulars know and dance only with each other—otherwise, a good dancer might get stuck wres-tling with someone who can't keep a simple beat. Some couples even go so far as to dress in matching outfits, with identical silver belt buckles, snakeskin boots, and glitzy cowboy shirts. It's almost a rule of thumb: the more conspic-uously dressed the female, the less need there is for the man to dress in flam-boyant style. A peroxide blonde in gingham miniskirt, laced bodice, and dar-ingly low-cut blouse needs only to be accompanied by a man in understated black T-shirt, black jeans, and good guy's white cowboy hat.

Other dancers are less concerned with appearances. One regular maintains that he does not set much store on changing into fancy outfits, unless he sweats so much that he needs to change his shirt. Tourists tend to dress down for the occasion, although maybe "undress" is a more accurate description. Guys might wear a baseball cap, cut-offs, and T-shirt. A woman wearing midriffs may accessorize with the latest in navel rings, which peek out over her too-tight Big Western belt buckle. Cowboy boots are *de rigeur* for the evening's attire. Some of the young women sport combat boots instead, and not a few non-locals wear dirty white sneakers onto the highly polished wooden floor.

Even when men and women dress alike, they definitely do not dance the same. Ginger Rogers once quipped that she did everything Fred Astaire did, except she did it backwards and in high heels. At the Wildhorse, macho men wear high heels on their cowboy boots, but they still steer their women back-wards across the dance floor. In time-honored tradition, the men keep the women off-balance in a series of twirls, dips, and complex cross-overs. It is "women's work" simply to be passive and follow in the man's footsteps.

Women, however, may use more extravagant gestures than men, just as they are allowed to dress in a more conspicuous manner. The guys loop their fingers in their belts, hold their arms behind their backs, and keep their gestures close to the body. Never do they display themselves in a suggestive manner, swing-ing hips or tossing hair about, as the women may. In short, women may make a statement about their feminine attractions while men display their power.

Dancing at the Wildhorse is not about dance prowess à la John Travolta cavorting on the disco floor. The level of dance complexity remains low, for the most part, and there's a reason for that. This is democracy in action, in a way, with the joys of dance accessible to all, young and old alike. The experience offers a brief glimpse of fame and glory to anyone who takes the trouble to show up on a weekday night and learn a few steps in tandem before stepping out in front of the cameras.

One thing, though. You do need to know your right foot from your left. You'd be surprised how many people don't.

CHAPTER 12

Swingin' Out:
Southern California's Lindy Revival (2000)

Juliet McMains and Danielle Robinson

We scuffle along the sidewalk in our sandals and vintage rayon dresses, clutching our notebooks as we hurry past sailors, bobby-soxers and GI's also headed for Culver City's Satin Ballroom. It is just past 8 o'clock on Saturday night, January 22, 2000, but already parking spots within four blocks of the dance hall are an impossible find. Tickets, which run us $15 apiece, grant us entry into the lobby where we gaze upon vendors displaying used shoes from 1942 with $90 price tags. An eager hairstylist stands by to mold women's hair into neatly pinned barrel curls for a mere $8. Chicklet-colored zoot suit imitations are displayed next to CD racks filled with the jazz greats of yesteryear. Inside the auditorium, eager-eyed neophytes struggle to control their flailing limbs, while more poised bodies expertly mirror each other in rhythmical foot flurry. The evening's main musical attraction is a 15-piece big band in class-B army uniforms ready to revive the musical classics of the 1940s. As the trumpets lead in the first set, one of us is swept onto the dance floor by a nineteen-year-old in a plaid sweater vest and a newsboy cap. The other takes the opportunity

Juliet McMains and Danielle Robinson wrote this essay specifically for this collection.

Jitterbugs, 1943. Leon James and Willa Mae Ricker perform "Air Steps." Photo by Gjon Mili, *Life Magazine,* Aug. 23, 1943, p. 100. By permission of Time/Warner Publications.

to slip back into the lobby in search of authentic wedge sandals, for which we have fruitlessly searched ever since we first awkwardly tried to lindy hop in spiked heels.

We found ourselves in the midst of this swing revival two years ago when we moved to Southern California for graduate study in dance history and theory. Both of us had considerable prior experience with partner dancing, but the movement we encountered on our first Monday night at the Derby, L.A.'s most renowned swing club, only slightly resembled the swing dance we had learned back home at Fred Astaire dance studios. These dancers were not transferring their weight in the bouncy triplet that is the hallmark of East Coast swing dancing. Instead, they were shuffling along the floor at fantastical speeds, moving deftly in and out of eight and six count rhythms, adding in their own syncopations and swivels every few bars.

This night at the Satin Ballroom marks our first entry into the community as deliberate scholars—we are armed with interview protocols and knowledge of swing's documented historical development. We find that we are not alone in this research endeavor, for we have been far outdone by the participants themselves. Indeed, one of the most unusual aspects of today's swing revival is that contemporary lindy hoppers are *obsessed* with their dance's history and its origins—theirs is a perpetual search for the ever-elusive, authentic "swing." The word "vintage" is a crucial term for this community, because dancers are fueled by a commitment to re-creating the past—the movement, mores, fashion, and music of the "swing era." Mainstreamers, newcomers, and scholar-dancers, in contrast, are instantly identifiable as novices by telltale signs such as '90s shoes, haircuts, and pseudo-swing skirts. We tried our best, with sparkling barrettes to distract from our very modern haircuts and heeled sandals that give the illusion of a wedge, but we cannot compete with those living the vintage lifestyle.

It is not long before we identify the "Cat's Corner," where the hippest dancers are jammin', challenging each other with their vintage moves and attire. Mr. and Ms. November, as pictured in our newly purchased Southern California Girls of Swing calendar, are swiveling and flicking in intricate syncopations which they claim to have reconstructed after hours of research at the UCLA film archives. Most dancers are expert researchers themselves, reconstructing the swing era with rigorous attention to historical detail and accuracy. Many women, for example, go so far as to sleep in pin curls and wear period underpinnings, including seamed hosiery. The men of the swing revival sport their grandfather's wing tips or two-toned spectator shoes with a pair of jaunty suspenders to hold up their loose fitting trousers. Swing has become a lifestyle in addition to a dance phenomenon. Hard-core devotees drive vintage cars, carry long-chained pocket watches, and listen to "real" swing music (big band music from the golden era). More than just a fashion show, this preoccupation with authenticity translates into a requirement that all committed swing dancers know its history.

As we interview our way across the ballroom floor, we realize that nearly every dedicated dancer we meet at the Satin Ballroom can recite a history of swing's origins and revival. One of the most common is that the lindy hop, the original swing dance, was born between 1927 and 1928 in New York City.[1] A Harlem Savoy Ballroom dancer named "Shorty" Snowden invented it to appease the boredom of a dance marathon contest. When a reporter asked him what he was doing, he replied "the lindy," naming it after Charles Lindbergh's recent "hop" across the Atlantic. He won the contest and took the dance back with him to the Savoy Ballroom, where it eventually became the most popular social dance of the '30s and early '40s, circulating under the name jitterbug as well as swing, lindy hop, and jive. Although swing music and dance emerged out of black cultural practices in New York City, by the '40s, swing had been appropriated by white bands, dancers, and the social dance industry to be championed as *the* American dance form. World War II played a key role in dissemination of the jitterbug, as GI's stationed on the West Coast and abroad indulged in America's "true national folk dance."[2] What made the lindy unlike any other mainstream American social dance up to that time was its "break-away" or "swing-out," which created a designated space for improvisation within the dance, mimicking the improvisational structure of the jazz music. So while it was still a partnered dance form in which the men led and women followed, moments of individual creativity figured prominently.

The quest to recover the past has characterized the swing revival from its earliest days. A favorite story of the revival begins in 1986 when Pasadena Ballroom Dance Association members sought out one of the original Savoy Ballroom swing dancers—Frankie Manning. As a result of their pilgrimage, Manning has become one of the most revered icons of the swing world today. After inventing swing's first aerial steps in 1936, he helped usher swing dancing into a new phase where it moved from social dance floors to Broadway stages and film screens. This new breed of professional swing dancers developed more athletic and spectacular moves to seduce audiences with their high-flying acrobatics and visually stunning tricks. For over a decade, Manning was a lead dancer and choreographer for Whitey's Lindy Hoppers, one of the African American dance troupes organized by former Savoy bouncer Herbert White, who negotiated their entry into mainstream American movies, nightclubs, musicals, and vaudeville, not to mention European and South American tours. But by the '50s, the swing era was tapering off as a result of pressures from wartime entertainment taxes and the rising popularity of bebop's new un-danceable rhythms, propelling Frankie Manning into retirement from the stage. Following his "rescue" from thirty years of work for the United States Postal Service, Manning has been elevated to the status of a demigod of the swing revival. At age eighty-six, he tours the world, giving workshops and sharing his love of lindy hop with a new generation.

Manning represents only one side of a tension-filled split in Southern California between two styles of lindy hop, the Savoy style (Frankie Manning at the helm) and the Dean Collins style (a.k.a. Hollywood, smooth, or GI style). Dean Collins, who was one of the many whites who flocked to the Savoy to absorb the energy and excitement of this new Harlem dance culture, moved from the East Coast to Los Angeles in 1937 and began choreographing lindy hop scenes for film.[3] The style he popularized on the West Coast is character-ized as more upright and smoother than the Savoy style, seeming to parallel categories used by some dance scholars to distinguish between African-derived and European-derived dance aesthetics.[4] Because the Hollywood-style danc-ers use each other's body weight for counterbalance, they are able to produce more dynamic and faster changes of body position. Savoy dancers, on the other hand, have a much looser connection that enables more space for individual improvisation for both the leader and the follower. Other characteristic dif-ferences include more bounce in the Savoy style as well as a more hunched-over body position, the use of kicks, and the incorporation of Charleston-derived patterns. In contrast, Dean Collins style dancers claim they are trying to produce the effect of a calm torso, undisturbed by the frenzy of the feet below. A Savoy breakaway is more playful and rounded than the whip of a Hollywood dancer's swing-out in which the leader sends his partner back out on a linear path or "slot."

Both camps are represented this night at the Satin Ballroom. The tension between them is articulated by the emcee who diplomatically points out the harmony symbolized by having both styles of lindy hop dancers sharing the floor peacefully. His exaggerated enthusiasm betrays the remaining rift between the two groups, and echoes the controversy that erupted at a recent dance contest sponsored by the Pasadena Ballroom Dance Association. Shortly be-fore the contest began, organizers announced that judges would base their decisions according to the aesthetics of "African American based" swing danc-ing. While swing dancers themselves seldom refer to the two styles in black and white terms (even though the forefathers they worship in each respective style may suggest such a racial divide), this move to privilege Savoy style as the "real" swing met with harsh criticism from Hollywood and Savoy dancers alike.

For all their careful research into movement, music, and fashion of the '30s and '40s, today's swingers tend to underplay the strained race relations, economic disparities, and social inequalities out of which swing dance and music emerged. While many African American legends of swing music and dance are worshiped, few white swing revivalists recognize their own possible participation in a legacy of appropriation. People tend to overlook swing's journey out of Harlem and into mass popularity, only *after* white big bands took to entertainment circuits, and its subsequent absorption in a largely white ballroom dance industry that no longer acknowledged swing's African American origins.

Indeed, they focus on its positive effects—an activity that transcends political concerns as peoples from almost every racial and ethnic group in the Los Angeles area come together under its auspices. However, the "past" swing revivalists tend to reinhabit is a distinctly white one that is filled with argyled co-eds and World War II GI's who are perpetually on leave, never quite at the front. They tend to overlook sentiments such as those expressed by Norma Miller, another of Whitey's Lindy Hoppers, who discussed the 1940s' absorption of African American lindy hop into mainstream American culture: "[The lindy hop is] part of our history. We sweated for that. We busted our butts to get that the way it was. And that's ours. We created it. It came out of the blood and sweat of Harlem."[5]

Yet, most of Southern California's primarily white (and Asian) swing practitioners, who tend to cluster between the ages of seventeen and twenty-five, imagine they are dancing themselves back into a so-called simpler time—a time when "men were men and women were women" and the gender roles in courtship were much more clear. "It was good times back then," insists an avid swing dancer at the Satin Ballroom who lives a vintage lifestyle as exemplified by his 1955 Bel Air. Another swing fanatic's Web site is headed by a banner that encapsulates this nostalgia: "My goal in life is to promote world peace by spreading the love of Lindy Hop!" These neo-swingers are reconstructing a romanticized past that neglects the racial strife that divided a segregated America at mid-century and continues to plague the United States today through more covert means.

When we ask people why swing is experiencing a renaissance today, the common quip is that swing never died. But no one denies that it went underground, out of popular circulation, or that it mutated into variants such as the East Coast swing taught in ballroom dance studios, the slower and more laid-back

West Coast swing, and the English jive known as the international dancesport competition standard. The past ten years have witnessed a surge of popularity in all forms of partner dancing—including ballroom, salsa, tango, hustle, and of course swing. This increase is often linked by journalists, cultural critics, and the dancers themselves to the isolation created by modern technology and visual culture as well as the health dangers of casual sex. A craving for physical intimacy is exemplified by a T-shirt logo we see emblazoned across the breasts of one young Satin Ballroom patron, "Lindy Whore." While lindy dancers may "dance around" with a selection of different partners during the course of an evening, their community is primarily based on an ethic of "good clean fun," safe partner swapping in the age of AIDS. Nineties swing dancers often cite contemporary movies that feature swing dancing (*Swing Kids* and *Swingers,* in particular) and the infamous 1998 Gap commercial set to Louis Prima's "Jump, Jive and Wail" as the impetus for their own embrace of swing. It seems more likely, though, that these films and commercials latched onto the coattails of a movement that was already underway and propelled by the emergence of early '90s neo-swing bands, such as the Brian Setzer Orchestra, Big Bad Voodoo Daddy, and Royal Crown Revue.

As we prepare to take our leave of the Satin Ballroom, we are introduced to Hal Takier, 1948 Harvest Moon Ball Jitterbug Contest winner. When we ask him to compare the swing revival to his experience in the golden era, he notes that they didn't have films or teachers as authorized experts, but "back then we had to make it up ourselves." Somehow in lindy hop's forty-year period of dormancy, its essence switched from invention to preservation. Ironically enough, the reconstruction of the past with letter-perfect accuracy has led some to miss the core tenet of pre-revival swing dancing—innovation, that is, improvisation. During the swing era, dancers abided by a tacit mandate never to copy exactly anyone else's steps. Yes, they borrowed ideas from each other but always varied each pilfered step slightly to make it their own, which ensured continual growth of the form. Perhaps the occasional merging of "authentic" swing moves and more contemporary movement practices (such as salsa and hip hop) is not "flawed" reconstruction that compromises the authenticity of the form but is in fact a step closer to the spirit in which swing was first practiced.

But the neo-swing obsession with authenticity is infectious. We can't seem to leave the club without tracking down just one more lead on '40s style wedge sandals. Almost an hour later, we exit clutching new swing CDs, a swing guidebook, and multiple Web addresses for vintage wear, optimistic that we will be able to return as true hepkittens. Unfortunately, a few modem calls later, we discover that although you can buy a variety of two-toned shoes named after some of the most memorable swing steps (boogie woogie, suzy-Q, balboa), wedge sandals are SOLD OUT. We resign ourselves to a hybrid existence, forever constrained by our modern bodies, our modern shoes, and an inescapable nostalgia signified by our continuing quest for white wedge sandals in a size six.

NOTES

1. Marshall Stearns and Jean Stearns, *Jazz Dance: The Story of American Vernacular Dance* (1968; reprint, New York: Da Capo Press, 1994), pp. 315–16.

2. *Life Magazine,* Aug. 23, 1943, p. 96.

3. Peter Loggins, "Los Angeles Area History of Swing Dancing," *The Hollywood Jitterbugs: Swing Preservation Club.* Online, Feb. 1, 2000. Degen Pener, *The Swing Book* (Boston: Back Bay Books, 1999).

4. Brenda Dixon Gottschild, *Digging the Africanist Presence in American Performance: Dance and Other Contexts* (Westport, Conn.: Greenwood Press, 1996), pp. 8–9.

5. Norma Miller, interviewed in *Dancing.* Created by Rhoda Grauer and produced by 13/NET in association with RM Arts and BBC-TV. Chicago: Home Vision videotape, 1993.

SUGGESTED BOOKS AND FILMS

Aldrich, Elizabeth. *From the Ballroom to Hell: Grace and Folly in Nineteenth-Century Dance.* Evanston, Ill.: Northwestern University Press, 1991.

Cashion, Susan V. "Dance Ritual and Cultural Values in a Mexican Village." Ph.D. diss., Stanford University, 1983.

Czarnowski, Lucile Katheryn. *Dances of Early California Days.* Palo Alto, Calif.: Pacific Books, [1950].

Dannett, Sylvia G. L., and Frank R. Rachel. *Down Memory Lane: Arthur Murray's Picture Story of Social Dancing.* New York: Greenberg, [1954].

Dodge, Roger Pryor. *Hot Jazz and Jazz Dance: Roger Pryor Dodge Collected Writings, 1929–1964.* Selected and edited by Pryor Dodge. New York: Oxford University Press, 1995.

Duke, Jerry. *Dances of the Cajuns: Louisiana and Texas.* San Francisco: Duke Publishing Company, 1988.

Emery, Lynne Fauley. *Black Dance from 1619 to Today.* 2d rev. ed. Princeton, N.J.: Princeton Book Company, 1988.

Gottschild, Brenda Dixon. *Digging the Africanist Presence in American Performance: Dance and Other Contexts.* Westport, Conn.: Greenwood Press, 1996.

Griffiths, John. *The Gentleman and Lady's Companion; containing, the newest cotillions and country dances; to which is added, instances of ill manners, to be carefully avoided by youths of both sexes.* Newport: Oliver Farnsworth, 1799. Available on microfilm with numerous other early works on the dance: Early American imprints from the American Antiquarian Society, Worcester, Mass. First series, no. 48865.

Hazzard-Gordon, Katrina. *Jookin': The Rise of Social Dance Formations in African-American Culture.* Philadelphia: Temple University Press, 1990.

Ingber, J. B., ed. *Dancing into Marriage: Collected Papers on Jewish Wedding Dances.* CORD, *Dance Research Journal* 17, no. 2, and 18, no. 1 (1985–86).

Investigación Folklórica en Mexico Materiales. Mexico City: Instituto Nacional de Bellas Artes (Mexico), Departamento de Música, 1962.

Jones, Betty, ed. *Dance as Cultural Heritage.* 2 vols. Dance Research Annual, nos. 14–15. New York: Congress on Research in Dance, 1983–85.

Kmen, Henry. *Music in New Orleans: The Formative Years, 1791–1841.* Baton Rouge: Louisiana State University Press, 1966.

Lewis, Daniel, ed. "Dance in Hispanic Cultures." *Choreography and Dance* 3, no. 4 (1994).

Lomax, Alan. *Folk Song Style and Culture.* American Association for the Advancement of Science, publication no. 88 Washington, D.C.: American Association for the Advancement of Science, 1968.

Malone, Jacqui. *Steppin' on the Blues: The Visible Rhythms of African American Dance.* Urbana: University of Illinois Press, 1996.

Marks, Joseph E., III. *America Learns to Dance: A Historical Study of Dance Education in America before 1900.* 1957; reprint, New York: Dance Horizons [1976?].

Martin, Carol J. *Dance Marathons: Performing American Culture of the 1920s and 1930s.* Jackson: University Press of Mississippi, 1994.

McDonagh, Don. *Dance Fever.* New York: Random House, 1979.

Millar, John Fitzhugh. *Country Dances of Colonial America.* Williamsburg, Va.: Thirteen Colonies Press, 1990.

Miller, Norma, with Evette Jensen. *Swingin' at the Savoy: The Memoir of a Jazz Dancer.* Philadelphia: Temple University Press, 1996.

Moreau de Saint-Méry, M. L. E. *Dance: An Article Drawn from the Work by M. L. E. Moreau de St.-Méry.* Trans. and introduction by Lily Hastings and Baird Hastings. Brooklyn: Dance Horizons, 1976.

Mueller, John E. *Astaire Dancing: The Musical Films.* New York: Knopf, 1985.

Nevell, Richard. *A Time to Dance: American Country Dancing from Hornpipes to Hot Hash.* New York: St. Martin's Press, 1977.

Parish, Paul. "A Revival in Full Swing." *Dance Magazine,* Sept., 1999, pp. 50–52.

Quirey, Belinda. *May I Have the Pleasure?: The Story of Popular Dancing.* London: BBC Publications, 1976.

Sachs, Curt. *World History of the Dance.* Translated by Bessie Schönberg. 1937; reprint, New York: W. W. Norton, 1963.

Schwartz, Paul. *Folk Dance Guide.* New York: P. Schwartz, 1953.

Seguin, Robert. *La danse traditionelle au Québec.* Sillery: Presses de l'Université du Québec, 1986.

Shaw, Lloyd. *Cowboy Dances: A Collection of Western Square Dances.* Caldwell, Idaho: Caxton Printers, 1939.

Stearns, Marshall, and Jean Stearns. *Jazz Dance: The Story of American Vernacular Dance.* 1968; reprint, Da Capo Press, 1994.

Stephenson, Richard, and Joseph Iaccarino. *The Complete Book of Ballroom Dancing.* Garden City, N.Y.: Doubleday, 1980.

Stewart, Doug. "This Joint Is Jumping." *Smithsonian Magazine,* Mar., 1999, pp. 60–74.

Thompson, Allison, comp. *Dancing through Time: Western Social Dance in Literature, 1400–1918.* Jefferson, N.C.: McFarland, 1998.

Wallace, Carol McD., Don McDonagh, Jean L. Druesedow, Laurence Libin, and Constance Old. *Dance: A Very Social History.* Foreword by Philippe de Montebello, preface by Diana Vreeland, and introduction by Yoshio Ohno. New York: Rizzoli and Metropolitan Museum of Art, 1986.

In addition, the Library of Congress digital collection has over two hundred dancing manuals as well as some eighty video clips of social dances. The "American Ballroom Companion: Dance Instruction Manuals, c. 1490–1920," can be directly accessed from the Library of Congress Home Page.

There are many sources that distribute movies on this subject, so check with your local distributor, regional colleges, or state archives for listings. Although the list could extend indefinitely and new titles are being added constantly, the following videos are currently available for purchase or rental. For addresses of distributors named below, and further suggestions, see the Dance Films Association's *Dance Film and Video Guide* named in Selected General Readings and References on Theatrical Dance.

And Still We Dance. 60 minutes, color. Searchlight Films. Documentary of the annual San Francisco folk dance festival. Demonstrations by California troupes of dances from Spain and Eastern Europe, Africa, the Philippines and Asia, North and South America.

Appalachian Spring: 22 minutes, black and white. In *Martha Graham in Performance.* Kultur. Graham herself dances to Aaron Copland's music in this 1944 modern dance piece in which she depicts the wedding day of a pioneer couple. Her duets and group dances "quote" from traditional country dance.

Ballet Folklórico Nacional de México. 110 minutes, color. Gessler Productions. The great folkloric ballet troupe of Mexico performs traditional dances that reflect their dual heritage from Spain and the Native Americans.

Canadians Can Dance. 22 minutes, color. National Film Board of Canada. Highlights of the folk dances performed by fifteen hundred entrants to the annual Canadian National Exhibition held in Toronto.

Dance Black America. 87 minutes, color. Dance Horizons Video. Contains historic footage of popular African American dances, such as the Charleston, jitterbug, cakewalk, as well as theatricalized re-creations performed with verve and exuberance.

Dancing: Dancing in One World (part 2) and *Sex and Social Dance* (part 6). 60 minutes each, color. PBS, 1993. Dances in part 2 were filmed at the Los Angeles Festival of 1990, which focused on Pacific Basin dances of the peoples of Los Angeles, Bali, Mexico, Native America, Hawai'i, and Oceania, as well as African Americans. Part 6 shows dance cultures as disparate as Morocco, Tahiti, and Hollywood, while the narrator generalizes in facile fashion about Elvis, rock 'n' roll, disco, and tribal dance.

Davidsbündlertänze. 43 minutes, color. Home Vision, 1985. Ballet choreographed by George Balanchine, consisting of variations on Schumann's piano waltzes and other traditional social dance forms popular in nineteenth-century North America.

Fiddler on the Roof. 3 hours, color. MGM/VA Home Video. The Hollywood movie of the Broadway musical with Zero Mostel as the keeper of the Jewish traditions.

Includes many dance scenes based on Eastern European folk dance, as choreographed by Jerome Robbins.

The Frankie Manning Collection. 5 videos, color/black and white. Available from Living Traditions, 2442 NW Market Street, Suite 168, Seattle, Washington 98107.

The Godfather, Part I. 171 minutes, color. Paramount. The quintessential Italian wedding feast in all its stereotyped glory, complete with pastel-colored wedding almonds and Mafiosi performing the tarantella.

The JVC/Smithsonian Folkways Video Anthology of Music and Dance of the Americas. 332 minutes, 6 cassettes, color. Victor Company of Japan; distributed by Multicultural Media, 1995. Folk music and dancing all over the Americas: Canada, United States, Caribbean, Central and South America. Titled excerpts of real people dancing in real downhome situations.

Kumu Hula: Keepers of a Culture. 85 minutes, color. Rhapsody Films. A documentary on the history of the hula; dancers demonstrate how they keep alive the spirit of the ancient chants and dances of the early Hawaiians.

Salsa. 96 minutes, color. Swank Distributors. A young dancer's attempts to win the title "King of Salsa" at the San Juan Festival held annually in Los Angeles.

Swing Kids. 112 minutes, color. 1993. In 1930s Nazi Germany, young adults, obsessed by American culture, are politically persecuted for their adherence to the "decadent" (meaning non-Aryan) cult of jazz. Great scenes of swing dance and lively music.

Tango Bar. 90 minutes, color, English subtitles. Warner Home Video. Raul Julia stars in this film set in an Argentine nightclub, which showcases many different kinds of tangos and depicts their historic evolution.

Top Hat. 97 minutes, black and white. Fox Hills Video. Fred Astaire and Ginger Rogers perform their classic foxtrot in *Cheek to Cheek,* he in the customary top hat and tails, she in a swirling gown trimmed with ostrich feathers.

The Wrecker's Ball. Color, 56 minutes. Great Performances, PBS. Paul Taylor's delightful romp based on swing dance and pop songs of the '40s through the '60s. This modern dance piece is an imaginative view of social dance as this old building would have seen it pass through its portals, from the time of GI's jitterbugging in a dance club to that of flower children stumbling about in a miasma of drug-induced fervor in an abandoned building.

PART 3

THE ANTI-DANCE BRIGADE

INTRODUCTION

Dancers posed problems for moralists almost from the very beginning of the Plymouth colony. As early as 1628, a dissident group set up a Maypole at Merry Mount and started to drink, carouse with Native American women, and dance about the pole. The authorities considered such practices to be of pagan origin and so ordered the profane pole to be removed, but difficulties with dancers did not necessarily diminish with time. Toward the end of that century, "Promiscuous Dancing," according to Reverend Increase Mather, "was openly practiced, and too much countenanced in this Degenerated Town."[1] In 1676 a certain M. Henri Sherlot set up a dancing school in Boston, only to be ordered out of the colony. Hot on his heels came Francis Stepney, who aggravated the matter with his insolent claim that he could teach more morality with plays than could preachers with sermons.[2] A few years after he ran into trouble with the law and ran away, yet another Maypole was erected.

If Mather hoped to stem the tide with his *Arrow against Profane and Promiscuous Dancing* (1685), the first selection in this section, he evidently did not succeed, and Cotton Mather was forced to follow in his father's footsteps with *A Cloud of Witnesses: Darting out Light upon a Case too Unseasonably Made Seasonable to be Discoursed on* (1700). Neither quarreled with dancing or leaping, which, as Increase Mather contended, is "a natural expression of joy: So that there is no more Sin in it, than in laughter, or any outward expression of inward Rejoicing."[3] "Not guilty!" was his verdict as to whether or not dancing per se is sinful, so long as the following conditions were met: that the sexes be kept separate, and that the dance be sober and performed in moderation. He and his son pointed to the commandment that forbade adultery in order to justify their prohibition of mixed or couple dancing, on the grounds that any activity that engendered impure thoughts or heightened sexual arousal was sinful. English country dances were evidently considered acceptable by Mather, because women could dance separately from men. The emphasis of the dance lay in the beauty of changing figures formed by long rows of dancers. All could enjoy the sociability of the dance and the improved sense of physical well-being that resulted, while at the same time avoiding the intimacy of touching a person of the opposite sex.

Two centuries later, Reverend Thomas Faulkner (represented in the next selection, "From the Ballroom to Hell") used many of the very same arguments as well as quotations from the Bible to condemn all dancing whatsoever, a position advocated by certain moralists particularly after the "Great Awakening," the religious revival that swept the American frontier in the early nineteenth century. At various times, Methodists, Presbyterians, Congregationalists, and Baptists, among others, have outlawed dancing. Some congregations enforced these prohibitions by expelling members who dared to flout the rules. Even today the issue is open to dispute: some orthodox rabbis forbid dancing at social events while others do not.[4]

The waltz, which made its way to North America prior to 1804, was virulently attacked by anti-dance moralists and at the same time scandalized dance enthusiasts due to the close embrace of the dancers. Today the waltz is viewed as the most staid of formalities, unpacked from mothballs for weddings or anniversaries, but in early America, most young women had never been held in public by a man, let alone looked deeply into his eyes and whirled about "like the wind, so that everything around us fades away."[5] This "closed-couple" dance was revolutionary in its social impact. Made giddy by so twirling, a young woman could shut her eyes to the chaperon's watchful gaze that followed her every move and listen intently while her partner dared to whisper sweet nothings in her ear. How could parental strictures possibly compete with such stirring enticements?

To the older onlookers, it seemed as if almost all social restraints were in danger of being jettisoned. The waltz involved such unseemly physical intimacy that, from the moment of its inception, it was labeled indecent, immoral, and even worse. By the end of the nineteenth century, the struggle to halt the waltz continued without abating. Moralists, growing ever more shrill, contended that "the degrading, lust-creating influence of the waltz" and its "voluptuous, sensual embrace" would automatically lead to a shameful career in prostitution for many a waltzing woman.[6]

Faulkner denied that "any woman can or does waltz without being improperly aroused." The woman was damned if she did respond, and damned if she did not: "any woman with a nature so cold as not to be aroused by the perfect execution of the waltz, is entirely unfit to make any man happy as his wife, and if she be willing to indulge in such pleasure with every ballroom libertine, she is not the woman any man wants for a wife."[7] As for its effects upon men, M. B. Williams asserted that "young men are driven by the ballroom to the brothel," an institution that he considered "a physical necessity for men" so long as dancers spin round the ballroom floor during the waltz.[8]

It is worth noting again that the seventeenth-century Puritan preacher Increase Mather did not express such a totally negative perception of dance as was held by these later writers; rather, he advocated dancing as conducive to health. He believed that it could improve "Poyse and Composure of Body," meaning poise and agility. The study of dance makes "the body active and strong, graceful in deportment, and a quality very much beseeming a Gentleman," so ran the defense originally set forth by John Playford, the dancing master who published the first English-language dance manual during Cromwell's Puritan regime.[9] Similarly, Victorian writers advocated dance as particularly valuable for women, who, perched on their pedestals, had little opportunity for physical exercise to improve their "delicate constitutions" and would often succumb to various "nervous" disorders.[10] Besides saving them from "vapors and melancholy," dance also rescued young women from "the evils of an over mental education."[11] Early in the twentieth century, American universities granted dance a home in physical education departments. Today aerobic dance has grown into a national sport, so that even anti-dance adherents may embrace it as a form of healthy exercise.

Mather anticipated a second defense of dance that remains current: he described dance as a manifestation of elite cultural forms, a "desirable Accomplishment" and useful for purposes of etiquette. He plainly stated, "Religioun is no Enemy to Good Manners." Dance and etiquette have long marched hand in glove in Western society. French dancing masters advertised in American newspapers that their curriculum included not only the latest *Meneut de la cour,* cotillions, and hornpipes, but also "the polite accomplishments of the graces so necessary to be observed in all genteel societies."[12] In the nineteenth century, ordinary citizens could purchase a variety of how-to-dance books designed to assist them in learning how to navigate around the perils of ultra-refined ballroom practices, since the smallest fault could lead to severe judgment concerning a person's poor "breeding" or undesirable social status. Today, commented one dancing master in 1879, "everybody who pretends to the slightest acquaintance with good society recognizes the necessity of learning to dance."[13] Some vestiges of this practice yet remain: most dance manuals published in the twentieth century also continued to deal with etiquette. Even

Break Dancing: Step by Step Instructions (New York: Beekman House, 1984) follows that tradition with advice on etiquette for dance competitions.

These two notions, dance as a form of healthy exercise and dance as conducive to learning proper manners, became fallback defensive positions when renewed attacks against dancing broke out early in the twentieth century.[14] Some critics singled out the latest dance fad and advocated legal sanctions against it. For example, according to headlines in the *New York Times* of June 13, 1926, a woman who danced the Charleston on public streets was arrested. Others viewed dance as healthful recreation, especially for women who were permitted few athletic outlets for their energies; yet others attacked, also by lawful means, the unhealthy environment of the dance hall itself in an attempt to reform the dance.

Pro-dance reformers and anti-dance moralists alike turned to the courtroom to enforce their particular agenda, and both agreed, too, that the weak needed to be protected. The object for intended rescue, however, changed with the times. On February 19, 1823, a letter to Philadelphia's *Union* fretted over "young men of our city [who] are ruined in these infernal . . . [dance] houses of destruction, and there associating with company the most vile, the most profligate, and the most abominable." By the end of the nineteenth century, Faulkner and a spate of other anti-dance moralists targeted women rather than men. John Dillon, for example, recounted melodramatic tales of thousands of unsuspecting female victims who were lured, as the title of his book put it, "from dance hall to white slavery" (meaning prostitution).[15]

Reformers in the early part of the twentieth century focused on symptoms, such as promiscuity or alcohol abuse. Belle Lindner Israels and members of the New York Council of Jewish Women advocated police regulation of existing dance halls, but also worked to substitute decent places, such as YWCA or city facilities, for commercial ones where liquor was sold.[16] Israels, in the third selection in this section, advocated dance as an healthy outlet and enjoyable recreation just as Mather had done over one hundred years previously. Let the public provide a licensed amusement place for young working women, she suggested, and so protect them from the dangers of free drinks and casual sex that abounded in this "dance mad" society. In 1911 her efforts won legislative support in New York, and other states followed.[17] Unfortunately, because underlying economic and social problems that affect poor working women have continued to fester, modern dance halls still spawn similar social problems. In Houston, for example, young women can earn up to $50 per night dancing and drinking with customers at Las Chenchas or El Mexico dance halls. Many admit that they don't like the practice of charging "a Dollar a Dance," but "it helps pay the rent" and besides "What else would I do on Saturday night?"[18]

African American dance forms have been the predominant influence in U.S. popular dancing throughout the twentieth century, ever since the cakewalk and ragtime put an end to European domination of the American ballroom. The black influence led to an overlay of disguised racism pasted onto the usual barrage of complaints from the anti-dance moralists, while dance defenders hastened to separate the new dances from their black social origins. In their foreword to *Modern Dancing* (1914), for example, dancing masters Irene and Vernon Castle aimed to "uplift dancing, [and] purify it," of all "vulgar [and] immodest" influences associated with ragtime. The Castles did not mention the blacks by name but promised to remove the following movement characteristics often associated with African American dance forms of the early twentieth century, including shoulder wriggles, hip shakes, body twists, and elbow flounces.[19] Similarly, in "The Twist: Brave New Whirl," Marshall Fishwick purported to place the dance in its social context of the day, a time when old fogeys disparaged the twist as "barbaric, erotic, inhuman, and satanic." Curiously enough, he overlooked the conjunction of such pejorative stereotypes with the dance's first stirrings in the black community even though his youthful jitterbugging had been similarly insulted. His father laughingly acknowledged that he had heard the same back in his Charleston days. Although Fishwick was evidently not aware of it, all three of these dances grew out of the black community and, not surprisingly, met with similar resistance from the establishment. Plus ça change . . .

The last selection, a news report printed in the *New York Times*, demonstrates that dance morality still remains a bone of contention between the generations. For decades the Purdy, Missouri, school board did not permit their graduating students to hold a senior prom. The students sued. In 1988 the U.S. district court ruled that such prohibition smacked of promotion of certain religious ideas, particularly in an area where many residents and half the school board members belonged to a church that held social dance to be "satanic," with a tendency to lead students to alcohol and drug abuse, not to speak of illicit sex.[20] The judge ordered the reluctant administrators to permit the event. Exiting from the decorated high school gym on prom night, jubilant seniors crowed about their "dance of the century," a cheeky reference to the fact that such dances had been forbidden from 1900 on. Their joy was short-lived, however. In 1990, the United States Supreme Court reversed the decision and left intact the school board's prohibition against dances on school property. This ruling signifies one more landmark along the way in the continuing battle of the anti-dance moralists that began in seventeenth-century America.[21]

NOTES

1. Thomas J. Holmes, *Increase Mather: A Bibliography of His Works* (Cleveland, Ohio, 1931), vol. 2, p. 569.

2. *The Diary of Samuel Sewall, 1674–1729*, ed. M. Halsey Thomas (New York: Farrar, Straus and Giroux, 1973), 1, p. 83.

3. Increase Mather, *An Arrow against Profane and Promiscuous Dancing Drawn Out of the Quiver of Scriptures* (Boston: Samuel Green, 1684); reprinted in *The Mathers on Dancing*, ed. Joseph E. Marks, III (Brooklyn: Dance Horizons, 1975), p. 31.

4. "Jews Struggle over Who Will Define the Nature of Orthodoxy," *New York Times*, Nov. 20, 1990.

5. The poet Goethe is quoted in Curt Sachs, *World History of the Dance*, trans. Bessie Schönberg (1937; reprint, New York: Norton, 1965), p. 430.

6. T[homas] A. Faulkner, *From the Ball-room to Hell* (Chicago: Church Press, 1894), p. 27; M. B. Williams, *Where Satan Sows His Seed* (Chicago: Fleming H. Revell Company, 1896), p. 91.

7. Faulkner, *From the Ball-room to Hell*, pp. 24–25.

8. He condemns the women who practice prostitution, however. See Williams, *Where Satan Sows His Seed*, p. 124.

9. Playford published *The English Dancing Master: Or Plaine and Easie Rules for Dancing of Country Dances, with the Tune to Each Dance* in 1651. See part 2, chap. 7 above: Kate Van Winkle Keller and Genevieve Shimer, "Playford's 'English Dancing Master' (1651) and Country Dancing in America."

10. M. Judson Sause, *The Art of Dancing embracing a Full Description of the Various Dances of the Present Day, together with Chapters on Etiquette, the Benefits, and the History of Dancing* (New York: Sause's Dancing Academy, 1880), p. 81; E. Woodworth Masters, *The Standard Dance Album* (Boston: author, 1883), pp. iv–vi; Edna Witherspoon, *The Perfect Art of Modern Dancing* (London: Butterick Publishing Company, 1894), pp. 1, 65.

11. Thomas Hillgrove, *A Complete Practical Guide to the Art of Dancing* (New York: Dick & Fitzgerald, 1863), p. 15; J. L. DeLortie, *Fashionable Dancing, Containing all the Last New and Fashionable Dances* (New York: Francis & Loutrel, 1867), p. 6.

12. [Philadelphia] *Pennsylvania Journal*, Jan. 7, 1786. See, for example, M. Martin-Foy, who offered to teach "the genteelest manners" as much as the Minuet (ibid.); Mrs. Byrne claimed "to pay particular attention to that very necessary part, *Polite Address*" ([Philadelphia] *United States Gazette*, Feb. 6, 1799).

13. *Cartier and Baron's Practical Illustrated Waltz Instructor, Ball Room Guide and Call Book* (New York: Clinton T. De Witt, 1879), p. 3.

14. During the 1920s, the number of anti-dance writings doubled over those of the previous decades, according to figures this author has extracted from the extensive, but

by no means conclusive, bibliography prepared by Joseph E. Marks, III, in *The Mathers on Dancing* (Brooklyn: Dance Horizons, 1975). The mean number of tracts per decade reported from 1685 to 1963 was 6.5, but the decade of the 1920s produced 23.

15. John Dillon, *From Dance Hall to White Slavery: The World's Greatest Tragedy* (Chicago: Charles C. Thompson, 1912).

16. An award-winning biography of Israels was written by her granddaughter Elisabeth Israels Perry: *Belle Moskowitz: Feminine Politics and the Exercise of Power in the Age of Alfred E. Smith* (New York: Oxford University Press, 1987).

17. Elisabeth Perry, "The General Motherhood of the Commonwealth, Dance Hall Reform in the Progressive Era," *American Quarterly* 37, no. 5 (Winter, 1985): 719–33. See also Ella Gardener, *Public Dance Halls: Their Regulation and Place in the Recreation of Adolescents,* U.S. Department of Labor, Children's Bureau Publication no. 189 (Washington, D.C.: Government Printing Office, 1929).

18. "In the Dollar Dances, Sadness Leads," *New York Times,* Jan. 31, 1989. Paul Cressey intensively studied the practice of "taxi dances," as they used to be called in the 1920s, in his *Taxi-Dance Hall* (Chicago: University of Chicago Press, 1932). The institution of paid dance hostesses has been made famous by the Depression-era song, "Ten cents a dance."

19. Irene Castle and Vernon Castle, *Modern Dancing* (New York: Harper & Brothers, 1914), p. 177. See also Marshall Stearns and Jean Stearns, *Jazz Dance: The Story of American Vernacular Dance* (1968; reprint, New York: Da Capo Press, 1994); Brenda Dixon Gottschild, *Digging the Africanist Presence in American Performance: Dance and Other Contexts* (Westport, Conn.: Greenwood Press, 1996).

20. "Missouri Students Fight Ban on Dancing," *New York Times,* Nov. 3, 1986; "Teenagers Are 'Footloose' over Judge Discarding Dance Ban," *Montgomery Advertiser,* Aug. 2, 1988.

21. For an extensive scholarly treatment of the tradition of opposition to the dance in America, see Ann Wagner's *Adversaries of Dance: From the Puritans to the Present* (Urbana: University of Illinois Press, 1997).

CHAPTER 13

An Arrow against Profane and Promiscuous Dancing Drawn Out of the Quiver of the Scriptures (1685)

Increase Mather

Concerning the Controversy about *Dancing*, the Question is not, whether all *Dancing* be in itself sinful. It is granted, that *Pyrrhical* or *Polemical* Saltation: i.e. where men vault in their Armour, to shew their strength and activity, may be of use. Nor is the question, whether a sober and grave *Dancing* of Men with Men, or of Women with Women, be not allowable; we make no doubt of that, where it may be done without offence, in due season, and with moderation. The Prince of Philosophers has observed truly, that *Dancing* or *Leaping*, is a natural expression of joy: So that there is no more Sin in it, than in laughter, or any outward expression of inward Rejoycing.

But our question concerning *Gynecandrical Dancing,* or that which is commonly called *Mixt* or *Promiscuous Dancing*, viz. of Men and Women (be they elder or younger persons) together: Now this we affirm to be utterly unlawful, and that it cannot be tollerated in such a place as *New-England* without great Sin. And that it may appear, that we are not transported by *Affection* without Judgment, let the following Arguments be weighed in the Ballance of the Sanctuary.

Arg. 1. *That which the Scripture condemns is sinful.* None but Atheists will deny this *Proposition:* But the Scripture condemns *Promiscuous Dancing.*

This *Assumption* is proved, 1. *From the Seventh Commandment.* [Thou shalt not commit adultery Ex. 20:14]. It is an Eternal Truth to be observed in expounding the Commandment, that whenever any Sin is forbidden, not only

Excerpts from Increase Mather, *An Arrow against Profane and Promiscuous Dancing Drawn Out of the Quiver of the Scriptures* (Boston: Samuel Green, 1684); reprinted in *The Mathers on Dancing*, ed. Joseph E. Marks, III (Brooklyn: Dance Horizons, 1975), pp. 31–59. Scholars today generally accept that the date of publication as given in the original text is a misprint, and the book was actually issued on Feb. 16, 1685, according to Thomas J. Holmes, *Increase Mather: A Bibliography of His Works* (Cleveland, Ohio, 1931), p. 22.

the highest acts of that sin, but all degrees thereof, and all occasions leading thereto are prohibited. Now we cannot find one Orthodox and Judicious Divine, that writeth on the Commandments, but mentions *Promiscuous Dancing,* as a breach of the seventh Commandment, as being an occasion and an incentive to that which is evil in the sight of God. Yea, this is so manifest as that the *Assembly* in the *larger Catechism,* do expresly take notice of *Dancing,* as a violation of the Commandments. It is said, that when in times of Reformations, Children have been taught in their Catechism, that such *Dancing* is against the Commandment of God, that now in *New-England* they should practically be learned the contrary. The unchaste Touches and Gesticulations used by *Dancers,* have a palpable tendency to that which is evil. Whereas some object, that they are not sensible of any ill motions occasioned in them, by being Spectators or Actors in such *Saltations;* we are not bound to believe all which some pretend concerning their own Mortification. But suppose it were so, if there be other persons, who are by *Mixt Dancing* drawn into sin; that's enough against it. . . .

2. Besides the seventh Commandment, *There are other Scriptures, which seem expresly and particularly to condemn the Dancing we plead against.* It is spoken of as the great sin of the Daughters of *Sion,* that they did walk with stretched-out necks, and with wanton eyes, *walking and mincing as they go, and making a tinkling with their feet,* Isa. 3.16. . . .

The summe is, that according to the judgment of most profound and accurate Interpreters; the Scripture does expresly, and by name condemn *Dancing* as a vicious practice. . . .

3. *There are many other Scriptures which do implicitly condemn them as sinful.* How often does the Scripture commend unto Christians, *Gravity* and *Sobriety,* in their behaviour at all times; and condemn all *Levity* in Carriage. When as *Dancing* is (as some have expressed it) a *Regular Madness.* . . . And truly such affected Levity, and Antick Behaviour, when persons skip and fling about like *Bedlams,* as they say, *Dancers* are wont to do; is no way becoming the Gravity of a Christian. . . .

Arg 2. If we consider, by whom this practice of Promiscuous Dancing was first invented, by whom patronized, and by whom witnessed against, we may well conclude that the admitting of it, in such a place as New-England, *will be a thing pleasing to the Devil, but highly provoking to the Holy God.* . . .

1. *Who were the Inventors of Petulant Dancings?* They had not their original amongst the People of God, but amongst the Heathen. Learned men have well observed, that the Devil was the first inventor of the impleaded *Dances,* and the Gentiles, who worshiped him, the first Practitioners in this Art. They did

honour the Devils, whom they served in this way; their Festivals being for the
most part spent in Play and Dances. And from them did the Apostatizing Idol-
atrous *Israelites* learn to behave themselves, as they did, when they worshipped
the Golden Calf. *They sat down, to eat and drink, and rose up to play,* or to dance.
I *Cor.* 7.10. . . .

2. *By whom have Promiscuous Dances been patronized?* Truly by the worst of
the Heathen. *Caligula, Nero,* and such like Atheists and Epicures were delighted
in them.[1] *Lucius* (that infamous Apostate) hath written an Oration, in defence
of profane and Promiscuous Dancings.[2] Amongst the Papists, some of their
more grave Writers, decry such a practice as a great Immorality. . . .

3. *Who are they that have faithfully testified against this practice?* Ignorant and
Profane Men say, no body is against it, but a few silly Precisians, who are more
precise than wise. But we certainly know, that the wisest, and the learnedest,
and the holiest men in the world have disliked it. The ancient Doctors (Fathers
as they are called) have thundred against this Sin. . . .

As for *the great Reformers of Religion,* and *Opposers of Antichristianism,* none
have gone beyond them, in an Holy Zeal against Profane and Promiscuous
Dancing. Let us in the first place, cite the *Waldenses:* They are in the Scripture,
honored with the names of *Saints* (Rev. 13.7).[3] These *Saints of God,* and *Mar-
tyrs of Jesus,* were haters of Mixt Dances. Because their words are Pathetical,
we shall here transcribe and insert them . . . "A *Dance is the Devil's Procession.
He that enters into a Dance, enters into his Possession. The Devil is the Guide,
the middle and end of the Dance. A man sinneth in Dancing divers wayes; as in
his Pace, for all his steps are numbered; in his Touch, in his Ornaments, in his
Hearing, Sight, Speech, and other Vanities. We will prove it first from Scripture,
and then by other Reasons, how wicked a thing it is to Dance.—He that Danceth
maintaineth the Devil's Pomp, and singeth his Mass. Again, In a Dance, a man
breaks the Ten Commandments of God. The very motion of the Body, which is
used in Dancing, giveth Testimony enough of evil.* Austin *saith,* "The miserable
Dancer knoweth not, that as many Paces as he makes in Dancing, so many steps
he makes to Hell." Thus (and much more to this purpose) do those faithful
Witnesses of Christ, declare against this Profane Practice. Moreover, the Ministers of the *Reformed Churches in France,* did above an hundred years ago (*viz.
Anno* 1581) concur in writing, and publishing a Book, against the vice we are
impleading. . . .

Arg. 3. *That Practice which the Graver sort of Heathen have condemned as
unlawful, Christians may well look upon as Sinful,* Rom. 2.14,15. *But this is true
concerning mixed Dancing;* as shall by Testimony be made to appear.

Macrobius informs us, that amongst the Ancient *Romans* skil in Dancing was reputed an infamous thing.[4] *Scipio Africanus* complains that some in his time would go with *impudent Dancers* (as he calls them) and learn to sing with them, Which practice their Ancestors looked upon as a disgrace to Gentlemen.[5] He therefore speaks of it as a great degeneracy of that Age, that some being Persons of Quality, sent their Children to a Dancing-school, and that he had himself seen at one of their Schools, a Boy of twelve years old Dancing, which he thought was a fitter employment for a lewd and foolish serving boy, than for the Son of a Gentleman. . . . And *Cicero* in his Oration *Pro Muraena* saith, that if a Man be a *Dancer,* he is doubtless either a Drunkard or a mad man.[6] . . . *Seneca* bewails it, that in his time young Ones were corrupted with *Obscene Dances;* and that *Dancing-schools* were tolerated in the City, and that some when they were inflamed at the *Dance,* went from the *Dancing-school* to the *Brothel house.*[7] . . . The Emperor *Tiberius* banished *Dancers,* not only from his Court, but out of the City of *Rome.*

Now, then, shall the *Gentiles,* who had only the dark Light of Nature to shew them what things were good & what evil, condemn *Petulant dancings?* And shall Christians who have the Scriptures and the Glorious Light of the Gospel to illuminate them, practise or plead for such works of Darkness? And shall that *Abomination* be set up in *New-England* (the place where the Light of the Gospel has shined so Gloriously) which *Moral Heathen* have detested? The Lord lay not this great sin to the charge of any, who have at all been guilty of it.

Arg. 4. *The practice which is not sanctified by Prayer, but is an Enemy to Religious Exercises, is surely an evil Practice. But this is true concerning mixt dancing.* It is a good Rule which *Practical and Casuistical* Divines are wont to give, *That work which a Man cannot pray over, let him not meddle with.* A Christian should do nothing wherein he cannot exercise Grace, or put a respect of Obedience to God on what he does. This in lawful Recreations may be done. 1 *Cor.* 10.31. But who can seriously pray to the Holy God to be with him when he is going to a Promiscuous *dance?* . . .

Arg. 5. *For Persons to Dance at a Time when God calls them to mourn, is certainly unlawful. But such is the case at this Day.* If the thing were in itself lawful (which the Arguments insisted on prove that it is not) yet to set upon such a practice at such a time, must needs be a great provocation to the sight of God. *Dancers* are wont to alledge that Scripture, *Eccl.* 3.4. *There is a Time to Dance* (though that does not speak a syllable for the Justification of such *Dancing* as we are writing against, nor indeed for any other *Dancing,* since the meaning of the place is not that there is a *lawful time,* but only a *limited time* to *Dance*). But they should consider that *There is a Time to mourn.* Now to set up *Dances* at a Time when God calls us mourn, is most certainly a provocation. . . .

Arg. 6. *That Practice against which the wrath of God hath been revealed from Heaven, may well be dreaded as unrighteous. Rom* 1.18. *But this is sadly true concerning mixt Dancings.* The Fruits and Effects thereof have been Tragical & Dismal. No doubt but that the *Promiscuous Dances* (for at their Sacrifices the Heathen used to do so) between the *Moabites* and the *Midianitish* Woman, proved a snare to the Children of *Israel.* But how terrible a Plague followed? . . . *Salome,* the Daughter of *Herodias* was notable at *Dancing!* But what end did she come to? *Nicephorus* relates that falling under the Ice, her feet *Capered* under the water; and her Head being cut off by the Ice, it danced above water. The Story of that Bishop is famous, who having a Mixed Dance in his House, he and the female in his hand hapned to be crush'd to Death. Also, in the City of *Magdeburg,* 24 Persons (Men and Woman) were struck dead with the Lightnings as they were *Promiscuously Dancing.* . . . It is known from their own Confessions that amongst the *Indians* in this *America,* oftentimes at their *Dances* the Devil appears in bodily shape, and takes away one of them alive. In some places of this Wilderness there are great heaps of Stones, which the *Indians* have laid together, as an horrid Remembrance of so hideous a fruit of their *Satanical Dances.* . . .

But let us hear what the Patrons of Dances have to plead. *Produce your Cause, and bring forth your strong Reasons, saith the Lord.* Say all that you have to say.

Plea. 1. *We read in the Scripture of* Dances. *Miriam Danced,* and *David Danced.*

Answer 1. Those Instances are not at all to the purpose; for they were Religious *Dances,* accommodated to the State of the Old Testament-Church. They had also Music in their worship, but such as have so in these dayes *Judaize* more than *Christians* ought to do; we shall divert into another *Question,* should we speak to that.

2. Neither were those mentioned, *Mixed dancings:* It is said of *Miriam, The Woman went out after her with Dances, Exod.* 15.20. But not that Men went out with them: Nor did *David* take a Woman by the hand to *Dance* with him before the Ark. In one Word, there is not so much as one Example in the whole Book of God concerning *mixt dancing,* except it be the Instance of that accursed and damned harlot the Daughter of *Herodias* [Salome].

Plea. 2. *The Design of Dancing is only to teach Children good Behaviour and decent Carriage.*

Answer. Religion is no Enemy to good Manners, to learn a due Poyse and Composure of Body is not unlawful, provided it be done without a provocation to Uncleanness, and be not a Nurse of Pride and Vanity. If therefore any be disposed to have their Children instructed in that which may be truly Ornamental, or a desirable Accomplishment in these respects, they may send them not to a Blasphemer, but to some Grave Person that will teach them Decency of Behaviour, not *Promiscuously,* but each Sex by themselves; so neither God nor Man will be offended.

This notwithstanding, Every thing is not *Good Carriage;* which Light and Vain persons shall call so. Why should *Pantomimical Gestures* be named good Carriage? There is a behaviour which Light Persons look upon as an accomplishment; but such as are grave and solid, and wise (whose esteem is most to be valued) have other thoughts of it. If the Holy Prophet *Isaiah* were alive in these dayes, he would not call *a stretched forth neck, and wanton eye, a Mincing as they go,* by the name of good carriage. It is one of the Devil's Wiles to Guild over corrupt Practices with Golden Names, that men may the more easily swallow them. . . .

Plea. 3. *Children are much pleased with this Exercise.*

Answer. That we believe: But if it suit with their corrupt natures, that's a sign it is evil. No doubt but if a Stage play were set up, many Children would be as much pleased with it, as now they are with the Dance. . . .

Plea. 4. *Such dancing is now become customary amongst Christians.*

Answer. Which cannot be thought on without horror. . . . But shall Christians follow the course of the World? They ought to swim against the stream, and to keep themselves pure from the sins of the Times of which this of *mixed dancing* is none of the least.

Plea. 5. *Some good men think it is lawful!*

Answer. We are not to walk by the Opinion of this or that good Man, but by the Scriptures. . . . We dare not deny, that there have been some good Men in the world, who have been so far misled as to justify Profanations of the Lord's Day. . . . But we cannot call to mind one Protestant Author who has been real for the interest of Reformation, that has set his Pen on work to plead for a practice so vile and infamous. This Objection turns upon Dancers thus, That practice with Holy Men in all ages have abhorred may well be suspected to be an evil practice: But it was shewed that this is true of promiscuous Dancing.

We shall then conclude this Discourse with a double *Corollary.*

Corol. 1. *It is the Duty of Churches to exercise the Discipline of Christ towards such of their Members as shall offend in this matter.* . . . Now they that frequent Promiscuous Dancings, or that send their Children thereunto, walk disorderly, and contrary to the Apostles' Doctrine. It has been proved that such a practice is a *Scandalous Immorality,* and therefore to be removed out of Churches by Discipline, which is the Broom of Christ, whereby he keeps his Churches clean. . . .

And shall Churches in *New-England* who have had a Name to be stricter and purer than other Churches, suffer such a scandalous evil amongst them? if all that are under Discipline be made sensible of this matter, we shall not be much or long infested with a *Choreutical Daemon*.

Corol. 2. *Such Church-Members in* New England, *as have sent their Children to be Practitioners or Spectators of mixt Dancing between young Men and Maidens, have cause to be deeply humbled.* But stand still a while! what a word is here! *Church-Members and their Children in* New England *at mixt Dances! Be astonished O ye Heavens!* without doubt *Abraham is ignorant of us, and Israel knoweth us not.* If our Fathers should rise out of their Graves, they would not own such Children. It has been observed by several learned & holy Men that *Job* giveth it as the Description and Character of ungodly ones: *They send forth their little ones like a Flock, and their Children Dance, they take the Timbrel and Harp, and rejoyce at the sound of the Organs,* Job 21.11,12. . . . The Catechism which Wicked men teach their Children is to Dance and to Sing. Not that Dancing, or Musick, or Singing are in themselves sinful: but if the Dancing Master be wicked they are commonly abused to Lasciviousness, and that makes them to become abominable. But will you that are Professors of Religion have your Children to be thus taught? The Lord expects that you should give the Children who are Baptized into his Name another kind of Education, that you should bring them up in the nurture and admonition of the Lord: And do you not hear the Lord Expostulating the case with you, and saying, you have taken my Children, the Children that were given unto me; the Children that were solemnly engaged to renounce the Pomps of Satan; but is this a light matter that you have taken these my Children, and initiated them in the Pomps and Vanities of the Wicked one, contrary to your Covenant? What will you say in the day of the Lord's pleading with you? We have that charity for you as to believe that you have erred through Ignorance, and not wickedly: and we have therefore accounted it our Duty to inform you in the Truth. If you resolve not on Reformation, you will be left inexcusable. However it shall be, we have now given our Testimony and delivered our own Souls. *Consider what we say, and the Lord will give you understanding in all things.*

FINIS

NOTES

1. Editor's note: Caligula ruled as Roman emperor from A.D. 37 to 41, and has been the object of vituperation ever since. Nero, Roman emperor from A.D. 54 to 68, was

infamous for his debauched and extravagant lifestyle, as well as persecution of the early Christians. Epicurus (341–270 B.C.) was founder of a school of philosophy that stressed pleasure as the ultimate good but that the life of pleasure must also be a life of virtue. Mather's use of "epicure" here reflects the tendency to omit this aspect of Epicurus's teachings.

2. Editor's note: Lucian of Samosata, circa A.D. 120 to 180, was author of as many as eighty prose works, many satirical, including *The Dialogues of the Gods.*

3. Editor's note: The Waldenses were members of a reform Christian sect that originated in twelfth-century France, in the Piedmontese Alps. They preached doctrines of poverty and simplicity.

4. Editor's note: Ambrosius Theodosius Macrobius was a Latin philosopher who wrote *Saturnalia.*

5. Editor's note: Two men of this name, one called The Elder and the other The Younger, were famous generals during the Punic Wars, second and third centuries B.C. Scipio Africanus the Younger was known as highly conservative in his views on morality.

6. Editor's note: Marcus Tullius Cicero is today remembered as one of the greatest of Roman orators, particularly in his letters. His writings range in subject from rhetorical to philosophical treatises.

7. Editor's note: Seneca enjoyed great fame among contemporaries in the first century A.D. for his philosophical writings and as an early tutor of the Emperor Nero.

CHAPTER 14

From the Ballroom to Hell (1894)

Thomas A. Faulkner

Since my conversion from a dancing master and a servant of the "Evil One" to an earnest Christian and a servant of the Lord Jesus Christ, the question has been repeatedly asked me: "Is there any harm in dancing?"

And letters innumerable have been coming in with questions to the same effect.

Selected excerpts from T[homas]. A. Faulkner, *From the Ball-room to Hell* (Chicago: Church Press, 1894), pp. 7–28.

First dancing; then drinking, smoking, and sex, 1912. This illustration depicts the "tragedy" of the unmarried mother. Published in John Dillon, in *From Dance Hall to White Slavery: The World's Greatest Tragedy* (Chicago: Charles C. Thompson, 1912), facing p. 62.

The more I mingle with people outside the dancing circle the more forcibly I am made to realize how many there are who are seeking to know the truth concerning the evil of dancing, and how many thousands more who, if they are not seeking that knowledge, certainly ought to have it.

Let me assure you in the first place that I am well aware that there are many church members and professing Christians who dance; but if on the strength of this you deem it a safe amusement, come with me for a few evenings, and when you have seen all that I can show you, let your judgment tell you, whether you can, with safety, place your pure beautiful daughter in the dancing academy or ballroom.

Let us first take an instance from the "select" dancing academy, and thus begin at the root of the matter.

Here is a beautiful young girl. Let me take her for an example.

She is the daughter of wealthy parents; they have been called to mourn the loss of two of their children; and this is their only remaining treasure, their darling, their idol almost, whom they love more than their own lives.

They wish to bestow upon her every accomplishment which modern society demands, so when it is announced that Prof. ———— will open his select dancing academy they hasten to place her under his instruction.

At first she seems shocked at the manner in which he embraces her to teach her the latest waltz.

It is her first experience in the arms of a strange man, with his limbs pressed to hers, and in her natural modesty she shrinks from so familiar a touch. It brings a bright flush of indignation to her cheek as she thinks what an unladylike and indecent position to assume with a man who, but a few hours before, was an utter stranger, but she says to herself: "This is the position every one must take who waltzes in the most approved style—church members and all—so of course it is no harm for me." She thus takes the first step in casting aside that delicate God-given instinct which should be the guide of every pure woman in such matters.

She is very bright and learns rapidly, but a few weeks have passed before she is able to waltz well, and is surrounded by the handsomest and most gallant men in the room, who flatter her until her head is quite turned. She has entirely overcome her delicacy about being embraced in public for half an hour by strange men. In fact she rather likes it now. She wonders all day, before dancing school, if that handsome man who dances so "elegantly" and says such nice things to her, will ask her to dance with him tonight, and finds herself dreaming of how delightful it would be to feel his arm about her.

The evening at last comes; the uninteresting square dances are gone through with, and the music of the waltz begins. Her partner is the Apollo of her day-dreams. He presses her close to his breast, and they glide over the floor together as if the two were but one.

When she raises her eyes, timidly at first, to that handsome but deceitful face, now so close to her own, the look that is in his eyes as they meet hers, seems to burn into her very soul. A strange, sweet thrill shakes her very being and leaves her weak and powerless and obliged to depend for support upon the arm which is pressing her to himself in such a suggestive manner, but the sensation is a pleasant one and grows to be the every essence of her life.

If a partner fails, through ignorance or innocence, to arouse in her these feelings, she does not enjoy the dance, mentally styles him a "bore," and wastes no more waltzes on him. She grows more bold, and from being able to return shy glances at first, is soon able to meet more daring ones until, with heart beating against heart, hand clasped in hand, and eyes looking burning words which lips dare not speak, the waltz becomes one long, sweet and purely sensual pleasure. . . .

She graduates from the academy and is caught into the whirl of society, and her life becomes what is called one round of pleasure—one round certainly of parlor dances, social hops and grand balls with champagne dinners and early goings home (early in the morning, *of course*).

This evening there is to be a ball of unusual grandeur. The last of the season of gaiety, and the closing of the dancing-school term. Our friend will surely be present. Let us attend. What a scene of beauty, gayety and splendor. . . .

But see, there is our friend of the dancing academy just entering on the arm of her devoted father. Three months have passed since we first met her. She is much changed, yet one can scarcely see in what the change consists. The face is the same, yet not the same. There is just the shadow of coarseness in it, a little less of frank innocence and true refinement, and a trace, not exactly of ill-health, but a want of freshness. This last is, however, well concealed by the use of cosmetics, and she is still a very beautiful girl, and the fond father's heart swells with pride as he sees the handsomest and most fashionable gentlemen of the ballroom press eagerly forward to ask her hand for the different dances of the evening.

Her father remains for a few of the square dances, but soon retires, knowing that his fair daughter will not want for attention from—gentlemen whose attentions he is sure must be desirable, certainly desirable, why not? Are these admirers not rich and handsome, and do they not move in the highest society? Ah, foolish father, how little he knows of the ways of ballroom society.

But let us turn our attention again to the dancers, at two o'clock next morning. This is the favorite waltz, and the last and most furious of the night, as well as the most disgusting. Let us notice, as an example, our fair friend once more.

She is now in the vile embrace of the Apollo of the evening. Her head rests upon his shoulder, her face is upturned to his, her bare arm is almost around his neck, her partly nude swelling breast heaves tumultuously against his, face to face they whirl on, his limbs interwoven with hers, his strong right arm around her yielding form, he presses her to him until every curve in the contour of her body thrills with the amorous contact. Her eyes look into his, but she sees nothing; the soft music fills the room, but she hears it not; he bends her body to and fro, but she knows it not; his hot breath, tainted with strong drink, is on her hair and cheek, his lips almost touch her forehead, yet she does not shrink; his eyes, gleaming with a fierce, intolerable lust, gloat over her, yet she does not quail. She is filled with the rapture of sin in its intensity; her spirit is inflamed with passion and lust is gratified in thought. With a last low wail the music ceases, and the dance for the night is ended, but not the evil work of the night.

The girl whose blood is hot from the exertion and whose every carnal sense is aroused and aflame by the repetition of such scenes as we have witnessed, is led to the ever-waiting carriage, where she sinks exhausted on the cushioned seat. Oh, if I could picture to you the fiendish look that comes into his eyes as he sees his helpless victim before him. Now is his golden opportunity. He must not miss it, and he does not, and that beautiful girl who entered the dancing school as pure and innocent as an angel three months ago returns to her home that night robbed of that most precious jewel of womanhood—virtue!

When she awakes the next morning to a realizing sense of her position, her first impulse is to self-destruction, but she deludes herself with the thought that her "dancing" companion will right the wrong by marriage, but that is farthest from his thoughts, and he casts her off—"*he* wishes a pure woman for *his* wife."

She has no longer any claim to purity; her self-respect is lost; she sinks lower and lower; society shuns her, and she is today a brothel inmate, the toy and plaything of the libertine and drunkard. . . .

But how is it with her ballroom Apollo? Does society shun him? Does he pine away and die? Oh, no, he continues in the dancing school, constantly seeking new victims among the pure and innocent. . . .

This tragedy, my friends, was acted out in real life, and is only a sample of hundreds and hundreds of cases of which I have had personal knowledge.

"But," some mothers say, "I know that I can trust my daughter. The waltz may be the means of leading astray some shallow, low-minded girls, and may arouse the lower nature of some of those whose lower nature lies very near the surface, but such girls would go astray anyway. My daughter is a pure, high-minded girl, and I am sure she is trustworthy."

I am glad she is. Keep her so, my friend, *keep her so*. Do not risk making her otherwise by placing her under the greatest temptation that can possibly come to a girl.

If you place her in the dancing academy or ballroom, she cannot and will not remain what you say she now is, and she has but a comparatively small chance of escaping ruin—comparatively only a small chance, I say.

It is a startling fact, but a fact nevertheless, that *two-thirds of the girls who are ruined fall through the influence of dancing*. Mark my words, I know this to be true. Let me give you two reasons why it is so. In the first place, I do not believe that any woman can or does waltz without being improperly aroused, to a greater or less degree. She may not, at first, understand her feelings, or recognize as harmful or sinful those emotions which must come to every woman who has a particle of warmth in her nature, when in such close connection with the opposite sex; but she is, though unconsciously, none the less surely sowing seed which will one day ripen, if not into open sin and shame, into a nature more or less depraved and health more or less impaired. Any woman with a nature so cold as not to be aroused by the perfect execution of the waltz, is entirely unfit to make any man happy as his wife, and if she be willing to indulge in such pleasures with every ballroom libertine, she is not the woman any man wants for a wife. It is a noticeable fact that a man who knows the ways of a ballroom rarely seeks a wife there. When he wishes to marry he chooses for a wife a woman who has not been fondled and embraced by every dancing man in town.

The second reason why so many dancing girls are ruined is obvious, when one considers how many fiends there are hanging about the dancing schools and ballrooms, for this purpose alone; some of them for their own gratification, and others for the living there is to be made from it. I am personally acquainted with men who are professional seducers, and who are today making a living in just this way. They are fine looking, good conversationalists and elegant dancers. They buy their admittance to the select (?) dancing school by paying an extra fee, and know just what snares to lay and what arts to practice upon the innocent girls they meet there to induce them to yield to their diabolical solicitations, and after having satisfied their own desires and ruined the girls they entice them to the brothel where they receive a certain sum of money from the landlady, rated according to their beauty and form.

Can you wonder when the degrading, lust-creating influence of the waltz itself is united with the efforts of such vile demons of men as I have described, that two-thirds of the dancing girls are ruined.

It is a greater wonder that any of them escape. . . . Dancing and drinking invariably go together. One rarely finds a dance hall without a bar in it or a saloon within a few steps of it, and sooner or later those who dance will indulge in drink, which is the devil's best agent in the carrying on of the vile business transacted in, and in connection with, the dance hall.

CHAPTER 15

Dance-Hall Reform (1909)

Belle Lindner Israels

The girls say that "carfare" is all it costs for a summer day at North Beach, admission fees the only "price" for a winter evening at a dancing academy. "With the voice of joy—with a multitude that kept holiday," they come and go at both places. In the summer the problem is what to do during enforced idleness; in the winter it focuses on where to go for relaxation. The beaches are summer types of amusement. The dancing academy of the winter months is at one end of slide, with stops *en route,* to the saloon where dancing is allowed as a thirst accelerator—where girls are an asset only in proportion to the amount of liquid refreshment that they can induce the men to buy.

The amusement resources of the working girl run the gamut from innocent and innocuous vacation homes and settlement dancing schools, sparsely furnished for those "well recommended," to the plentiful allurements of the day boat, with its easily rented rooms, the beach, the picnic ground, with its ill-lighted grove and "hotel," to numberless places where one may dance and find partners, with none too scrupulous a supervision.

Having made accusations, let us proceed to substantiate them.

It is an industrial fact that the summer months find thousands of working girls either in the position of compulsory idleness through slack season in the

Selected excerpts from Belle Lindner Israels, "The Way of the Girl," *Survey* 22 (July 3, 1909): 486–97.

trades with which they are familiar, or attempting "to kill time," through one or two weeks of a vacation, unwelcome because it bears no definite recreative fruit. . . . Active participation in athletics gives a natural outlet for the boy. The recreative desire of the young girl leads not to Sunday baseball—except as "he" may be playing—nor is it able to content itself with a comparatively expensive and therefore infrequent visit to the theatre. Her aspirations demand attention from the other sex. No amusement is complete in which "he" is not a factor. The distinction between the working woman and her more carefully guarded sister of the less driven class is one of standards, opportunities, and a chaperon. Three rooms in a tenement, overcrowded, with the younger children, make the street a private apartment. The public resort similarly overcrowded, but with those who are not inquisitive, answers as her reception room. . . .

The range of summer amusements around New York city covers first, beach resorts; second, amusement parks; third, the picnic park utilized for the outing, the chowder, and the summer night's festival; fourth, the excursion boat; fifth, the vacation home or camp provided by settlements, churches, and girls' clubs.

Of the beach resorts, Coney Island and Rockaway [New York] are naturally in the van of public thought. Rockaway is expensive to reach. Its clientele is of the upper class of saleswomen and office workers. They enjoy the ocean bath and spend a comparatively simple day at the beach; and, being better provided with the world's goods than the average girl whom we wish to consider, are not seeking the same kinds of excitement.

Coney Island—the people's playground—where each year "everything is new but the ocean" is the most gigantic of the efforts to amuse.

A dancing master said: "If you haven't got the girls, you can't do business! Keep attracting 'em. The fellows will come if the girls are there."

Coney Island does attract them. It only costs fare down and back, and for the rest of it the boys you "pick up," "treat."

When the girl is both lucky and clever, she frees herself from her self-selected escort before home-going time, and finds a feminine companion in his place for the midnight ride in the trolley. When she is not clever, some one of her partners of the evening may exact tribute for "standing treat." Then the day's outing costs more than carfare. With due recognition of the simpler amusement places on the island—such as Steeplechase Park, where no liquor is sold, and also of the innocent pleasure along the beach front, not even belittling the fact that "nice" people dance in the Dreamland ballroom, the fact remains that the average girl has small powers of discrimination. So many hundred places abound on the island to counter-balance the few safe ones, that "careers" without number find their initial stage in a Raines law hotel at this resort.

The danger is not in the big places on the island, where orderly shows and dance halls are run, and where young persons may go unattended. But the greatest number of musical halls and dance resorts are along the side streets of the Bowery, and with the exception of one or two semi-respectable places, are thoroughly disreputable. On Saturday and Sunday nights many young working girls are attracted to these places. They know the bad reputation of some of them, but the dancing floor is good, there are always plenty of men, and there are laughter and liberty galore. . . .

The town is dance mad. If you walk along Grand Street on any night in the week during the winter months, the glare of lights and the blare of music strike you on every side. It might be an esplanade at Dreamland instead of a business street. Columbia Street, Delancey Street, Stanton Street, Allen Street, Houston Street, all have their quota of places, good, bad, and indifferent. Further uptown, the dance places hold sway in almost every locality, and the problems which this dancing mania presents vary from the moral issues of the lower East Side to the drink temptations that beset the girl further uptown. This is essentially the winter problem. Down on the East Side, dancing is cheap. Twenty-five cents a couple is all it costs—ten cents for girls, because, as I have said before, the girls are the desirable quantity. Throughout the city the rule obtains that it shall cost the girl less to enter the hall than the man. Downtown, the dancing academy presents its worst features. It is frequently located in rooms not adapted for such purposes, and very often unsafe and unsanitary. It is called a dancing academy, because on at least four nights a week, instruction in dancing is actually given. It pays to have the classes as a basis for the crowds which it is hoped to attract on "reception nights." Usually Wednesday, Saturday and Sunday nights are set aside for receptions and Sunday afternoons for matinee dances. This is the rule everywhere in the dancing academies, not only on the East Side. These receptions are really public dances, which anybody with the price of admission may attend. In a few places, on the payment of admission, one may enter any night, and provision is made for these transients, by having every other dance a general dance, the one in between being given up to the pupils and their instruction. The downtown hall is infested with the "spieler." This refers not to his style of dancing, but it is a generic term covering many youths who have no other apparent means of livelihood than assisting the dancing master with his pupils. It is the business of the spieler to attract and interest young girls. He dances with the wall flowers, and he is expected to keep everybody happy and everybody busy. He makes it his duty also to point out to those seeking them, the girls whose "good time" can be prolonged beyond the dancing floor. He is acquainted with the moral character of every girl who enters the place, and in all too many instances, he is probably responsible for it. Whether the spieler is part of an organized system for supplying girls to houses of prostitution is questionable, but he is part of that underworld which spreads its network for that most attractive of captures—the young and innocent girl. Spielers will tell you in moments of confidence that no girl comes to the dance hall night after night and remains what she was when she began coming there. You cannot dance night after night, held in the closest of sensual embraces, with every effort made in the style of dancing to appeal to the worst that is in you, and remain unshaken by it. No matter how wary or how wise a girl may be—and she has enough things in her daily life in factory and store to teach her—she is not always able to keep up the good fight. It is always a matter of pursuit and capture. The man is ever on the hunt, and the girl is ever needing to flee. It does not necessarily mean that these girls become prostitutes, but they belong in one of the many hundred classes into which the social evil divides itself. In the uptown dancing academies, the liquor selling that goes on assists in the weakening process. It helps to becloud the vision and to make distinctions between right and wrong a little more puzzling. In many instances, especially in the light-hearted Irish boys and girls, there is no deliberate intention to seek out the girl for wrongful purposes, but the girl is pretty and happy, and she wants a good time, and she does as the other girls do. She takes soft drinks at first, but later she begins to like being just a bit sporty. At this stage of the game, the cocktail is introduced, and boy and girl frequently leave the warm hall where they have been dancing together and drinking, none too clear in their minds as to their relations towards each other. The girls of this type rarely go very far on the downward path, but they are only too apt to lose the bloom of their youth in the course of these promiscuous amusements.

Dancing is offered in another class of place. Many saloons have as adjuncts a dance floor in a room set aside for that purpose. Here, without any attempt at concealment, the drink is the thing, and it can truly be said, "they have cast lots for my people and have sold a girl for wine." Dancing is carried on for three minutes, and then there is an intermission of fifteen to twenty minutes, when the waiter urges you to drink. If you don't drink, and if you don't get other people to drink, you are not welcome, and the waiter very frankly tells you so. The saloon dance hall has no good features. A method must be found to stamp it out altogether. No effectual means has yet been found. The evils are masked under a semblance of giving pleasure. It is the most insidious form of enticement. It must be said for these places that good girls go there by accident more than by design. The good girl is more apt to go to the dancing academy, but even the percentage that does go to these places should be kept away.

Girls do not of intention select bad places to go to. The girl whose temperament and disposition crave unnatural forms of excitement is nearly beyond the bounds of salvation; but ninety out of one hundred girls want only what they are entitled to—innocent relaxation. The moving picture show is on the wane. The skating rink had its day long ago. The dance is destined to be the next feature in popular amusement.

Let us provide it plentifully, safely, and inexpensively. Then the winter problem will be taken in hand. The bill to regulate and license academies meets only a few of the most apparent evils. How to legislate out of existence the bad features of the summer amusement places seems almost unanswerable, since there are so many political and other interests that work underneath in these enterprises. An ex-governor of the state controls one of the excursion boats of which we have spoken, and a state senator is most deeply interested in Coney Island. It is a fetching argument against any attempted betterment to say that the people's amusements are being interfered with. It is hard to realize that interference is necessary for social betterment. It is not beyond the bounds of possibility that a municipal scheme of amusement could be evolved. . . .

Van Cortlandt Park, now made so accessible by the subway, is filled on Sundays with young men and women, who apparently ask nothing more than the doubtful pleasure of sitting quietly on the benches or the grass eating peanuts. Why not a public dance platform, to which admission is charged, and which is properly conducted? They have them in France and in Germany—and they work and they pay. Why not a public carrousel? Why not other amusement features in some corners of the great new parks which we are acquiring? These things do no harm, and they offer innocent diversion of the kind which the multitude seeks.

We must recover from the idea that the public is intrinsically bad. It needs instruction in the fine art of using, not abusing its privileges, and a little faith in the great American proletariat will develop a marvelous return.

Let us frankly recognize that youth demands amusement. When the cities begin to see their duties to the little ones, playgrounds come. Youth plays too. Instead of sand-piles give them dance platforms; instead of slides and see-saws, theaters; instead of teachers of manual occupations, give them the socializing forces of contact with good supervising men and women. Replace the playground, or more properly, progress from the playground to the rational amusement park.

Denial of these privileges peoples the underworld; furnishing them is modern preventive work and should be an integral part of any social program.

CHAPTER 16

The Twist: Brave New Whirl (1962)

Marshall Fishwick

History suggests that there is one clear manifestation of approaching middle age: when you and your closest friends conclude that the younger generation is "going to the dogs." So it is in every culture, every clime. Plato's friends are a case in point. So are Dante's. My favorite story on this theme is much closer to home, however, involving two tight-lipped Vermont farmers sitting around a winter stove. The first one complains that there's been far too much he-ing and she-ing going on in the valley lately. To which his neighbor gives a sparse answer: "'Bout same as usual, Jake. Only other people are doing it now."

The favorite parental target in 1962 is the new dance rage, the Twist. Not even the Russians come in for such violent denunciation in some quarters. Parents forbid it individually, and some towns communally. The dance draws such descriptive epithets as barbaric, erotic, inhuman, and satanic. Listening to a group of local ladies sound off recently, I realized that I had heard a remarkably similar description myself once—when I learned how to jitterbug! So did my father, he admitted privately—when he did the Charleston.

Actually I do not intend to debate the merits or demerits of the Twist. Whether or not the American girl has sacrificed romance for sex appeal I am not prepared to say; but if anyone thinks sex didn't appeal before the days of the Twist, I'll take my stand and slug. If this be treason, I am prepared to make the most of it.

As a student of American culture, I am willing to argue more: that the Twist is a valid manifestation of the Age of Anxiety; an outward manifestation of the anguish, frustration, and uncertainty of the 1960s; an effort to release some of the tension which, if suppressed and buried, could warp and destroy.

In our dancing, as in our ideology and diplomacy, we show who we are, and what America is in the twentieth century.

Marshall Fishwick, "The Twist: Brave New Whirl," *Saturday Review,* Mar. 3, 1962, pp. 8–10. Reprinted by permission of General Media International, Inc., *The Saturday Review,* © 1979.

The same can be said, of course, for other people in other ages. The smug, rationalistic, Cartesian eighteenth century danced the minuet. The aroused, romantic, Darwinian nineteenth century waltzed. The tempo of the times is mirrored in the tempo of the music. Can this be applied to the twentieth century, and the "wild" outbursts of our musicians and dancers? I think so. My case would run something like this:

Around the turn of the century—historians will always argue about just when—there was a notable quickening in the American tempo. "Everybody knows that at *some* point in the twentieth century America went through a cultural revolution," writes Henry F. May in "The End of Innocence." "Glance at a family album, or pick up a book or magazine dated 1907. You will find yourself in a completely vanished world." . . .

To tell it fully in a short article, or long book, is out of the question. We are too close to the transformation either to recognize or evaluate all that has happened. Sociologists have begun to document the change from the Protestant ethic to the social ethic; from individualism to togetherness. . . .

The art form which has been most successful at capturing the essence of contemporary America is jazz. Here, if anywhere, we can sense the meaning of process. Musicians grope for a line, follow it, explore it, soar with it. They are, as our children claim, "way-out"—as much in space in their own particular way as our astronauts.

By superimposing syncopation and polyrhythm, jazz gives us unending variety and a tension of counterpurposes. Whereas the traditional European rhythms are chordal or vertical, those of American jazz are linear or horizontal. No wonder jazz has been our most important cultural export, and Louis Armstrong our best diplomat, in the last generation. The testimony on this point is impressive. Speaking of World War II, the German pianist Jutta Hipp wrote: "I remember nights when we didn't go down to the bomb shelter because we listened to jazz records. We just had the feeling that you are not our enemies, and even though the bombs crashed around us . . . we felt safe [Fishwick's ellipsis]."

Taken almost as a religion by many abroad, jazz has encountered stern opposition from some at home. The basic reason will illuminate the current condemnation of the Twist. The psychiatrist Dr. Norman Margolis has explained this tendency by noting that an essentially free and uninhibited art form ran into a stratum of society that put high values on properness, control, and restraint. The remnants of the Puritan tradition dictated a rigid cultural conscience repressing those impulses with which jazz has associated, and which it symbolized. A new generation, anxious to achieve its own independence and expression, has adopted new sounds and gyrations as its red badge of courage. Thus the implications of the matter are social and psychic as well as musical.

Add to that list theological implications, too. Thoughtful churchmen realize that they can no longer evade this embarrassing question: why has jazz won more converts than either the Christian Church or the Communist party in the last fifty years?

Wilson Wade, professor of religion at Dartmouth College, has suggested an answer: "Jazz shows us the image of the twentieth century man—in search of his humanity." In its honesty and ability to mirror our times it offers advantages traditional music lacks. To know and participate in the life of the Man of the Sixties, we must open ourselves to the sound of jazz, and the sight of the Twist. In neither is there a clear-cut distinction between good and evil, or any delusions about categories. Instead, there is despair and hope, ecstasy and cacophony, frustration and fulfillment. "If we in the Church are really open to the gifts which God continually sets in our midst," Dr. Wade adds, "we may find that jazz is the long-awaited symbol for the renewed affirmation we so desperately need." To this strong affirmative statement Father Kennard, of the philosophy department of Loyola University in Los Angeles, adds five words: "To swing is to affirm." . . .

Schools and styles come and go—Dixie, ragtime, swing, bop, cool—but the implication of jazz remains. It is no passing fad, to be corrected as American taste improves. Jazz is in the main stream of American culture; a recoil from the loneliness of a fragmented culture; a device to heal the psychic alienation that separates and corrodes. "Where lucidity reigns," the existentialist leader Albert Camus wrote, "a scale of values becomes unnecessary."

I am aware that in all the areas we have mentioned (art, music, entertainment) the woods are full of hucksters and phonies. We all know about that donkey that tied a brush to its tail and painted a prize-winning abstract painting, and the singing star who had his faulty adenoids removed and lost his contract on TV. What age *hasn't* had its phonies and pretenders? What cultural revolution has ever swept a people without confusion, pretension, and exhibitionism? Should that which is genuine be condemned because it is surrounded by that which is spurious?

Before you reject the sights and sounds of the Sixties, think back on the days when *you* were a rebel; when all the "old fogies" (that is, people over 26) complained that you were going just a little too far, a little too fast. By listing a score of "crazes" that have swept our nation since 1900, I think I'll elicit smiles of admission and nostalgia from all but the *ancien régime* among *Saturday Re-*

view readers: Cake Walk, Camel Walk, Eagle Rock, Shimmy, Black Bottom, Charleston, Snake Hips, Lindy Hop, Shim Sham, Truckin', Susie Q, Shorty George, Peckin', Boogie Woogie, Big Apple, Shag, Sand, Apple Jack, Mambo, Cha cha cha.

"But none of them," you may argue, "is like the Twist." Did you expect them to be?

Only a man braver and wiser than I would claim to know where the line between experimental and eccentric, new and neurotic, significant and silly must be drawn. In art as in life, those who tend to "like it all" and those who "hate it all" tend to obstruct true issues and merit. Ralph Waldo Emerson told us over a century ago what type of people we needed in the democracy which would fulfill the American dream: "Men and women of original perception and original action, who can open their eyes wider than to a nationality . . . men of elastic, men of moral mind, who can live in the moment and *take a step forward* [Fishwick's ellipsis]."

We move forward in doubt, and sometimes in fear. Viewing the mechanization of life, the acceleration of pace, and the mobility of people, we cannot help it. Too often we meet, have surface contacts, and ricochet on, like billiard balls tapped aimlessly by an infant. By losing our identity, we lose our community, in a land of hard, inhuman ambitions. The pioneers of our time are Prometheans, and the less sensitive among them have enthroned a new trinity: mechanism, militarism, and money. Instead of going Onward and Upward, we have moved from Progress to Perplexity. Yet that which is *essentially* American remains; and continues to be the hope of Western civilization. No one has ever isolated this essential ingredient, and probably no one ever will. Scott Fitzgerald tried and came up with a memorable metaphor. "France has a land," he said, "England has a people, but America, having about it still the quality of the idea, is harder to utter. It is the frozen limbs at Valley Forge, the graves at Shiloh, the tired drawn faces of its great men. . . . It is a *willingness of the heart* [Fishwick's ellipsis]."

Thomas Wolfe saw the voyage from the Old World to the new and easily twisted America as one of the exciting truths of human history. "There is no other experience that is remotely comparable to it," he wrote in "Of Time and the River," "in its sense of joy, its exultancy, its drunken and magnificent hope which, against reason and knowledge, soars into a heaven of fabulous conviction, which believes in the miracle and sees it invariably achieved."

The defense rests. Vive le Twist!

CHAPTER 17

The Dance of the Century (1988)

New York Times, *Dec. 12, 1988*

DANCE OF THE CENTURY "WAS A BLAST"

PURDY, Mo., Dec. 11 (AP) Although it took a Federal judge's intervention to produce the first high school dance in this century-old Ozarks town, the students needed a little encouragement to do the rest Saturday.

Nancy Fox, Purdy High School's Student Council president, said the students were shy about taking the floor when the homecoming dance began until she reminded them of the attention the dispute over the event had received around the country.

She said she told them, "They say we can't dance." After that, the floor was crowded for the rest of the evening, she said.

"It was a blast—we had a great time," Miss Fox said.

Outsiders were not allowed into the gymnasium, but rock music, shouts and claps could be heard throughout the dance.

RULING UNDER APPEAL

Sheldon Buxton, superintendent of the Purdy school system, said about 85 of the 161 students at the school attended the dance. He said it went smoothly, but he refused to comment on whether other dances would be held.

Longtime residents say Purdy has always had a ban on social dancing in the schools. But Federal District Judge Russell Clark ruled this summer that the school board's written policy against dancing unconstitutionally promoted the values of those who oppose dancing for religious reasons.

The four-member school board appealed Judge Clark's order, but the United States Court of Appeals for the Eighth Circuit allowed the dance to go on while it considered the issue. The appeals court is not expected to rule in the case any time soon.

"Dance of the Century Was a Blast," Associated Press release, *New York Times,* Dec. 12, 1988. By permission of AP.

Miss Fox's mother, Joan, a spokeswoman for the 21 students and parents who sued the school board, said board members had warned that the students might have this dance "but they won't have another one."

Board members refused to comment.

NOT "WORTH ALL THAT"

Miss Fox said board members attended the dance. But the board members, who sat on the sidelines talking among themselves, apparently did not cramp students' style.

"It was really fun, everybody's dancing," said Shannon Francisco, a senior.

But Miss Francisco, 17, added that the dance had caused controversy and bitterness in the town. "I don't think it was worth all that," she said.

Students leaving the dance answered with choruses of "awesome" when asked about their evening.

SUGGESTED BOOKS AND FILMS

Adams, Doug, and Diane Apostolos-Cappadona, eds. *Dance as Religious Studies.* New York: Crossroad Publishing Company, 1990.

Brookes, James H. *May Christians Dance?* St. Louis, Mo.: J. W. McIntyre, 1869.

Dillon, John. *From Dance Hall to White Slavery: The World's Greatest Tragedy.* Chicago: Charles C. Thompson, 1912. Reprinted as *From Dance Hall to White Slavery.* New York: Padell Book and Magazine Company, 1939.

Cressey, Paul. *The Taxi-Dance Hall: A Sociological Study in Commercialized Recreation and City Life.* Chicago: University of Chicago Press, 1932.

Gardner, Ella. *Public Dance Halls: Their Regulation and Place in the Recreation of Adolescents.* U.S. Department of Labor, Children's Bureau Publication no. 189. Washington, D.C.: Government Printing Office, 1929.

Gross, J. B. *The Parson on Dancing as It is Taught in the Bible, and Was Practiced Among the Ancient Greeks and Romans.* 1879; reprint, Brooklyn: Dance Horizons, n.d.

Hart, Oliver. *Dancing Exploded: A Sermon Shewing the Unlawfulness, Sinfulness, and Bad Consequences of Balls, Assemblies, and Dances in General.* Charlestown, S.C.: David Bruce, 1778. Microfilm. Early American Imprints. First series; no. 15848.

Hazzard-Gordon, Katrina. *Jookin': The Rise of Social Dance Formations in African-American Culture.* Philadelphia: Temple University Press, 1990.

Hubbert, James Monroe. *Dance and Dancers: A Calm and Rational View of the Dancing Question.* Nashville, Tenn.: Cumberland Presbyterian Publishing House, ca. 1901.

Malone, Jacqui. *Steppin' on the Blues: The Visible Rhythms of African American Dance.* Urbana: University of Illinois Press, 1996.

Marks, Joseph E., III. *America Learns to Dance.* 1957; reprint, Brooklyn: Dance Horizons, [1976?].

Mather, Cotton. *A Cloud of Witnesses; Darting Out Light Upon a Case, Too Unseasonably Made Seasonable to be Discoursed On.* Boston: B. Green & J. Allen, c. 1700. Reprinted, along with Increase Mather's *An Arrow Against Mixt Dancing,* in Joseph E. Marks, III, ed., *The Mathers on Dancing.* Brooklyn: Dance Horizons, 1975. This edition also includes a selected bibliography of anti-dance tracts published in the United States.

Perry, Elisabeth. "The General Motherhood of the Commonwealth: Dance Hall Reform in the Progressive Era." *American Quarterly* 37, no. 5 (Winter, 1985): 719–33.

Rust, Ezra Gardner. *The Music and Dance of the World's Religions: A Comprehensive, Annotated Bibliography of Materials in the English Language.* Westport, Conn.: Greenwood Press, 1996.

St. Denis, Ruth. "Dance as Spiritual Expression." In *Dance: A Basic Educational Technique,* ed. F. R. Rogers, pp. 100–110. New York: Macmillan, 1941.

Stewart, Iris. *Sacred Woman, Sacred Dance: Awakening Spirituality through Movement and Ritual.* Rochester, Vt.: Inner Traditions, 1998.

Troxell, Kay, ed. *Resources in Sacred Dance: Annotated Bibliography from Christian and Jewish Traditions.* Peterborough, N.H.: Sacred Dance Guild, 1991.

Wagner, Ann. *Adversaries of Dance: From the Puritans to the Present.* Urbana: University of Illinois Press, 1997.

There are many sources that distribute movies on dance, so check with your local distributors, regional colleges, or state archives for listings. Titles for new videos are expanding constantly. For addresses of distributors named below, or further suggestions, see the Dance Films Association's *Dance Film and Video Guide* named in the Selected General Readings and References on Theatrical Dance.

Acrobats of God. 22 minutes, color. Pyramid. Martha Graham effectively addresses the anti-dance moralists in this joyous celebration of the dancer as one who is blessed by God.

Dirty Dancing. 100 minutes, color. Swank Distributors, 1987. Mather, Faulkner, and the Castles themselves would no doubt have condemned Johnny Castle, the dancing master portrayed in this movie. Dances from the 1950s are divided into two types: old-fashioned and "dirty." The young people, it should be no surprise, prefer those that shock their elders.

Footloose. 106 minutes, color. Paramount, 1984. High school students attempt to persuade a conservative school board to sponsor a high school prom; during the 1990s it saw new life when it was made into a Broadway musical with expanded music.

The Joy of Bach. Either 16 or 30 minutes, color. Vision Video. Five Bach pieces are choreographed by Manfred Schnelle and performed by Jacob's Pillow Dancers. An example of the trend to use dance for liturgical purposes; produced by the Lutheran Film Associates.

Revelations in *An Evening with Alvin Ailey American Dance Theatre.* Approximately 30 minutes, color. RM Arts. *Revelations,* Ailey's masterpiece, became the signature piece of his dance company. Set to African American spirituals, it depicts his own experiences of baptism by immersion and portrays churchgoers on a hot summer Sunday.

Speaking in Tongues. 60 minutes, color. Paul Taylor's condescending depiction of rural southern life, complete with the preacher, the prostitute, gang rapists, and a parcel of village folk.

The Story of Vernon and Irene Castle. 90 minutes, black and white. RKO, 1939. Fred
   Astaire and Ginger Rogers whirl their way through dances popular before World
   War I when the dance hall reformers were very active. The Castles were held up as
   models of deportment and grace.

Tzaddik. 30 minutes, color. Electronic Arts Intermix. Eliot Feld choreographs a study
   that evokes memories of Hassidic Jewish rituals; performed to Aaron Copland's
   Vitebsk.

PART 4

PIONEERS OF THEATRICAL DANCE IN AMERICA

INTRODUCTION

The first wave of the invasion of professional French theatrical dancers arrived on American shores during the 1790s. The occasional English actor or dancing master, who appeared in American theaters from the 1730s on, found it difficult to compete with these graceful invaders and, with rare exceptions, retired from the stage in short order. Jean Baptiste Francisqui, whose contributions are recounted in the second selection, was but one example of the French dancers who fled Haiti during the slaves' revolt and arrived in the United States prior to 1800.[1]

American theatrical dance was never the same after the French dancers' arrival. From 1791 on and for the next fifty years, French dancers, teachers and their students, choreographers, and ballet masters were employed, and a French-derived ballet repertoire was produced annually on the New Orleans and Philadelphia stages.[2] Ballet became an integral part of stage entertainments from New York to New Orleans. The first selection illustrates the significant impact these dancers had on John Durang (1768–1822). America's first native-born professional dancer recalls how he learned ballet by watching French dancers as they performed or taught. He danced the gavotte à la Vestris, which was modeled after a dance performed by the great Paris Opéra dancer Gaetano Vestris. So, too, were the ballet steps with which he interlaced his sailor's hornpipe.[3]

A large part of the French dancers' impact stemmed from their ability to assemble an "instant" repertoire drawn directly from that of the theaters of Saint-Domingue (today known as Haiti), their last stop on the theatrical circuit before they fled to the United States. As the French dancers arrived, they sought each other out and called on French musicians to play for them or composers to create for them. They found French singers to perform in opera-ballets with them and French designers or machinists to create the necessary stage illusions. Their repertoire, which consisted of pastoral ballets, comical ballets, harlequinades, and ballet-pantomimes, had first been given either at the Paris Opéra or popular Parisian theaters, where they had originally appeared before coming to the West Indies. In addition, many members of their audience had immigrated along with them from France via Haiti.

From 1791 almost up to the Civil War, dancers who had trained and performed in Paris monopolized the American stage: some stayed to settle and teach a new generation of American dancers while others, such as Fanny Elssler (1810–84), toured on circuit to great applause only to return to Europe with her pockets full of gold. Elssler, one of the most celebrated ballerinas from the Paris Opéra, brought with her a contagious disease called "Elsslermania." "Fanny Elssler is all the word—all the rage—all the mania—all the talk of the town," according to the *New York Morning Herald* on May 2, 1840. The third selection reprints two contemporary descriptions of the woman who became the personification of desire for her audiences, one a review of her debut performance at the Park Theatre in New York City and the other a private journal entry written by the eminent literary figure Ralph Waldo Emerson. Emerson and the newspaper were not alone in the attention they devoted to this renowned ballerina. All imaginable fashions and fetishistic objects were named after her: there was hair worn à la Elssler, Elssler champagne, sugar candies, boats, boots, shoes, hats, bootjacks, and even lozenges at the pharmacy.[4] Gentlemen wore Elssler boots, ladies were seen in Elssler cuffs, and both ate Elssler bread. It got so that "everything and all things are now Fanny Elssler."[5] In her two-year tour, she performed slightly over two hundred times in the United States or Cuba, and reportedly amassed a fortune of nearly $140,000.[6] Her tour marked the culmination of a fifty-year period that saw many French dancers come to North America. After she left, Italians began to invade in substantial numbers around the mid-century and dominated dance in North America up until World War I, when the Russians, in the guise of "Diaghileff's *Ballet Russe,*" toured America coast to coast.

In the meantime, young American dancers grew tired of waiting in the wings, and seized whatever opportunities they could find to take center stage for themselves. The number of American dancers, most trained by French performers, expanded rapidly during the first half of the nineteenth century until Italian ballet masters came to take up much of the slack. Juvenile dancers dominated dance activities in Philadelphia from 1800 to the early 1820s, and growing numbers of American children featured as dancers appeared each year, particularly after the Paris Opéra dancers proved that dancers could earn a good income. The statistics reflect an astonishing progression: In 1784, John Durang, the first American professional dancer, performed his hornpipe for the Philadelphia theater. By 1830, as many as thirty children were dancing in the corps de ballet at only one Philadelphia theater, while yet other theaters boasted substantial numbers of what they termed "juvenile" or "infant" dancers.[7] By 1853, George Washington Smith, a Philadelphia-born choreographer, could direct a corps de ballet of 150 dancers, whom critics praised for their "evolutions [that] add quite a grace and charm to the performance."[8] By 1893, as will be seen in part 5, Kiralfy, the choreographer for *America,* could brag that he had directed over 150 dancers and 650 other performers in that one stage production alone.

Some Americans developed into stars in their own right, such as Mary Ann Lee and George Washington Smith, who toured the United States year after year. Others toured the world, for example, the Ince sisters who went on tour to Australia and la petite Celeste who sailed to Peru and California, while the Vallee sisters, the Wells (a brother and sister team), and Julia Turnbull all performed in Cuba. Some became dancing masters, most prominently John Durang's son Charles, who wrote several books on dance. A handful developed into choreographers, such as George Washington Smith, who staged ballets right up through the end of the nineteenth century. Augusta Maywood even triumphed at the Paris Opéra Ballet, and an African American dancer named William Henry Lane ("Juba") performed to the applause of English royalty. These accomplishments and many others illustrate positive phases in the establishment of ballet as an art form in nineteenth-century America.

While some American dancers were proving that they could master elite art forms associated with the Old World, others were involved in creating a new type of American theatrical art. By the late 1820s and 1830s, solo dancers who impersonated blacks became fashionable, such as the infamous character of Jim Crow as portrayed by Thomas Rice. Minstrel shows, a northern urban phenomenon of the 1840s, replaced these solo acts by collective impersonations performed by whole troupes. When this "new, uniquely American popular culture form, the minstrel show, emerged on the scene, it became an instant rage and a national institution virtually overnight," according to Robert Toll.[9] Within a few years of minstrelsy's birth in 1843, one writer reflected its widespread public acceptance when he asserted that the minstrel "deserves to be fostered and cherished" by Americans.[10] Some nineteenth-century admirers touted the minstrel show as "the American National Opera," "the only true American drama," or "this, our only original American institution."[11]

These shows, in line with the general trend toward lavishly spectacular entertainment, grew larger and larger. What had begun as small troupes of six grew to as many as one hundred by 1878. The minstrels lasted until the early 1930s on the Mississippi River showboats, and into the 1960s in amateur vaudeville shows for the benefit of local American Legion halls and similar institutions. By the 1880s African Americans themselves formed minstrel show troupes and took advantage of one of the rare opportunities for blacks to find lucrative, albeit inherently degrading, stage employment. One tragic effect of the minstrel shows was that demeaning stereotypes of African Americans became deeply embedded in popular culture, a development which contributed to the deep divisions in American society between rich and poor, black and white. Sad to say, they remain with us to this day.

The old-time minstrel show settled into a rigid format that survived well into the twentieth century. It began with the Walk-about, a characteristic floor pattern in which the performers, two by two, circled the stage in a kind of strut or cakewalk dance. They sat down while the Interlocutor greeted the audience and engaged in comical repartee with the End Men named Tambo and Bones.[12] The show next moved into the olio, a series of comical skits and monologues, musical interludes, acrobatics, and dance. The performers often poked fun at elitist cultural traditions; for example, Mr. Christy was famous for his *Black Bayadere,* in which he imitated Fanny Elssler. He went so far as to dance in toe shoes and an identical copy of her pink and black lace tutu. A chorus might sit in the bleachers at the back of the stage and sing or comment, in pantomime form, on the action. They would point in unison to some dramatic action on stage, then slap their knees and grin as if amused, for example.[13] It ended with a dramatic afterpiece, generally a parody or farce such as is reprinted in the fourth selection, the Christy Minstrels' *Black Crook Burlesque,* which featured white men masquerading as black men pretending to be white women pretending to be French ballerinas. The finale was the structural obverse of the beginning, with farewells by the Interlocutor and a Walk-about by the cast.

The minstrel shows, with their gratuitous insults and stereotyped characters, lasted until the 1970s in the United States. Now they are dead and gone. *The Black Crook Burlesque,* an 1867 farce that poked fun at a very popular dance spectacle described in the final selection for this section, has been included in this book as a reminder of how far American society has come. Our modern sensibility finds such blatant racism to be excruciatingly discomforting. Yet we still have far to go, for the bigotry that fuels this kind of humor has not disappeared.

The last selection consists of two newspaper descriptions of the most famous homegrown spectacle of the nineteenth century. This extravaganza premiered in 1866 in New York and ran continuously on American stages until 1909. *The*

Black Crook was basically an expensive hodgepodge of worn-out Romantic conceits, complete with melodramatic plot and an assortment of heroes who sell their souls, villains who lock up helpless heroines in dungeons, and so on. However silly the plot, the spectacle is important in the history of American musical theater, for it reached a huge, nationwide audience with the best ballet dancing available during that period. Although many recent scholars argue against such a simplistic proposition, it has long been accepted as an important "landmark for the beginning of American musical comedy."[14]

The Black Crook's success was founded on a formula that emphasized lavishness and lots of legs. Even prior to the Civil War, one reviewer in *Porter's Spirit of the Times,* June 25, 1859, commented that ballets with a "lot of tiresome children" had recently been supplanted by those with "some really very good-looking women and a principal dancer of actual talent and personal attractiveness." *The Black Crook* magnified that trend. It employed eighty dancers, only half of them American—and the latter scarcely danced but simply paraded about in revealing outfits. The manager exploited his dancers by advertising in the *New York Clipper,* September 29, 1866, a timetable of salacious attractions for male voyeurs. He suggested that any man who is a "lover of natural beauties" might wish to "drop in, take a peep at a favorite scene, or dancer, or leg, or something, and, after enjoying the sight, return to the bosom of his family."

The three-tiered structure discriminated against American dancers, once able to aspire to stardom but now relegated to the background. Italians who had trained at La Scala were hired as ballerinas, while minor soloists were recruited from English music halls. *The Black Crook* production thus perpetuated the myth of European dancers' supremacy even after some Americans had already achieved high levels of international renown and scores of others had proved capable of performing in various capacities as soloists or lowly corps de ballet members. Americans continued to lose ground before the onslaught of the Italian dancers, later to be followed by the Russians. By the time Isadora Duncan arrived on the dance scene in 1896, many young American dancers were easily persuaded to join her artistic revolution and reclaim center stage for themselves.

NOTES

1. For descriptions of others, see Maureen Needham on Placide, Douvillier, and Gardie in the *International Encyclopedia of Dance,* ed. Selma Jean Cohen (New York: Oxford University Press, 1998).

2. Maureen Needham [Costonis], "Ballet Comes to America, 1792–1842: French Contributions to the Establishment of Theatrical Dance in New Orleans and Philadelphia" (Ph.D. diss., New York University, 1989).

3. Several written versions of "Durang's Hornpipe" have survived. Charles Durang published his father's solo version in *Ball-Room Bijoux and the Art of Dancing* (Philadelphia: Fisher & Brother, 1856), p. 158. The other, a social dance for four couples, can be found in a school notebook kept by Elizabeth and John Crawford of Massachusetts and now in the collection of Houghton Library, Harvard University, MS. thr 286. Much simplified, the social dance was still extant as late as 1918 and published in George C. Gott, *Old Familiar Dances with Figures* (Philadelphia: Oliver Ditson Company, 1918), p. 27.

4. *Daily Picayune* (New Orleans), Nov. 10, 1840, and Apr. 18, 1841; *New York Morning Herald,* June 3, 1840. I am indebted to Mary Grace Swift for some of these references.

5. *New York Morning Herald,* June 3, 1840. See also Needham [Costonis], "The Personification of Desire: Fanny Elssler and American Audiences," *Dance Chronicle* 13 no. 1 (1990): 47–67.

6. Ivor Guest, *Fanny Elssler* (Middletown, Conn.: Wesleyan University Press, 1970), p. 185.

7. See Needham [Costonis], "Ballet Comes to America." These findings run counter to the canard that ballet "was almost nowhere taught in America, and Mlle. Elssler's ballet master, James Sylvain, had a desperate time trying to find girls just to fill the stage and stand correctly for her corps de ballet," according to Elizabeth Kendall, *Where She Danced* (New York: Alfred A. Knopf, 1979), p. 5. This tale would appear to have its origin in an ersatz "memoir" of Fanny Elssler (actually written by Henry Wikoff), in a section that dealt with Havana, not the United States. [Henry Wikoff], *Letters and Journal of Fanny Elssler* (New York: H. G. Daggers, 1845), p. 62.

8. [New York] *Spirit of the Times,* June 25, 1853.

9. Robert Toll, *Blacking Up: The Minstrel Show in Nineteenth Century America* (New York: Oxford University Press, 1974), p. 139.

10. *Spirit of the Times,* Jan. 6, 1855.

11. Quoted in Toll, *Blacking Up,* p. v.

12. See Jeff Branen and Frederick Johnson, *How to Stage a Minstrel Show: A Manual for the Amateur Burnt Cork Director* (Chicago: T. S. Denison & Company, 1921).

13. Interview with Nell Brandon, who was fortunate to see a performance on one of the last Mississippi River boats, Hilton Head Island, N.C., May 6, 1988.

14. Julian Mates, in *America's Musical Stage: Two Hundred Years of Musical Theatre* (Westport, Conn.: Greenwood Press, 1985), p. 123.

CHAPTER 18

John Durang (1768–1822), First American Theatrical Dancer

John Durang

I saw [a Mr. Rusell (Roussel)] dance a hornpipe which charmed my mind. I thought I could dance as well as any body but his stile set it off, with his dress. I practised at home and I soon could do all his steps besides many more better hornpipe steps. He was a Frenchman and the French seldom do many real ground steps. The pigeon wing[1] I never saw done by any other person, and I could not make that out from the front of the house. I contrived to get Mr. Rusell to board at my father's house that I might have the opportunity to dance more correct than I had been used to. I learned the correct stile of dancing a hornpipe in the French stile, an allemande, and steps for a country dance. Except the pigeon was the only difficulty I had to encounter: he could not show me the principle and the anatomy of the figure of the step, nor I never met with a dancer since that could show it to me. The mystery of the figure occured to me in bed, for my thoughts where constant on that object. I dream'd that I was at a ball and did the pigeon wing to admiration to the whole company; in the morning, I rose in the confidence of doing the step. By this strange circumstance on trial I was master of the step, and could explain the anatomy of the figure, and by a certain rule and method I never failed in teaching it and make my pupils master of it. . . .

Music and dancing was my attraction; I was noticed for my dancing. A man whose performance I would sometimes go and see exhibited in a house the corner of the little street running from South, to Shippen Street, between Front and Second Street. This house is part of the oldest and the first theatre that was build in Philad'a by old Hallam and Douglass;[2] it is a large old red frame building at the corner of South and the little street, and stands there yet to this day occupy'd in tenements. This man whose name I forgot, his performance

Selection excerpted from the original manuscript held at York County Historical Museum and Library as printed in John Durang, *The Memoir of John Durang, American Actor, 1785–1816,* ed. Alan S. Downer (Pittsburgh: University of Pittsburgh Press, 1966), pp. 11–13, 16–19. Durang's idiosyncratic grammar and spelling have been retained. By permission of York County Historical Museum.

John Durang was best known for his hornpipe performed in the guise of a jolly American sailor. Watercolor by John Durang. Used with permission courtesy of the Historical Society of York County, Pennsylvania.

consisted of a miscellaneous collection: transparencies, the magic lantern, sea fights in machinary, singing—all bad enough, but anything was thought great in those days. As I had a mechanical genious, and a turn for music (I could play on several instruments of music), by his flattering and promises, I consented to go with him from this to Boston, on the conditions he was to pay my whole expense while I chuse to stay with him, and to give me one night's performance to my profit, and not publish my name, and pay my journey home. A desire for travelling, and in the hope of improveing myself, and gain a better knowledge of the world, I consented to go with him. This was the first and only thing I ever done without the consent and knowledge of my father, in obedience to his will while under his command.

And now the ups and downs of my life begin. I was just in the age of 15, active, industrious, full of health and cheerfulness. I was preparing to make my first tour, to leave my father's house and mingle with the multitude of the world. My confidence in God was the security and hope in my chance of fortune; my aversion to vice, couplet with prudence, was my guide thro' life. My association was confined to partial select company; I could allways pass my time better in my chamber than in company; I was doing while some only talk of it. Idleness, resorts to taverns, low company, drinking, smokeing, gaming &c., was always my detestation. With a clear, independent spirit, I set out with this man in the stage by way of New York to Boston. . . .

[Upon returning home to Philadelphia], I met with an old school fellow who was rejoiced to see me. He revived my spirits by insisting to carry my baggage tho' but small and accompany me to my father's house. I approached the house with timorous steps and fluttering heart. Like the Prodigal Son returned, I entered the house, and with submissive reverence approach'd my father, who stretch'd forth his hands and with transport embraced me in his arms with a parental affection. Our tears where our substitute for words; they express'd at once a welcome and reconciliation with my father.

At this time, 1785, Lewis Hallam, Mr. Allen[3] and wife, and Mr. Moore, where performing in the old Theatre, South Street, under the head of "Lectures on Heads." Mrs. Allen sung; they gave scenes of plays and scraps of pantomimes.

I had an invitation to a ball. I dress'd in costume of the times, a blue coat cut in the French stile, a white tissue vestcoat, white casemere small clothes, white silk stockings, French shoes, stitch'd heels, with small sett buckles in the knee and shoes, ruffle on the wrist and bosom; the hair full dressed with the toupee, the hair tied in a fantail club with a black rose, two curls each side well powdered; a cock'd hat, gloves, and small cane, a gold watch with gold trinkets on the chain. I attended the ball. On entering the hall, I saw a large assemblage of ladies and gentlemen, many of my acquaintance, and here it was, the only time I ever could be prevaild on to dance a hornpipe in a private company. The next day commendation where bestow'd on my dancing thro' the city. The report reach'd Mr. Hallam's ear, who waited on my father to negotiate on liberal terms for me to dance on the stage, which with my father's consent I excepted.

Mr. Hallam wish'd me to rehearse my hornpipe in the morning on the stage, to get used to it—I expect a desire on his part to see a specimen of my talents. When I came on the stage, Mr. Hallam introduced me to Mr. and Mrs. Allen. The presence of them setting in the front of the stage to see me rehearse rob'd me of my best powers. A kind of fright seized me and weaken'd my better strength, which will allways be the situation of a novice on his first examination, especially when before such sterling old actors; you dread the criticism of their judgment. Mr. Hallam play'd the "Collage Hornpipe" on the violin. I dancet a few steps and made an apology, and hoped he would be satisfy'd, with my dancing at night. He encouraged me by assurance that he was already satisfied with the certainty that I would please. Mrs. Allen gave me a compleat discription of the suitable dress, with the advise to finish every step beating time....

My dress was in the caracter of a sailor, a dark blue round about full of plated buttons, paticoat trousers made with 6 yeard of fine linnen, black satin small clothes underneath, white silk stockings, a light shoe with hansome set buckle, a red westcoat, a blue silk handkerchief; my hair curled and black, a small round hat gold laced with a blue ribband, a small rattan.

With anxiety I waited the result of the night. The theatre on this occasion was crowded to see a fellow townsman make his first appearance on any stage. I had contrived a trample[4] behind the wing to enable me to gain the centre of the stage in one spring. When the curtain rose, the cry was, "Sit down, hats off!" With the swiftness of Mercury I stood before them, with a general huzza, and dancet in busts of applause. When I went off the stage, I was encored. They made such a noise, throwing a bottle in orchestre, apple, &c. on the stage, at last the curtain was raised again and I dancet a second time to the general satisfaction of the audience and managers, and gained my point.

My dress for fancy dances was in the costume of the celebrated dancer, Vestry [Vestris[5]], in England: the coat or fly with out sleeves made of white or colored silk, the small clothes the same trimed with flowers or ribband, white silk stockings, red pumps with a beau; a shirt with French sleeves, very fine trunk sleeves from the shoulder to the elbow, tied with a ribband in the centre, a laced shirt collar and bosom, a silk sash and shepherd's hat to correspond with the dress, the hair tied with a ribband. The first thing I did in pantomime was Scaramouch in *Harlequin Tutchstone*.[6] Mr. Hallam was the Harlequin, and Mr. Allen the clown in pantomimes, both very great.

NOTES

1. A dance step executed in part by jumping up and striking the legs together.

2. Since the first Lewis Hallam died before David Douglass joined the Old American Company, Durang must be referring to the Southwark (1766), which replaced Douglass' first theater, erected in 1760. Lewis Hallam the Younger played principal roles in Douglass' company.

3. From the Theatre Royal Edinburgh, Allen joined with the younger Hallam in presenting a miscellaneous entertainment. The comic "Lecture upon Heads" had been originally devised and performed by George Alexander Stevens at the Haymarket in London, January 8, 1755. It was freely plagiarized by Stevens' contemporaries and successors.

4. A canvas sheet tightly stretched on a frame, a primitive trampoline.

5. Editor's note: Gaetano Vestris, originally of Italy, was known as "le dieu de la danse" or the god of dance when he performed at the Paris Opéra. His son Auguste succeeded him as leading dancer at the Paris Opéra. Durang's ambitions reached high when he chose Vestris as his model.

6. Since the authors of eighteenth-century pantomimes are rarely identified, and since American versions frequently are (from Durang's own accounts) what we would call today "improvisational," no attempt has been made at attributions. Editor's note: Alan Downer is incorrect when he states that harlequinades' authors are rarely identified; over three hundred pantomimes are to be found in the collection of Harvard College, many of them attributed to the eighteenth-century authors. Harlequinades, such as *Harlequin Touchstone* mentioned by Durang, were great favorites of American audiences. Some were composed by French authors and traveled to England and America; others were taken directly from the traditional Italian commedia dell'arte and adapted to local tastes. For example, *Harlequin Skeleton* (originally *Arlequin Squelette*) was performed by Lewis Hallam in New York, March 4, 1754, and remained a staple of the American Company's repertoire throughout that century. The tradition continues. That piece is even today performed by the Danish pantomime troupe in the Tivoli Gardens at the Peacock Theatre.

CHAPTER 19

The American Career of Jean Baptiste Francisqui (1793–1808)

Maureen Needham

Jean Baptiste Francisqui, adept theatrical entrepreneur and public relations expert that he was, doubtless had not intended to make his United States debut in quite so dramatic a fashion as he did. In fact, he had most likely not intended to visit the newly established republic at all. However, no one would have been foolish enough to stay and debate the matter with 452,000 enraged Haitian slaves armed with machetes, sharpened sticks, and flaming torches, when only a few gold pieces could persuade a Yankee ship captain to squeeze in a few more passengers as he departed for the mainland. Once on board, Francisqui and his three friends scarcely had time to breathe freely from their narrow escape before the group, as he explained in the *Charleston City Gazette and Daily Advertiser* (Feb. 8, 1794), was "plundered by privateers and conducted to Providence, where they experienced a number of misfortunes." Shortly afterwards they made their theatrical debut in Savannah. It was an inauspicious opening to the American phase of the extraordinary career of Jean Baptiste Francisqui, the most gifted and prolific of the French dancer-choreographers to immigrate to the United States in the eighteenth century.

Francisqui volunteered little information concerning his European career other than that he had once danced at "the Opera House, Paris," and the only dancer of that name was a "M. Francisque" enrolled at the Royal Academy of Music as a student in 1777 and 1778.[1] By 1783 the *Almanach* lists his promotion to an "élève" or apprentice who danced on a daily basis at the Paris Opéra, and the next year he was placed at the head of his class in that list. He joined the corps de ballet in 1785 and continued to dance at the Paris Opéra for one more year.

The young Francisqui was engaged as *premier danseur* at the Théâtre de Saint-Pierre at Martinique in July, 1788. He danced in the French colony until

Abridged and adapted by the author from Maureen Needham [Costonis] in New York Public Library *Bulletin of the Humanities,* Winter, 1982, pp. 430–42. The notes have been cut considerably; see the original for complete documentation.

April, 1789, but sometime after that he traveled to Saint-Domingue.[2] There he met with the dramatic adventures previously recounted, and arrived in Savannah, Georgia, sometime in October, 1793. He hastened to announce an "exhibition" of Jean Jacques Rousseau's lyric drama, *Pygmalion;* a comedy; a pastorale ballet; and a well-known comic ballet from the Comédie Italienne, *The Two Chasseurs, or Hunters, and the Milkmaid.* His cast included the tiny band who had followed him from Haiti: Jean Baptiste Val, a "clever" actor-dancer who had played the Haitian opera houses since 1783, his wife, evidently a proficient but ill-proportioned ballerina, and M. Dainville, a French actor highly regarded by critics for his "cultivated talent."[3]

Francisqui opened a new theater in Charleston on February 8, 1794, a few months later, and merged with a rival troupe of French dancers who also came to Charleston that spring. "The French Theatre," as it became known, offered an ambitious program of "dancing, pantomime, ballets or dances, harlequin pantomimes, rope dancing, with many feats and little amusing French pieces; and to satisfy many who wish it, the grand pieces of the French theatre." All this, four times per week.[4] Within weeks they opened before a bilingual audience drawn from local English-speaking citizens, the numerous French-speaking Huguenot settlers, refugees from Saint-Domingue, and even an enthusiastic contingent of pirates.

His new partner, Alexandre Bussart Placide (1750–1812), was one of the most celebrated French theatrical performers of the eighteenth century. He danced on the tightrope, played Pierrot in pantomimes, and composed five highly successful harlequinades while a star of Nicolet's Grand Danseurs du Roi, the Paris theater where he began the brilliant career which was to take him throughout Europe, the United States, and the West Indies.[5]

Their leading ballerina was Mme. Placide, actually Susanne Théodore Taillandet (1778–1826). She danced in Placide's ballets throughout most of his American career. Under the name of Mlle. Théodore, she had danced at the Comédie Française from 1784 to 1786. Then she moved on to the Paris Opéra as a fellow student with Francisqui, while she also earned her reputation at Nicolet's as one of the most beautiful and popular dancers in all of Paris.[6] The other members of the troupe—such as Louis Duport, Louis Douvillier, and Laurent Spinacutta—could also claim impressive credentials in France and in the United States.

The Charleston French Theatre reflected a true partnership of Placide and Francisqui. Placide specialized in acrobatics but also directed harlequinades and comical ballets, drawing upon his experiences at Nicolet's in Paris and Sadler's Wells in London. Francisqui complemented those skills in that he knew the sophisticated *ballets en action* of Noverre, Dauberval, and Gardel taken from the Paris Opéra repertoire and could adapt them to a small cast and stage.

The English dancing masters who once staffed the American theaters found it difficult to compete with these graceful French invaders. In fact their popularity was such that dance in the United States was no longer the same after the French dancers arrived. English gigues and reels, sailors' hornpipes, and mock French court dances gave place to melodramatic three-act pantomime ballets, comical *"ballets villageoises,"* or charming pastorale ballets. Francisqui, on the other hand, began to devote his talents to devising American patriotic pantomimes, such as *American Independence; or the Fourth of July.*

He and his various friends toured up and down the eastern coast of the United States. He began in Savannah in 1793 and remained in Charleston throughout 1794 and 1795, visiting Richmond, Norfolk, and other smaller southern cities. For unknown reasons, Francisqui's troupe divided from Placide's by the end of 1795 and, early in March of 1796, Francisqui and the Vals made their New York City debut. He immediately was invited to join the American Company, where he danced with Mme. Gardie for the rest of the season. He traveled to Newport with a contingent of actors for the summer season.

In Boston Francisqui was appointed ballet master for the new Haymarket Theatre during the winter of 1796 and spring of 1797. He shared the position with Jean-Marie Lege, who had once danced with the Placides at Nicolet's theater in Paris. Then he abruptly transferred to the rival theater where Mme. Gardie had appeared during that season. Lege let it be known publicly in the *Massachusetts Mercury* ([Boston] Feb. 10, 1797) that Francisqui's jealousy had prevented him from demonstrating his true talents, and a choreographer's war broke out. The repertoire of both theaters suddenly increased in volume, while newspaper advertisements grew in exaggerated puffery. The critic in the *Massachusetts Mercury* judged Lege to be the winner in "low comedy," whereas Francisqui was more impressive in the *danseur noble* and *demi-caractère* roles.

Still in Boston, Francisqui switched his allegiance once again, this time to a wholly French troupe operated by Philippe Lailson, complete with a circus, which offered lavishly appointed spectacles of opera and ballet performances alternating with horseback and tumbling entertainments. He rode the circuit from Boston to New York to Philadelphia and back again during 1797 and 1798. Francisqui choreographed a new ballet in honor of President John Adams's visit to the theater. The Adamses would hardly have been aware of it, but Francisqui and his partner Susanne Taillandet Douvillier, formerly Mme. Placide, were likely the same dancers whom John and Abigail Adams had seen dance at the Paris Opéra when they attended it many years before. According to Charles Durang, "the [Lailson] company was far superior to any which had visited the country, but it was too expensive."[7] The company folded in July of 1798—sets, costumes, even the horses were put up for sale.

At this point we lose track of Francisqui briefly, but pick up his trace again in the then-Spanish colony of Louisiana. A tantalizing fragment of a playbill, dated September 3, 1799, refers to a ballet choreographed by the wandering choreographer, who settled in New Orleans.[8]

Francisqui was not only the founder of the New Orleans opera-ballet company but also one of the earliest directors of the troupe itself. He even led the group on a series of international tours at a time when East Coast theatrical companies had to import English singers and actors to fill their stages. Contemporary observers in New Orleans left no evidence that they knew Francisqui had led the company on annual pilgrimages to Havana, Cuba, where he presented French opera and ballet; consequently most theater historians have assumed that the New Orleans theater was closed during most of 1800 through 1803. However, Francisqui took his company abroad on three successive occasions that coincided with the close of the New Orleans theatrical season.[9] They presented French operas as well as his regular repertoire of ballets and pantomimes. He premiered at least sixteen new pantomime ballets and six pantomimes, as well as duets and solos. The critic of *El Reganon* praised Francisqui highly for his professional expertise: "What agility and poise in treading the boards and presenting themselves to the public! Come, there can be no doubt that these actors, particularly the principals, have worked for a long time in the theater and have seen good originals."[10] The critic was accurate in his perceptions: Francisqui's training at the Paris Opéra ballet school was the best offered at that time.

Francisqui remained a citizen of New Orleans for nine years, the longest that he had ever settled in his adult life. He must have prospered. He lived in a large double house on Toulouse Street staffed by four servants. He evidently was successful enough that he never needed to dragoon his wife or any of his three children onto the stage, as was the custom then.

He opened a dancing school, which was acknowledged to be the city's finest. He had opened his first dancing school in Martinique, and continued to teach in practically every city in which he stayed for any length of time. In New Orleans he sponsored public subscription balls designed for his young students. He announced in *Le Moniteur* (Dec. 14, 1805) a series of "Grand Balls for Children," which "will begin at three o'clock in the afternoon and will finish at eight in the evening." These balls were so popular that uninvited adults crowded the youngsters off the ballroom floor. Francisqui finally acquiesced to popular demand and permitted adults to dance at either end of the hall, but he begged the public to leave open the central space for the children, "For whom the balls are *expressly* given" (Jan. 18, 1806).

One reason for the popularity of his balls was his ingenious selection of music. In January of 1807 he invited General Wilkinson and his brass militia to play a round of waltzes. Soon the brass band alternated sets with the traditional string orchestra on a regular basis. The transition from string orchestra to brass dance band could be viewed as one of the earliest steps in the formation of the jazz band in New Orleans. If jazz—to put it simply—can be described as dance music played by a brass band and flavored with "swing" or African American rhythms, then two of the main ingredients were thus combined by 1807 in Francisqui's ballroom. As for the third significant element, the development of jazz music by black musicians, it is not known whether or not Francisqui's orchestra included the African American violinists or other instrumentalists who often performed in another New Orleans ballroom during that period.[11]

One of Francisqui's last recorded appearances in New Orleans occurred at the newly organized St. Philippe Street theater. The program for his own benefit performance (announced in *Le Moniteur* on May 11, 1808) was unusual in that it relied primarily on ballet rather than the usual variety of opera, farce, and ballet pantomime. The daring program featured Berquin's comedy, *Petit jouer au violin,* which included dances as well as poetry; Beaunoir's two-act *Temple de l'Hymen, ou, La Rose et la bouton* (ballet pastorale with song and dialogue that concluded with a *Contredanse des cerceaux*). Other short dances rounded out the evening: *La Gavotte de Venus, Pas de caractère* for four dancers, and an *Anglaise* danced by a ten-year-old girl. The sole American offerings were Francisqui's solos to the tunes of *O Columbia, Happy Land* and the *Marche du Président des Etats-Unis.* His students were soloists as well as in the corps de ballet; it was the first occasion in which his students, rather than professional dancers, dominated the stage.

The theater folded shortly after his last appearance there on May 19, and his possible partner in the enterprise, Louis Douvillier, filed a petition for bankruptcy in the fall of that year. Francisqui and his family mysteriously disappeared, never again to be seen on American soil as far as can be ascertained. If this adventuresome entrepreneur continued to dance and teach elsewhere, his whereabouts have not yet come to light.

Keen professionalism was perhaps the most dominant aspect of Jean Baptiste Francisqui's personality. He was a prolific choreographer who produced over 125 ballets and pantomimes during the fifteen years of his American career. No other ballet master in the country even approached the size and variety of his choreographic output. Francisqui was invariably a valued member of the companies with whom he worked, according to William Dunlap, a claim substantiated by the large headlines that were accorded his choreography in the newspaper notices.[12]

Francisqui was impressive as a performer for his highly refined style, his "agility and poise."[13] The critic in the *Columbian Centinel* (Dec. 28, 1796) proclaimed that "the eye never witnessed more taste, elegance and ease than were exhibited by the performers in the pantomimes." On December 31, the same critic extolled Francisqui's "style of dancing and pantomime exhibitions" as "the most elegant ever seen by an American audience."

Francisqui and his dancing partners imported the most sophisticated forms of French theatrical dance yet seen in the United States, and the American theater was considerably enriched by his presence. He educated an audience to appreciate the refinements of French ballet and trained native students in the art. His most enduring contributions were the establishment of the New Orleans opera ballet and his directorship of the troupe that later became famous as the New Orleans French Opera Company, which endured from 1792 to 1919.

The American phase of Francisqui's professional career began under unfavorable circumstances and apparently ended as it had begun. The American dance world profited a great deal from his many contributions, although Francisqui may have considered himself personally unfortunate in that he chose to sail west toward the New World. In contrast, his Paris Opéra classmate Charles Louis Didelot journeyed east to Russia and encountered a czar who gladly funded his lavish productions as well as supported an entire ballet academy. Jean Baptiste Francisqui could unearth no such patron in the youthful republic of the United States. American support for ballet has remained a touch-and-go proposition ever since.

NOTES

1. Martin Shockley, *The Richmond Stage, 1748–1812* (Charlottesville: University Press of Virginia, 1977), p. 98. *Almanach des Spectacles,* vol. 26 (Paris: Duchesne, 1777), p. 20; ibid., vol. 37 (Paris: Duchesne, 1778), p. 19. According to published libretti at the Opera House in Bordeaux, the city where Francisqui was said to have been born (Francis Wemyss, *Chronology of the American Stage from 1752 to 1852* [New York: Wm. Taylor, 1852], p. 53; and Thomas Allston Brown, *History of the American Stage* [New York: Dick

and Fitzgerald, 1870], p. 134), a family of dancers with that name was active there in 1785. The problem of identification is compounded by a birth certificate for a much younger "Jean Baptiste Francisquy" (born 1777) discovered by Mary Grace Swift in the Municipal Archives of Bordeaux.

2. Maurice Nicholas, "Le Théâtre de Saint-Pierre au XVIIIe siècle; les Années difficiles," *Annales des Antilles* 1 (1955): 57.

3. Charles Durang, *History of the Philadelphia Stage between the Years 1749 and 1855,* MS arr. and illus. by Thompson Westcott, 1868, University of Pennsylvania Library, vol. 2, p. 45, available on microfilm. Jean Fouchard, *Artistes et Répertoire des scènes de Saint-Domingue* (Port-au-Prince: Imprimerie de l'Etat, 1955), pp. 84, 20. (Boston) *Columbian Centinel,* Dec. 28, 1796. Henri Lyonnet, *Dictionnaire des comédiens français* (ca. 1910?; reprint, Geneva: Slatkine Reprints, 1969), p. 415.

4. *Charleston City Gazette and Daily Advertiser,* Mar. 26, 1794.

5. Emile Campardon, *Les Spectacles de la Foire, 1595–1791* (Paris: Berger-Levrault et Cie., 1877), vol. 2, pp. 227–29 and 238–41. Fouchard, *Artistes,* p. 71; and his *Plaisirs de Saint-Domingue* (Port-au-Prince: Imprimerie de l'Etat, 1955), pp. 173–81.

6. Campardon, *Spectacles,* vol. 2, p. 430. The name on her death certificate was misspelled as "Vaillande"; see the St. Louis Cathedral Archives, *Book of Funerals, 1824–28,* Act 630, p. 140.

7. C. Durang, *History of the Philadelphia Stage,* p. 66.

8. Original in the Notarial Archives of New Orleans. René Le Gardeur, Jr., "En Marge d'une affich de théâtre de 1799," *Comptes rendus de l'Athenée Louisianais,* Mar., 1955, pp. 24–26.

9. Edwin Teurbe Tolon and Jorge Antonio Gonzalez, *Historia del teatro en la Habana* (Santa Clara: Universidad Central de las Villas, 1961), pp. 36–49.

10. Ibid, p. 40.

11. Henry Kmen, *Music in New Orleans: The Formative Years, 1791–1841* (Baton Rouge: Louisiana State University Press, 1966), pp. 38, 226–45.

12. William Dunlap, *History of the American Theatre and Anecdotes of the Principal Actors* (1792–97; reprint, New York: Burt Franklin, 1963), pp. 274–84.

13. Tolon and Gonzalez, *Historia del teatro,* p. 40.

CHAPTER 20

Critics React to Fanny Elssler's American Debut (1840–41)

New York Mirror: A Weekly Journal of Literature and the Fine Arts, *May 30, 1840*

FANNY ELSSLER

Our hopes have been realized. The beautiful, the noble, the graceful Fanny Elssler, has been received in a manner worthy of her, and of the nation to whom she came to offer the homage of her talent. It was a great solemnity for the city of New-York. The Park theatre never saw so great a triumph. This narrow and dirty building bore the traces of something marvellous. Mlle. Elssler has done what no other dramatic power had ever done before her; not even Malibran—this lyric giant, whose cradle was the United States. In the best days of Malibran, the feminine aristocracy of New-York never became plebeian enough to sit on the last seats of the second gallery of the Park. Fanny Elssler has effected this miracle. Powerful magician! she destroyed all demarcations, humanized the most savage affectation, and, thanks to her, that part of the theatre called "the hell," was transformed into an Eden, where sparkled the most fastidious and disdainful houris of New-York. The parterre also had a new skin on it; its rags were exchanged for the most fashionable costumes. We saw there a count and two chargé d'affaires; the places were sold from ten to fifteen dollars instead of fifty cents, the ordinary price.

It would be impossible to describe the emotion, the ardour, the religious expectation, with which this crowd opened its soul and eyes to Fanny Elssler appearing before it. The breath of the whole audience was suspended. But it would be still more difficult to give an idea of the transport, the exaltation, the cries, the vociferations, the hurras which accompanied Fanny Elssler when she

Review from *Courier des Etats Unis*, translated from the French by an unnamed "lady correspondent," for the *New-York Mirror: A Weekly Journal of Literature and the Fine Arts* 17, no. 49 (May 30, 1840). Ralph Waldo Emerson, "Journal Entry," Oct., 1841; in *The Heart of Emerson's Journals*, ed. Bliss Perry (Boston: Houghton Mifflin, 1926), pp. 167–68.

Fanny Elssler in *La Voliere*, lithograph by P. Gauci after J. Deffett Francis, London, August, 1838.

appeared and followed her from her first step till her last. . . . Fanny Elssler, this timid child, was alarmed at the unparalleled celebrity she had acquired. She said to us, some hours before she was to encounter the trial, "I shall not content the public unless I dance on my head." You have only danced on your feet, Fanny, and the public is content! You have accomplished—what do I say? you have surpassed all that its most extravagant hopes had dared to conceive! And what could it hope or desire more delightful, more intoxicating, than you? Notwithstanding you were parsimonious to this public, famishing to see you! You only threw unto them a small portion of your attractions! The piece that you chose did not show you to advantage; you, only, made the piece! La Tarantule is a ballet without vivacity, etc. etc. But what do you want of a troop or ballet there, when you appear yourself? The drama, the action, the spirit, the emotion, the laugh; it is you—nothing but you! Is there a piece or a theatre, or rather will there not always be a piece and a theatre, there, where Fanny Elssler appears? What work of the mind, or the hand of man, will ever compare to this work of the divine creation?

The Americans proved this, in changing the judgment they had already formed against the Tarantule. Their first condemnation was transformed into an unbounded admiration. When the piece was finished, or rather when Fanny Elssler finished, they groaned with regret; they loudly called for the vision which escaped their fascinated eyes; and when Mlle. Elssler re-appeared, we feared for a moment that she would be crushed with the flowers that the public showered on her head. Mr. James Silvain placed one of these thousand flower-crowns on the brow of Mlle. Elssler, who advanced before the public, bowing under the weight of her triumph and trembling with emotion; with her graceful hands crossed on her bosom, which could hardly contain the beatings of her heart, she said, "a thousand thanks—my heart is too full for words."

We register, with pride, this magnificent triumph of Mlle. Elssler, not only on account of the justice rendered to her talent, but on account of the influence it will have in propagating the delightful art in this country. The dance, as Mlle. Elssler practices it, is not a useless spectacle—a fruitless curiosity; it is the most beautiful hymn that nature can receive from woman, the most beautiful of its creatures. All work of art is a divine beam which attaches heaven to earth.

These sentiments would soon become national here; they would be religiously kept in this country, open to all religions, if they had for missionaries such priestesses as Fanny Elssler. She exhibits to the eye and the mind the type of beauty without example, whether she dances or walks, whether she is seated or negligently leaning. The American public were fascinated with the sight of the new unparalleled grace, with which this woman is gifted; her person bearing the marks of a divine stamp. Fanny Elssler is the incarnation of what is beautiful; through her, you are made to worship dancing, and the theatre becomes the school of statuary, where its marvels are displayed in all the pomp of life, action and youth.

The piety that we feel for the magnificence of her corporeal structure, induces us to make her a reproach, which yesterday all intelligent spectators made with us. Carrying to the extreme the fear of the American public, whose modest susceptibilities are probably greatly exaggerated, Fanny Elssler elongated so much her dancing dress, that her beautiful limbs, so marvellous in their shape, disappeared under this importunate veil. This is a profanation, a want of courage. We honour chastity, but whoever thought of putting a petticoat on the Venus of Medicis. We protest against this mutilation, which was generally blamed. Let this be said to the timorous conscience of Fanny Elssler.

Fanny Elssler is the first theatrical celebrity who comes from France to salute the United States. This example will no doubt be followed—it ought to be—and America will have the right to enter into that great council of intelligences that create fame—all will wish to be adopted by the new world—Fanny Elssler will be the Lafayette of the opera.

Ralph Waldo Emerson's Journal, Oct., 1841

I saw in Boston Fanny Elssler in the ballet of *Nathalie*. She must show, I suppose, the whole compass of her instrument, and add to her softest graces of motion or "the wisdom of her feet," the feats of the rope-dancer and tumbler: and perhaps on the whole the beauty of the exhibition is enhanced by this that is strong and strange, as when she stands erect on the extremities of her toes or on one toe, or "performs the impossible" in attitude. But the chief beauty is in the extreme grace of her movement, the variety and nature of her attitude, the winning fun and spirit of all her little coquetries, the beautiful erectness of her body, and the freedom and determination which she can so easily assume, and, what struck me much, the air of perfect sympathy with the house, and that mixture of deference and conscious superiority which puts her in perfect spirits and equality to her part. When she courtesies, her sweet and slow and prolonged salaam which descends and still descends whilst the curtain falls, until she seems to have invented new depths of grace and condescension,—she earns well the profusion of bouquets of flowers which are hurled on to the stage.

As to the morals, as it is called, of this exhibition, that lies wholly with the spectator. The basis of this exhibition, like that of every human talent, is moral, is the sport and triumph of health or the virtue of organization. Her charm for the house is that she dances for them or they dance in her, not being (fault of some defect in their forms and educations) able to dance themselves. We must be expressed. Hence all the cheer and exhilaration which the spectacle imparts and the intimate property which each beholder feels in the dancer, and the joy with which he hears good anecdotes of her spirit and her benevolence. They know that such surpassing grace must rest on some occult foundations of inward harmony.

But over and above her genius for dancing are the incidental vices of this individual, her own false taste or her meretricious arts to please the groundlings and which must displease the judicious. The immorality the immoral will see; the very immoral will see that only; the pure will not heed it,—for it is not obtrusive,—perhaps will not see it at all. I should not think of danger to young women stepping with their father or brother out of happy and guarded parlors into this theatre to return in a few hours to the same; but I can easily suppose that it is not the safest resort for college boys who have left metaphysics, conic sections, or Tacitus[1] to see these tripping satin slippers, and they may not forget this graceful, silvery swimmer when they have retreated to their baccalaureate cells.

It is a great satisfaction to see the best in each kind, and as a good student of the world, I desire to let pass nothing that is excellent in its own kind unseen, unheard.

NOTE

1. Editor's note: Emerson refers here to the Harvard University students, who, he assumed, would be distracted from their studies of philosophy, mathematics, and Latin by Elssler's charms.

CHAPTER 21

The Black Crook Burlesque (1867)

G. W. Griffin with Mr. Christy for Christy's Minstrels

CAST OF CHARACTERS[1]

Wolfgang Hedgehog (Black Crook)	G. W. H. Griffin
Lucifer	C. F. Shattuck
Molly Bonfanti	Christina
Betsy Regalia	Husietta
Lucalico	Burbankiana
Ducklegs	Hodgkiniana
Ritalanda Somegallus	Lesliana
Misery	Boycetta
Gossiper	Nobodiana

SCENE 1. *A wood—den of the BLACK CROOK. At rise of curtain, wild music, allegro.*

(*Enter BLACK CROOK right, 3E. He is dressed in black tights—black blouse reaching to the knee—black belt—black shoes with buckles—black wig with hair standing in all directions. If done in black face the forehead should be washed clean with a sponge, leaving it perfectly white; rub a little of the black off from under the eyes, so as to give the face a wild expression. If done in white, the forehead must be painted green. He carries a cane to lean upon—it should be an old fashioned one with a cross piece for handle. He is nearly bent double as he enters leaning upon cane. He walks around two or three times, then stops in center of stage. Music stops.*)

G. W. Griffin with Mr. Christy for Christy's Minstrels, 1867. Reprinted in Gary D. Engle, *This Grotesque Essence: Plays from the American Minstrel Stage* (Baton Rouge: Louisiana State University Press, 1978), pp. 122–27. The editor has added some notes to this selection as well as quoted from some of Engle's citations.

Male minstrel show performers would dress in Fanny Elssler's Cachucha costume and pose en pointe as they imitated the great ballerina. Sheet music cover of "Campbell's Melodies" (New York: Wm. Hall & Son, 1848). Author's personal collection.

B.C. Now to conjure up the spell
      That shall do my bidding well!
      More of riches I must have,
      More of pleasure still I crave.
      But should the spell impotent prove,
      While the sprites of earth I move,
      Then my power on earth is done!
      Then I'll invoke the Evil One!

(*Music repeats. BLACK CROOK takes cane and draws circle on stage, then uses cane in flourishes, as if invoking evil spirits. Music ceases. BLACK CROOK walks down left in despair, then putting his hand to his forehead, speaks:*)

B.C. Alas! I fear I have no power
      To aid me in this trying hour.
      What shall I do? My brain grows wild.
      And through the air on fire I ride!
      I'll call to aid the Evil One,
      He'll just come on from Washington.
      He'll aid me in my dire distress,
      Then send me on to con-ge-ress!

(*Wild chord by the orchestra. LUCIFER appears, either through trap, or from right, 3E. Flash of lighting and sound of gong. He is dressed in red tights, with red hood on his head, and two horns. In his right hand he holds a scroll with which he points at BLACK CROOK, who shrinks from him in fear.*)

Luc. Well, here I am! all right, you see,
      Now what is it you want of me?
B.C. (*creeps up to him*)
      I want a dozen magic lamps,
      To aid through life in picking up stamps.
Luc. Thou hast thy wish, fool, even now,
      The stamp of Cain is on thy brow.
      Come, tell me what thou does desire—
      I'm getting cold without a fire.
B.C. Well, then, I s'pose I must tell all,
      The best of men will sometimes fall.
      The people call me the "Black Crook,"
      Because I read the "Magic Book."
      They've robbed me of my magic spell,
      And now myself to you I'll sell.

Luc.   Out with it, knave! name the condition
       On which you'll join me in perdition.
       You are the kind I wish to see,
       For such as you resemble me.
B.C.   Then, first, I want the privilege
       To be the first on "Broadway Bridge,"
       Then I'd be pointed out to all,
       As the young man, graceful and tall,
       Who was the first to cross the street
       Without wading through mud twelve inches deep.
Luc.   The first I grant! Now name the other,
       Come, hurry up! I've no time to bother!
B.C.   Then first I'd know, as you're a resident,
       About what time they'll impeach the President?[2]
Luc.   Bosh!
B.C.   Another thing I wish you'd tell,
       As you are bound to go to quell
       Disturbance in this land of ours,
       Who, at the next election, will hold the bowers?
Luc.   You shall know all, avaricious fool,
       If you'll bring to me each year a soul;
       Each year, when the clock strikes the hour of night,
       A soul from you shall be my right.
B.C.   Enough! Each year a "sole" I'll steal,
       And with it bring you a toe and heel,
       And, if your majesty it suits,
       Next year I'll bring you a pair of "boots."
Luc.   'Tis well, now I must be a going,
       Methinks, I hear some "rooster" crowing:[3]
       Now don't forget, on land or sea,
       That crooked trunk belongs to me.

(*LUCIFER vanishes right through flames of red fire. BLACK CROOK hobbles off, left 3E.*)

SCENE II—A garden

"GRAND ENSEMBLE DE BALLET."

In this scene can be introduced as many Ballet Girls as you please; however, six or eight is the usual number. They are all dressed in burlesque style, excepting one, who is to be a good dancer in order to show a contrast between herself and the others. The ladies who compose the Grand Ballet are dressed in white gauze dresses, reaching nearly to the knee; without hoops. The waists are red or blue satin, abundantly stuffed to form immense bosoms—large heavy shoes—white stockings stuffed, to form "big limbs"—fashionable lady's wig, with tremendous waterfall—green wreaths upon the head.

At change of scene they come from all the entrances upon their toes, with hands elevated; moving to "slow music." Move around awkwardly for about thirty-two bars, then change to:

SECOND MOVEMENT—WALTZ BY BALLET.

THIRD MOVEMENT.

The leading dancer comes from right, 3E dressed in beautiful style, and executes LA ARIEL. Moving over to each corner alternately, and tending gracefully back, each Ballet Girl, as she approaches, strikes a comical attitude. At end of dance, she retires back.

FOURTH MOVEMENT.

LA SYLPHIDE is burlesqued by one of the comedians, after which someone from the gallery throws a large cabbage, with large envelope stuck in it. Dancer takes it, kisses envelope, looks up at gallery, and puts envelope in his bosom.

FIFTH MOVEMENT.—VILLAGE HORNPIPE, *Burlesque*[4]

SIXTH MOVEMENT.—LA BAYADEN, *Burlesque*[5]

SEVENTH MOVEMENT.—MAY POLE DANCE

MAN brings on May Pole and holds it on stage—it has six strings of different colored muslin hanging from the top. Each Ballet Girl takes one, and they all dance MAY POLE DANCE. They finally get entangled in the muslin, winding up the man's head, etc., and all run off with the May Pole. They immediately re-enter and form for the last scene.

PALACE OF DEW DROPS.[6]

With real water streaming from EMERALD FOUNTAINS, Members of the "Corps de Ballet" form on each side of the stage in comical attitudes. Fancy Dancer is placed upon a soap box, center. Two little demons, dressed in red, rush out from either side with pans of red fire, and form each side of Fancy Dancer; forming Tableaux on their knees, in front of the stage. At each corner is placed two Irish women upon boxes, pouring water from green watering-pots into a tub. A string of stuffed legs, boots, strings of onions, little dolls, cabbages, old clothes, bottles, etc., is let down from above by means of a rope held by someone in 3d entrance, and kept moving slowly up and down. LUCIFER and BLACK CROOK swing off, holding onto ropes suspended from beams above. They swing back and forth. Music appropriate.

THE END

NOTES

1. Editor's note: The names of three famous ballerinas who appeared in the original *Black Crook* are satirized in this list of characters: Maria Bonfanti becomes Molly Bonfanti, Betsy Rigl is Betsy Regalia, and Rita Sangalli's name is changed to Ritalanda Somegallus. Bonfanti and Sangalli both trained at La Scala, Milan. See Barbara Barker, *Ballet or Ballyhoo: The American Careers of Maria Bonfanti, Rita Sangalli and Giuseppina Morlacchi* (New York: Dance Horizons, 1984).

2. Gary D. Engle notes that "The impeachment of Andrew Johnson occurred on February 24, 1868." See *This Grotesque Essence: Plays from the American Minstrel Stage* (Baton Rouge: Louisiana State University Press, 1978), p. 125.

3. Engle notes that "Before the cartoons of Thomas Nast saddled the Democratic party with the image of a donkey, the party was associated with the figure of a rooster. Thus, the crowing of a rooster often meant the oratory of a Democrat" (ibid., p. 126).

4. Editor's note: By 1867, when this burlesque played for over three months at the Fifth Avenue Opera House in New York City, hornpipes were still popular on the variety stage, including those identified with firemen as well as sailors.

5. Editor's note: The opera-ballet of *La Bayadere or the Maid of Cashmere* was associated with the French ballerinas who came to the United States prior to Fanny Elssler and was considered a satiric target on American stages from the 1830s on. Augusta Maywood made a triumphant theatrical debut in the leading role and then departed for Paris, where she danced in starring roles at the Opéra. See Maureen Needham [Costonis], "'The Wild Doe': Augusta Maywood in Philadelphia and Paris, 1837–1840," *Dance Chronicle* 17 no. 2 (1994): 123–48.

6. Editor's note: Augusta Maywood played the role of the Dew Drop Fairy in 1838, before she left for Paris; Mary Ann Lee later added the role to her repertoire.

CHAPTER 22

Critics React to *The Black Crook* (1866)

New York Times, *Sept. 13, 1866*

NIBLO'S GARDENS.—MR. WHEATLEY opened his beautiful theatre last night after a prolonged recess, during which the house has been cleaned, redecorated, regilded, and put in apple-pie order. A new stage, of the most modern and best approved construction, has been made at great expense, and a vast amount of new scenery procured. The house was densely packed with a critical and appreciative audience, additional interest being imparted to the opening by the announcement of a new and original spectacular drama, entitled the "Black Crook."

The "Black Crook" is a story of sorcery, demonism and wickedness generally, in which one *Hertzog* (Mr. MORTON), a deformed and ill-natured, but very learned man, grows desperate in spirit, makes a compact with *Zamiel* or Satan, by which he agrees to win over to perdition one human soul for each year of life to be granted to him, the account to be settled on the last day of the year, before the clock strikes midnight. The lover-hero *Rodolphe*, is enamored of *Amina;* he is a poor painter—she a rural beauty. *Count Wolfenstein* sees her, and by force of feudal power takes her for himself, locking her lover in a dungeon. The *Black Crook*, in search of a soul for his next New Year, visits *Rodolphe*, tells him of a cave of gold in the forest, also that his love, *Amina*, is noble and induces him to go in search of the treasure. On the way *Rodolphe* sees a dove pursued by a serpent, kills the reptile and saves the bird, who proves to be the *Fairy Queen Stalacta*. She exposes *Hertzog's* trick, and assists *Rodolphe*. The reader will now readily see that the Count is slain, *Amina* rescued and married to *Rodolphe*, and the *Black Crook (Hertzog)* himself very justly sent to the Devil, instead of sending the gay young lover.

The house was fairly packed with a mass of humanity, exceeding the crush at any time, even at that house of crushes. The first act is trashy, but affords ample scope for fine spectacular display, and introduces the English and French ballet troupes, who were received with enthusiasm. Mlle. BONFANTI, the *premier danseuse,* is as light as a feather, and exceedingly graceful. She, with Mlle. SANGALLI and Mlle. RIGL, was *encored* twice during the *Pas de fleurs.* The *Pas de Sabot* is also a charming arrangement, in which Mlle. ROSI DEL-VAL received the well-merited applause of the house. Miss MILLY CAVEN-DISH . . . was *encored* in her song of "The Naughty Men." The act closed with a grand incantation scene laid in a wild glen, whose weird and unholy look was quite *apropos* to the devilish business there inacted. The curtain went down on the second act at 10:45 o'clock. The features of this act were the dances held in the gorgeous grotto of Stalacta. Mlle. SANGALLI and the full ballet appeared in the *Pas de Naiad,* after which came the ballet success of the night, the witching *Pas de Demons,* in which the Demonese, who wear no clothes to speak of, so gracefully and prettily disported as to draw forth thunders of applause. No similar exhibition has been made in an American stage that we remember, certainly none where such a combination of youth, grace, beauty, and *elan* was found. The curtain was rung up three times at the close of this act, in compliance with peremptory demands of the house. The late hour, not far from morning, at which the "Black Crook" closed, prevents a further notice of its merits. Mr. WHEATLEY, who has made an actual outlay of not far from $30,000 in preparation of the piece, is to be congratulated upon its success. It will be repeated every night, and is well worth seeing, as it is decidedly the event of this spectacular age.

New York Daily Tribune, *Sept. 17, 1866*

"THE BLACK CROOK AT NIBLO'S GARDEN"

Niblo's Garden opened in a literal blaze of glory on Wednesday evening. The audience assembled on that occasion was so large that it filled the house in every part, overflowed into the lobbies, and, in the shape of frequent and large detachments, extended to the street and pervaded the neighborhood. Great enthusiasm prevailed before the curtain, and great excitement behind it. A livelier scene than was thus presented could not well be imagined. "The Black Crook" was played by easy stages, from 7[:45] o'clock until 1[:15]. Most of the auditors remained till the gorgeous end. Hopes were entertained, at one time, that the performance would last until the merry breakfast bell should "wake the snorting citizens." But these proved fallacious. By dint of great energy on the part of Mr. Wheatley and the mechanics, "The Black Crook" was at length played through; and a patient multitude, dazed and delighted, went to brief dreams of fairy-land. It takes time to digest so much radiance, and we have not, therefore, been in haste to describe this extraordinary drama. Having swallowed the rainbows, however, it is now our very pleasant duty to say that they are very good to take. The scenery is magnificent; the ballet is beautiful; the drama is—rubbish. There is always a bitter drop in the sweetest cup; a fly in the richest ointment. Mr. Barras's drama is the bitter drop and the superfluous fly, in this instance. Several very fine names are applied to "The Black Crook" in the bill of the play. It is called "grand," "romantic," "magical," "spectacular" and "original." To approach such a production in any other than a spirit of reverential awe, is, perhaps, to fail in proper respect for genius. Mr. Barras is understood to have devoted several of the ripest years of his scholastic life to this stupendous drama. But awe is a spirit that cannot be summoned as easily as Zamiel. Besides, we have read Lord Byron's "Manfred" and Goethe's "Faust" and Hoffman's stories, and even Mr. Reynold's "Romance of Secret Tribunals." Then, too, we have seen so many spectacles, in which the fairies war on the demons, and conquer for love's sake and in the holy name of virtue! Mr. Barras, an old reader and an old actor, has picked up a good many literary and theatrical properties, in his time, and they have been more or less useful to him, we dare say; but it must be remembered that the fields of literature are open to all gleaners, and hence that plenty of people will infallibly recognize Mr. Barras's properties. To call "The Black Crook" "original" is merely to trifle with intelligence. Herein, for example, we encounter our venerable and decrepit friend, the Alchymist, who wants to live forever, and is perfectly willing to give, not only his own soul to the Devil, but every other soul that he can possibly send to Avenus. Here, too, is the humble youth, torn from his peasant maid and shut up in "the lowest cell," ha! ha! by the Baron, cruel and bold. And then the Fiend's Minister, the Alchymist, surnamed "The Black Crook," is on hand to release him and send him on the road to avarice, vengeance, and perdition. Here are the old manorial or baronial servitors, the red-nosed steward and the high-capped dame; and along with them comes the arch and piquant little village-maid, who sings a song, and smiles, and shows her pretty ankles to the sheepish swains. There are fairies, too, and demons; and, in the upshot, of course, the former conquer the latter, and the parted lovers are joined in happiness, and the Baron bold is run through his bold body, and the Fiend is cheated of his prey, and the Black Crook is removed, through a dreadful hole in the earth, to a region of great heat and many dragons.

And that Mr. Barras calls an original drama! For the construction of it, we can only say that the literary materials, stage business, etc., appear to have been put into an intellectual bag and vigorously shaken up together. And there we leave the high dramatic theme. There was, in fact, no need of the pretense of a drama, in this instance; or, if there was, almost any old spectacle would have been preferable to "The Black Crook." All that was needed was a medium for the presentation of several gorgeous scenes, and a large number of female legs; and it was only necessary that the medium should not be tedious. And this brings us to the real merits of the entertainment that is now nightly offered at Niblo's Garden, and which, we presume, will be nightly offered for many weeks to come. Some of the most perfect and admirable pieces of scenery that have ever been exhibited upon the stage are employed in the illustration of this piece. . . .

The last scene in the play, however, will dazzle and impress to even a greater degree, by its lavish richness and barbaric splendor. All that gold, and silver, and gems, and lights, and woman's beauty can contribute to fascinate the eye and charm the sense is gathered up in this gorgeous spectacle. Its luster grows as we gaze, and deepens and widens, till the effect is almost painful. One by one curtains of mist ascend and drift away. Silver couches, on which the fairies loll in negligent grace, ascend and descend amid a silver rain. Columns of living splendor whirl, and dazzle as they whirl. From the clouds droop gilded chariots and the white forms of angels. It is a very beautiful pageant. . . . But all the scenes are excellent; and though we cannot say that anything has been done for the dramatic art, by the production of "The Black Crook," we can heartily testify that Scenic Art has never, within our knowledge, been so amply and splendidly exemplified.

In respect to the Ballet, it is the most complete troupe of the kind that has been seen in this country. To discriminate between the dancers would be as difficult as to distinguish one rose from another amid a wilderness of roses. But if either be more fascinating than another, it is Mlle. Rigl. The greater share of applause on Wednesday fell to the lot of Mlle. Sangalli. Marie Bonfanti, too, was welcomed with cordial enthusiasm. We have not space to descant upon the beauties that were so liberally revealed on the occasion—nor is there need. The town will take care to see for itself what treasures of grace Messrs. Jarrett and Palmer have lured from the opera-houses of Europe. Mr. Costa, however, is to be especially congratulated on his directorship of the Ballet. . . .

SUGGESTED BOOKS AND FILMS

Barker, Barbara. *Ballet or Ballyhoo: The American Careers of Maria Bonfanti, Rita Sangalli and Giuseppina Morlacchi.* New York: Dance Horizons, 1984.

Branen, Jeff, and Frederick Johnson. *How to Stage a Minstrel Show: A Manual for the Amateur Burnt Cork Director.* Chicago: T. S. Denison & Company, 1921.

[Costonis], Maureen Needham. "Ballet Comes to America, 1792–1842: French Contributions to the Establishment of Theatrical Dance in New Orleans and Philadelphia." Ph.D. diss., New York University, 1989.

———. "The Personification of Desire: Fanny Elssler and American Audiences." *Dance Chronicle* 13, no. 1 (1990): 47–67.

———. " 'The Wild Doe'—Augusta Maywood in Philadelphia and Paris, 1837–1840." *Dance Chronicle* 17 no. 2 (1994): 123–48.

de Laban, Juana. "The Dance in American Theatre: An Analytical History Based on the New York Stage from 1751–1821." Ph.D. diss., Yale University, 1947.

Durang, Charles. *History of the Philadelphia Stage between the Years 1749 and 1855.* MS arranged and illustrated by Thompson Westcott. Philadelphia: University of Pennsylvania library, 1868. Available on microfilm.

Emery, Lynne Fauley. *Black Dance from 1619 to Today.* 2d rev. ed. Princeton, N.J.: Princeton Book Company, 1988.

Gintautiene, Kristina. "*The Black Crook:* Ballet in the Gilded Age (1866–1876)." Ph.D. diss., New York University, 1984.

Guest, Ivor. *Fanny Elssler.* Middletown, Conn.: Wesleyan University Press, 1970.

Loney, Glenn, ed. *Musical Theatre in America.* Westport, Conn.: Greenwood Press, 1984.

Magriel, Paul, ed. *Chronicles of American Dance.* New York: Henry Holt and Company, 1948.

Mates, Julian. *The American Musical Stage before 1800.* New Brunswick, N.J.: Rutgers University Press, 1962.

Moore, Lillian. *Echoes of American Ballet.* Ed. Ivor Guest. New York: Dance Horizons, 1976.

Swift, Mary Grace. *Belles and Beaux on Their Toes: Dancing Stars of Young America.* Washington, D.C.: University Press of America, 1980.

Thomas, Tony, and Jim Terry with Busby Berkeley. *The Busby Berkeley Book.* Greenwich, Conn.: New York Graphic Society, 1973.

Toll, Robert. *Blacking Up: The Minstrel Show in Nineteenth Century America*. New York: Oxford University Press, 1974.

Winter, Marian Hannah. "American Theatrical Dancing from 1750 to 1800." *Musical Quarterly* 24 (Jan., 1938): 58–73.

There are many sources that distribute movies on dance, so check with your local distributors, regional colleges, or state archives for listings. Titles for new videos are expanding constantly. For addresses of distributors named below, or further suggestions, see the Dance Films Association's *Dance Film and Video Guide* named in the Selected General Readings and References on Theatrical Dance.

Although it may be difficult to obtain, the movie series entitled *The Magic of Dance—Reflections by Margot Fonteyn*, part 2: *The Ebb and Flow* (60 minutes, color) includes a reconstruction of John Durang's famous hornpipe and Mary Skeaping's re-creation of a typical eighteenth-century pastorale ballet such as Francisqui and the earliest French ballet dancers may have brought to America.

The Ballerinas. 108 minutes, color. Kultur. Segment on Fanny Elssler with a reconstruction of her famous *Cachucha* dance as notated by Zorn and performed by Carla Fracci.

Creole Giselle. 88 minutes, color. Mary Ann Lee was the first American ballerina to dance *Giselle*, the classic of the Romantic period; it premiered in Boston in 1846. This poetic version, by the Dance Theatre of Harlem, sets the ballet in ante-bellum Louisiana. There are numerous other filmed versions of *Giselle* performed by famous artists.

Dance Black America. 87 minutes, color. Dance Horizons Video. Includes documentary materials on nineteenth-century dances. Features a re-creation of the buck and wing by William Henry Lane (Juba), a famous African American dancer who dazzled London audiences with his skills, plus demonstrations of cakewalk from minstrel shows as well as rare footage of early Edison films.

La Fille mal Gardée. 98 minutes, color. National Video Corp. Dauberval's delightful comical romp is the only example of the Noverre-influenced eighteenth-century *ballet en action* or dramatic ballet that is in the current repertoire worldwide; it was popular in the United States from 1824 on. Frederick Ashton's historically inaccurate but charming re-creation features soloists from the Royal English Ballet.

Golddiggers of 1933. 96 minutes, black and white. 1933. One of the most exquisite of Busby Berkeley's Hollywood productions, the choreography features identical smiling beauties tapping and kicking their hearts out. Berkeley's visual imagination overflows in surrealistic beauty.

Goldwyn Follies. 120 minutes, color. Embassy, 1938. Probably the closest thing to a modern version of *The Black Crook* in terms of hodgepodge plot with beautiful, talented ballerinas and lots of legs. George Balanchine choreographed this Hollywood film. For shame!

The Jolson Story. 129 minutes, color. RCA Columbia, 1946. The story of Al Jolson's rise from the ranks of minstrelsy; it includes some production numbers with song and dance. Far more authentic is the original 1927 *The Jazz Singer,* with Al Jolson himself playing the lead; however, due to its racist stereotyping *au courant* during that period, it is difficult to obtain at most video stores.

Living American Theatre Dance. 11 minutes, color. Phoenix Films, 1982. The American Dance Machine rehearses different Broadway musical routines, the staple of their company's performing repertoire.

Minstrel Man. Black and white. 1977. This full-length movie includes the historically accurate re-creation of a WWI-era minstrel show, complete with white gloves, striped pants, and demeaning stereotypes. Hard to obtain and also hard to stomach.

The Romantic Era. 89 minutes, color. Kultur, 1980. Includes excerpts from *Nathalie,* ballet for which Fanny Elssler was lauded in North American and Cuban theatres, as well as *Robert le Diable,* in which she danced in the United States. Includes performances and conversations by Carla Fracci, Alicia Alonso, and others.

West Side Story. 155 minutes, color. United Artists, 1961. After this Romeo-and-Juliet love story set in Spanish Harlem won the Academy Award, Jerome Robbins changed the look of Broadway musical theater. Music by Leonard Bernstein and lyrics by Stephen Sondheim.

PART 5

THE CREATORS:
VISIONS OF AMERICA

INTRODUCTION

The French dancers who came to America in the 1790s brought with them not only their dancing shoes but also their ballet repertoire. American audiences were already familiar with short comical dances, such as "the Dwarf dance" or "mock minuet," with hornpipes featured during the *entr'acte,* or with country dances in the finale. Previously in the eighteenth century, these were most often performed by English dancing masters or provincial actors. After 1791, troupes of highly trained French dancers introduced serious dramatic ballets, and American audiences grew to be enchanted with these melodramatic mixtures of pantomime and dance.

Although he has never been so credited, Jean-François Arnould-Mussot (1734–95) was author of a dozen ballets presented in the United States during this time by Francisqui, Madame Gardie, and others, which were the first "serious" dramatic ballets (as opposed to "comical") offered to American audiences.[1] Henry Lyonnet called Arnould-Mussot "the true creator of melodrama," and he was an important transitional link between Noverre's *ballet d'action* and the later French Romantic period.[2] *The American Heroine,* the initial selection in this section, was typical of his work in its blend of dance with dramatic pantomime, as well as its reliance on stereotyped characters such as the virtuous heroine, the outcast hero, the innocent victim, and manipulative villain. The author, who never set foot on American shores, skillfully included authentic details of Indian life, anticipating the romantic penchant for "local color."

The American Heroine represents an early—and highly sympathetic—portrayal of Native Americans on the United States stage, based on a supposedly factual account of an English sailor who sold his Indian sweetheart into slavery after she saved his life. In the preface, Arnould-Mussot expressed righteous indignation at the villain's avarice and perfidy.

The heroine of *The American Heroine,* called Jarika, illustrates the widespread diffusion of Jean Jacques Rousseau's vision of the "noble savage," a shining example of natural morality uncorrupted by civilization. In the excerpt translated in this next selection, she proves her extraordinary generosity by saving, for the second time, the sailor's life even after he attempted to sell her into slavery. Jarika dismisses the traitor from her sight with a disdainful gesture and accepts the Chief's marriage proposal. Her emotional responses on stage were communicated via pantomime gestures performed rhythmically to music. The dramatic action, as was inevitable with many *ballets d'action,* ended with a final dance of celebration.

Over the next one hundred years, particularly when the romantic impulse began to wane, theatrical emphasis gradually came to focus more and more upon lavish spectacle rather than on plot or character development, as exemplified by advertisements for "Imre Kiralfy's Grand Operatic Historical Spectacle, *America*" that heralded its "Magnitude and Pomp Unparalleled." Even for the Gilded Age, a time when theatrical managers succumbed to spectacle fever, this was an extravaganza to end all extravaganzas, with over seven hundred singers and dancers featured in the Chicago World's Fair Exposition in 1893. Just prior to the Civil War, ballet had declined to the point where it was included in theatrical productions mainly, as the *Spirit of the Times* (Mar. 14, 1857) commented, in order to make a "grand display of pretty faces, forms, and legs." Imre Kiralfy (1845–1910), *America*'s creator, belonged to a Hungarian family dance troupe who toured the United States with *The Black Crook* and other spectacles.[3] He was enamored of lavish scenic effects with large casts and elephants on stage, all of which obscured the efforts of individual dancers.

America differed from many other nineteenth-century spectacles in its preference for a certain realism over fairy-tale fantasy. Kiralfy selected historically accurate costumes, and downplayed the outrageously revealing costumes seen in *The Black Crook.* This is not to say that his vision of America can be considered as anything but subjective, for events were tailored to fit his optimistic notions of evolutionary progress. The Cherokee Trail of Tears, for example, was conspicuously missing, as were any references to the dominant majority's historic mistreatment of other racial, social, and ethnic groups. The Civil War, which had occurred only a few years previously, was glimpsed as mere background to a melodramatic love story written from the Yankee point of view. According to the scenario, peace was declared just in time to save the southern heroine, who was about to be shot as a spy. The contrived finale, where "Union and Confederate soldiers now appear in fraternal amity," eschewed the political reality of the bitter Reconstruction period. Despite Kiralfy's historically accurate trappings of costume, chronology, and setting, then, *America* reflected a highly selective vision of life in the United States.

The California-born author of our next selection, Isadora Duncan (1877–1927), differs in that she was as inclined to criticize her native country as to praise it. She anticipated many modern-day issues of feminine sexuality. She chose to live openly with several lovers and castigated American women for, as she put it, drugging their souls with matrimony. Duncan was also concerned with feminist issues of health. She danced in free-flowing tunics and urged women to jettison their corsets, a notion greeted with ridicule similar to that accorded the so-called bra-burning liberationists of the 1960s. She preached the beauty of the bare foot, which scandalized audiences who sat at her feet with their own pinched in high-button shoes. And she predicted the coming of "the new woman," a free and intelligent spirit who "shall dance the freedom of women."[4]

Duncan was outraged at what ballet training did to dancers. Look closely at the pretty opera *corphyée,* she suggested, because a "deformed skeleton is dancing before you."[5] So, too, she dismissed European dance genres, attacking them because they cramped the free expression of emotions with their fairy-tale escapism. Worst of all, as far as she was concerned, Duncan felt that ballet was decidedly nonspiritual in its inspiration and educational practices. She aspired to create a dance, as we see in the next selection entitled "Isadora Duncan's Vision of America Dancing," where children would be left free to express American virtues, where democracy would be reflected in their movements, and the natural beauty of America would be symbolized in their gestures. She advised dancers to create a new art and throw away "the servile minuet," which she considered mere refuse from an unfortunate tendency of Americans to copy European dance forms. In addition, she critiqued jazz as "sensual" rather than "spiritual" in its effect. Her vision of America proclaimed the coming of a new age. Even taking into account Duncan's penchant for hyperbole, her vision has been fulfilled in that millions of young Americans have followed in her footsteps.

Duncan sincerely believed in her reforms and was deeply hurt at the reception accorded her last American appearances. For example, by October of 1922, the Bostonians lifted their eyebrows at her bare legs, and they walked out of Symphony Hall when she "disarranged" her garments so as to expose her shoulder. She justified her conduct by demanding, "What should I care what part of my body I reveal? Why is one part more evil than another?" When the mayor of Boston banned her from the stage, she defended herself indignantly and fired her guns at a city in "rigor mortis because of its fearful conceptions of life and culture." Or should I "call it 'cul choor'?" she jibed in a final parting shot.[6] Admittedly, the case was complicated by Isadora's publicly expressed sympathy for the Bolsheviks, sentiments not calculated to endear her to many. She shook the dust from her sandals and went into exile, haunted by newspaper headlines that screamed rumors of how the U.S. secretary of labor intended to strip away her citizenship. The founder of American modern dance never again returned to her native land.

While Duncan remained active in Europe, others stepped forth to capture the spotlight. The eminently practical Ruth St. Denis (1879–1968) was quick to comprehend that spirituality could be a commercially viable entity in American theater. She combined an utterly sincere mysticism with awesome arm ripples in her dramatic dance entitled *Incense,* for example. Reports about Duncan filtered back across the Atlantic, while St. Denis, in company with her young husband Ted Shawn (1891–1972), founded dancing schools in Los Angeles, New York, and Jacob's Pillow. She taught thousands, including those destined to become the great pioneers of American modern dance. Their Denishawn Company introduced countless thousands more to dance concerts as the group crisscrossed the country on a series of tours from 1914 to 1926.

Although his contributions have often been slighted, Shawn played more than stage partner for his glamorous wife in her favorite role of goddess. He administered the school in Hollywood; he taught the advanced classes; he directed the rehearsals; together they auditioned students and maintained constant vigilance backstage during the performances. He choreographed almost twice as many ballets for the company as St. Denis did; today his choreography is perhaps more often revived than hers.[7] A number of his early pieces utilized American thematic material, locales, characters, and music, whereas St. Denis primarily relied upon an eclectic collection of oriental exotica for her inspiration.

"Papa" Shawn, as he liked to be called, justifiably felt that men had been given short shrift by Americans insofar as dance was concerned, and in "Dancing for Men, 1926," the fourth essay of this section, he single-handedly attempted to redress the imbalance. He attacked the lopsided proportion of female to male dancers on American stages and defended every man's inalienable right to dance without harassment or attacks upon his masculinity. He cited unnamed authorities to support his chauvinist claim of male supremacy in the dance, and then proceeded to devalue woman to the status of mere decoration or "accompaniment." Furthermore, he claimed, "the essential qualities necessary for success in the dance are masculine qualities," such as physical strength, endurance, controlled precision, and discipline. Shawn thus turned the tables on women dancers by denying *their* femininity, just as his own masculine identity had once been questioned. Not long after publishing *The American Ballet,* the book from which this essay is taken, Shawn founded his popular company of All-Male Dancers, which toured the country from 1933 until the beginning of World War II and did much to overcome public prejudice against male dancers.

The early pioneers of American modern dance who earned their stripes dancing in the highly theatrical productions at Denishawn reacted to St. Denis's attempts to replicate another culture's aesthetic experience. Most agreed that such efforts were misguided and preferred to break with the past. Martha Graham may perhaps have protested too much when she asserted, "We deny their influence over us, and embark upon our own art-form."[8] Dancers, whom Doris Humphrey called the Sleeping Beauties of the world of ballet, awakened from a long nap to observe, "We belong to the twentieth century; we have something to reveal about it in the light of contemporary experience."[9] These pioneers and others began to search for relevant themes and idiosyncratic ways of dancing to express these concerns. From the late 1920s to the early 1940s, many dancers began to explore American subject matter, just as did the American regionalist writers such as Robert Penn Warren and other Agrarians, American scene painters such as Grant Wood and Thomas Hart Benton, and composers such as Aaron Copland who utilized American folk tunes in concert music. In just ten short years, Martha Graham choreographed her beloved *Appalachian Spring* and at least nine other American pieces. Within the space of eleven years, Doris Humphrey created *Shakers* and nine other dances that dealt with American society. Also during the same period, Charles Weidman produced *Flickers,* while Helen Tamiris composed *Walt Whitman Suite.* Lew Christensen created the ballet *Filling Station,* and Eugene Loring set *Billy the Kid.* These pieces, and scores of others, were characterized by the use of American themes and subjects, folktales or literary works, regional settings, characters, and music.

During the decade of the '30s, American dancers and choreographers became increasingly self-conscious about their mission as "American" artists. Earliest to lead the charge (at least in print) was Helen Tamiris (1905–66), who urged in her "Manifest" of January, 1928, that an artist's "principal duty" was to express the spirit of her nation. As seen in these next two selections, dance concert programs could provide a platform for revolutionary pronouncements. Martha Graham (1894?–1991) issued a "Platform for the American Dance" in which she advocated that "the American dance owes a duty" to the American audiences. Doris Humphrey (1895–1958) likewise issued a "Declaration" of principles for American dance as "an expression of American life." Not just the avant-garde modern dancers but also the ballet folk seem to have been struck by the need to issue aesthetic manifestos of a patriotic persuasion. For example, Lincoln Kirstein, today revered as the founder of the New York City Ballet, wrote his *Blast at Ballet: A Corrective for the American Audience,* in which he detailed a "Program and Manifesto" to be used to break up "the Great Conspiracy" of Russian dancers who dominated ballet in the United States at that time.

A common theme for these various manifestos of the 1930s is a commitment to the creation of a revolutionary form of dance, totally new and unbeholden to Europe, that would be quintessentially American. "This new dance of action," Doris Humphrey enthused in her "Declaration," "comes inevitably from the people who had to subdue a continent, to make a thousand paths through forest and plain, to conquer the mountains, and eventually to raise up towers of steel and glass." The artistic aspirations of these revolutionaries were deeply rooted in their political vision of America, a breadth of vision that echoes Isadora Duncan's scorn for the nineteenth-century ballerinas posed on their pink satin pedestals, as much as it does Duncan's exhortations for the modern dancer to leap over the barricades and fight for the avant-garde cause.

American Document (1938), the libretto seen in the next selection, illustrates how the aspirations described above could be put into practice. It is taken from an early large-scale ensemble piece of Americana choreographed by Martha Graham.[10] Commentators at its premiere immediately and almost unanimously agreed upon its significance. Lincoln Kirstein, for example, heralded it as a "dance-drama of the first importance."[11] Many critics noted that the piece was a radical departure for Martha Graham and suggested that it marked a significant shift in her development as an artist.

The dance itself was an unusual combination of speech (with excerpts read aloud from the Declaration of Independence, the writings of a Seneca chieftain, a sermon by Reverend Jonathan Edwards, and the Emancipation Proclamation), music and dances set within the traditional minstrel show format of processional, cross fire, olio, and afterpiece. Characters included the two End Men, the Interlocutor, and so on. However, the blatant forms of parody typically found in a minstrel show changed in Graham's hands, so that, in the end, the sympathies of the audience were directed at those who had formerly been mocked.[12] *American Document* thus acknowledged the slaves' suffering as well as their joy on the day of emancipation. In essence, then, Graham took a form that, for eighty years, had been associated with racial insults and radically transformed it into a vehicle to portray instances of injustice and suffering.

Katherine Dunham (1912–), in the next selection, examined the African American experience from the point of view of one who has suffered from racial discrimination. She used the theme of racial violence as focus for her dramatic ballet *Southland* (1951), which depicted a black man's lynching by a southern mob after he is falsely accused by a white woman. Later writers cite Dunham as recalling that the piece was inspired by the 1955 murder of sixteen-year-old Emmett Till after a white Mississippi woman accused him of "wolf-whistling" at her, but actually its premiere in Santiago de Chile occurred five years prior to Till's death. Her ballet might be better described as an anticipation of the increasing numbers of violent acts during the 1950s and 1960s directed against African American citizens who dared to demand justice under the Constitution during the civil rights movement.

The first section ended with an eerie dance of jubilation performed by the white female protagonist while the hero's charred corpse swung from a bough. "Strange Fruit," a song Billie Holiday made famous, played in the background. Its title referred to a lynched corpse as this "strange fruit hanging on the old magnolia tree." This same theme was used by Charles Weidman (1936) for his *Lynchtown* and inspired Pearl Primus (1943) in yet another piece on the subject, this one named after the original Langston Hughes poem, "Strange Fruit."

Dunham's ballet was never performed in the United States, an omission that she regretted for the rest of her life. According to the choreographer, the Chileans greeted its premiere warmly, although unnamed persons at the American embassy pressured her not to perform it again.[13] Dunham attributed her later difficulties with the State Department, under whose auspices she toured as a goodwill ambassador, to their having blackballed her after this incident.[14] The ballet was performed for the last time in Paris.

Although produced in the same decade but otherwise a total about-face from Dunham's devastating critique of American racism, the Russian-born ballet choreographer George Balanchine (1904–83) created a red-blooded-American ballet that celebrated the American flag and other contemporary icons—or perhaps mocked them. No one was quite sure, as will be evident in a contemporary review reprinted in this next selection. *Stars and Stripes* (1958) came complete with a surfeit of red, white, and blue tutus; parades of marching bands; loud Sousa music; long-legged baton twirlers; grinning drum majors, and an enormous American flag that unfurled to cover the entire back wall during the grand finale. The ballet, as George Balanchine described it, was "a kind of balletic parade, led by four 'regiments.'"[15] It was divided into five sections termed "campaigns" so that each regiment marched onto stage in turn, some in wedge-shaped drill formations and others in traditional two-by-two lines. The fourth movement featured a *pas de deux* danced to the strains of a tuba, which Balanchine envisioned as a lugubrious tribute to President (formerly General) and Mrs. Eisenhower. The fifth movement, a sea of primary colors and quicksteps, brought out the entire company for a rousing finale.

As with Dunham's *Southland,* this ballet, which seems on the surface to be an almost simpleminded, xenophobic celebration of Balanchine's adopted country, gave rise to instant controversy. Some in the audience were insulted by a ballet originally "conceived as a musical joke," and charged that Balanchine, in a fit of "sheer perversity," had concocted the whole thing as a "parody of patriotism."[16] The critic Lillian Moore, as will be seen in "A Critic Reacts to Balanchine's *Stars and Stripes,* 1958," worried how other cultures would react if the piece, called "a discomforting touch of chauvinism" by some of her peers, was to be taken overseas on a forthcoming international tour by the New York City Ballet.[17] Dag Hammarskjold, secretary general of the United Nations, was so offended by its "shameless exhibition of chauvinist sentiment" and "the blatant effrontery of [its] imperialist gesture" that he was said to have requested it be omitted from the tour repertoire.[18] He was seconded by John Martin, dance critic for the *New York Times,* who termed it a "colossal piece of cynicism," and begged, "Please, Mr. Balanchine, leave 'Stars and Stripes' at home" (*New York Times,* Feb. 2, 1958).

Nevertheless, the ballet seems to have survived well enough, despite the fact that its choreography lacked the exquisite craftsmanship and subtle elegance for which Balanchine's best ballets were noted. One moment in its performance history stands out: late one Sunday night, a New York City Ballet audience, rising with their coats to leave, was puzzled to see the curtains lift again for an unexpected performance of *Stars and Stripes.* The dancers froze in place, and a terse announcement followed that American hostages had only just been released by their Iranian captors. The audience, myself among them, went wild. Everything, even the shamelessly manipulative waving of yellow ribbons by each member of the corps de ballet, was cause for more cheers.[19]

Yvonne Rainer (1934–), as we see in the next selection called "Flag Dance, 1970," choreographed a radically different kind of flag dance. Hers was grounded in the heyday of the Vietnam protest movement, a time of draft-card destruction in front of army induction centers, Buddhist monk self-immolation in Saigon public squares, and, rather than waving, burning flags in full view of the White House. Rainer, incensed by the arrests of war protesters, plotted her own performance protest. As she told the story, she decided to join two taboo themes exquisitely calculated to offend the mores of middle-class Americans: public nudity and desecration of the American flag. Her *Judson Flag Show* followed from that confluence.

The dance consisted of nude dancers decked out in huge American flags tied like bibs about their necks. They performed two repetitions each of *Trio A,* a work that has since come to achieve the status of a "classic" in modern dance. Unlike many choreographers who view their work as personal property, Rainer taught *Trio A* to anyone who wanted to learn it. Moreover, she encouraged anyone to teach it, no matter whether the dancers were "skilled, unskilled, professional, fat, old, sick, amateur."[20] It continues to be taught and performed, settling comfortably into its role as an icon of the rebellious '60s and '70s. She herself set it for solo dancer in jeans and sneakers, a tap dancer, ballet dancer in tights and ballet shoes, ensembles moving in unison outdoors on the streets, duos moving out of synchrony at a party, or, as in this selection, solos performed separately by nude dancers at the Judson Church in Greenwich Village. Rainer envisioned herself "as a post-modern dance evangelist [who would] bring movement to the masses, watching with Will Rogers-like benignity the slow, inevitable evisceration of my elitist creation."[21] Generations of dancers later, innumerable versions of the same dance can be found, but, fortunately for dance historians, a film is available with Rainer performing a definitive version—or at least *one* of hundreds of others that she might define as equally definitive despite certain transfigurations inherent in the process of being handed on. In a certain sense, then, Rainer has answered Isadora Duncan's call for an American dance form, accessible to dancers and nondancers everywhere, that would reflect our democratic commitment to America. Instead of togas and bare feet, though, the dancers dressed in scruffy jeans and sneakers. Or, as in this case, American flags and bare bottoms.

Trio A made its premiere at Judson Church on January 10, 1966, under the title *The Mind Is a Muscle, Part I.* The only "musical" accompaniment was the resounding crash that wooden slats made as they were thrown off the balcony with relentless regularity. Rainer, inspired by her ambivalent "love of, and contempt for dancing," succinctly described *Trio A* as "Details executed in a context of a continuum of energy."[22] The dancer's body moved in a slow, controlled fashion throughout a continuous series of smoothly flowing and unfolding movements. Unlike ballet dancers, the performer never repeated any of these movement patterns and eschewed the standard dance vocabulary of steps, poses, fake smiles, and stereotyped combinations. All movements confirmed rather than fought against the pull of gravity.

Following in the footsteps of Isadora Duncan, Helen Tamiris, and Doris Humphrey, who proclaimed their aesthetics in print and urged a break with past practices, Rainer published a 1965 manifesto that called for rejection of all stage artifice: "NO to spectacle no to virtuosity no to transformations and magic and make-believe no to the glamour and transcendency of the star image no to the heroic no to the anti-heroic no to trash imagery no to involvement of performer or spectator no to style no to camp no to seduction of spectator by the wiles of performer no to eccentricity no to moving or being moved."[23] *Trio A,* which was greeted with critical catcalls as well as yawns, has come to be accepted as an important statement of the avant-garde canon for the Judson Church movement of the '60s and '70s generation. The movement was centered at the Judson Church in New York's Greenwich Village, and, as with many another successful avant-garde movement, was later incorporated into the mainstream. It had lost the power to shock any longer.

Not so others who have come after. It is characteristic of avant-garde art that shock value is much sought after as an aesthetic consideration in and of itself.[24] The down side of this desire to astonish is that, once astonishment is attained, it is all too easy to lose one's place at the helm. Soon, the latest jolt is replaced by some other, yet more outrageous conceit: for example, classical ballet choreographers have set *Giselle* in an insane asylum, *Coppélia* in a housing project or *Romeo and Juliet* as a hip-hop ballet in present-day Philadelphia.[25] Audiences quickly become jaded and rush after the next novelty: a *Swan Lake* danced by an all-male chorus of swans.[26] The line between provocative and passé all too quickly blurs.

Perhaps one exception to this generalization is the career of William Forsythe (1949–), who has managed to remain preeminent among the avant-garde for over twenty-five years. As did Isadora Duncan, this "bad boy" choreographer of American ballet paid for his success by exile. American reviewers had a field day with the blond, blue-eyed choreographer who once excelled as the best rock 'n' roll dancer at his Long Island high school, an influence still evident in his work as director of the Frankfurt Opera ballet since 1984. Establishment critics originally greeted his work as the "latest specimen of overkill and pretentiousness," "excessively violent and even nihilistic," "provocatively pseudo-intellectual," as demonstrating "formalistic creative rigidity" and filled with an "overload of paraphernalia and timeworn theatrical devices."[27] His audiences, who even today in the decorous Parisian Chatelet Theatre react with raucous enthusiasm to his audacious originality, have been insulted as mere pawns in these hostilities—Forsythe, as Linda Small of the *Village Voice* said some years ago (July 28, 1987), "is accepted as a wild, interesting innovator by those who neither think nor see." Time has passed, however, and finally a few American critics have started to sing a different tune, most notably Roslyn Sulcas in the *New York Times* (Nov. 29, 1998), who acknowledged that "Forsythe is widely considered the most important dance maker on the planet" even though his name is scarcely known in the United States. His American renown will likely increase, albeit gradually, because outrageous behavior of the avant-garde variety tends to antagonize the critics—and Forsythe has definitely alienated the New York dance establishment.

Forsythe's European exile is indicative of a trend that led talented American dancers and choreographers far from their native shores. During the 1980s alone, John Neumeier directed the Hamburg ballet, Mark Morris was appointed ballet director at the venerable Théâtre de la Monnaie in Brussels, Carolyn Carlson worked at La Fenice theater in Venice, and Glen Tetley has been with the Netherlands Dance Theatre, among many others. A National Endowment for the Arts study reported that, in 1989, the average income for a choreographer in the United States came to the grand total of $6,000. That was the good news: the bad was that their expenses hit $13,000.[28] It should be no surprise that almost all of these artists had to support themselves by other means. Government-funded opportunities in Europe generally offered stable situations. Mark Morris commented, "We had a building, we had six studios, we had offices, we had a full-time physical therapist, we had health insurance. We had money."[29] Given what is necessary to enhance talent, it was no wonder that the émigré choreographer became the sign of the times during the 1980s and well into the 1990s.

American dancers, teachers, and choreographers continued to spend a great deal of their time traveling abroad through the 1990s. Trisha Brown and David Parsons found ready welcome in France, season after season, as had Alwin Nikolais before them. Bill T. Jones was appointed ballet master at the Lyon Opera House in France. Madonna, Michael Jackson, and MTV dancers were beamed via satellite around the world. Even artists who specialized in the ancient Hawaiian hula were exported to Japan for weekend seminars. The trend was so dominant that as much as 42 percent of modern dance companies' earned income was gained through international tours.[30]

But this changed. The impact of international economic instability began to be felt in the dance world and, around the same time, funds from home began to dry up. When Jesse Helms locked horns with the National Endowment for the Arts, threatening its very existence in 1995, administrators caved in to the congressman. Grantees were asked to sign the equivalent of loyalty oaths and proclaim their intention not to violate so-called community standards of decency in their creation of artistic works. Bella Lewitzky, long active in California's modern dance world, was incensed and successfully sued the NEA for violating her First Amendment rights. In the end, though, Congress won. The politicians simply tightened the noose around NEA's budget.

NEA changed its rules to restrict its grants to individual choreographers, and the bureaucrats fanned the flames between so-called elitist and populist arts as a matter of policy.[31]

With the diminution of foreign tours as a source of income, and particularly with the closing down of the National Endowment connection, many American dance companies were hard put to survive at all.[32] During 1995 to 1999, from the very start of the NEA controversy, companies that folded or were placed in financial jeopardy included the Los Angeles Ballet, the Joffrey Ballet (with over half a million dollars in dues collected but unpaid to the union), Cleveland–San Jose Ballet (so far behind on bills that the landlord chained its doors shut and the utility company turned off its electricity), the Ohio Ballet (which had lost significant funding from NEA), and Ballet Arizona (over one million dollars in debt). Ruth Page's *Nutcracker,* a Chicago tradition that began in 1965, closed its doors in 1998. Also in 1998, Dance Aspen filed for bankruptcy due to escalating debt, including its well-regarded festival. Likewise, the Hartford Ballet folded, over one million dollars in debt, but quickly reorganized under a new name and director. City Ballet of New York refused to discuss its financial problems but quietly cut its dance troupe from ninety to seventy-five. Other small companies may not have made the headlines, but they, too, hit shaky times, begging and borrowing as best they could to get by. All this happened at the time of the biggest bull market in American history, with more millionaires per square inch in the United States than ever before. Where have all the patrons gone?

But money, after all, is only money and is the least of performers' problems compared to the plague of AIDS, which rampaged unimpeded through the dance community during the 1980s and early 1990s. Elke Solomon, an artist who lived in New York's loft district, lamented to me that "All we do, every day, is go to funerals, sometimes three times a day." Who knows how many potentially great works of art were buried during that time?[33] The dying gave witness and the living were inspired to pay tribute, which led to a whole new category of art, by and about people who were suffering—"victim art" as Arlene Croce of the *New Yorker* disparaged it. Genevieve Oswald, curator emerita of the Dance Collection at Lincoln Center, responded by initiating an oral history interview project to capture the voices and concerns of those dance professionals afflicted with HIV and AIDS.

Last Supper at Uncle Tom's Cabin/The Promised Land (1990), the last selection in this book, shows how Bill T. Jones (1965–) uses dance to address the existential meaning of this devastation, a personal issue for him because he fully expects that his own life will be cut short as that of his partner had been.

In response to Croce, he claims that he does not obsess on death and decline but rather celebrates "the resourcefulness and courage necessary to perform the act of living."[34] Jones's sprawling, epic work has been controversial from its inception. He interweaves the personal lives of his performers with their artistic representation on stage, and, in the end, they and the audience are impacted by the artistic event itself. An ex-convict named Justice, a retired stockbroker, Jones's own mother—these are simultaneously characters in the play as well as real people walking about the stage. Jones faces head-on the existential meaning of Evil, in the person of Job who demands to know why God has sent the plague of AIDS to his people. Jones also takes on questions of nudity and Puritanism, racism and classism, homophobia and gay pride. In short, he looks directly into the lion's den of social issues current in the 1990s, and so follows the tradition of other choreographers who depict their individualistic vision of America through the dance.

By the close of the twentieth century, American choreographers and dancers were no longer so eagerly sought after on the international market (although some, such as Trisha Brown or David Parsons, continue to be invited abroad). The world was locked in the doldrums of economic recession, except for the American dollar that climbed ever higher and higher in value. What to do?—Not surprisingly, the prodigal sons and daughters returned home. Even Mark Morris, who had outraged the proper Brussels bourgeois with his avant-garde shenanigans, made an American comeback as director of a commercial Broadway musical.

Former expatriates were not alone in recognizing the United States as the land of artistic opportunity. Impoverished Russian and other Eastern European ballet dancers leapt the Atlantic to invade countless American companies, bringing technical skills that helped to revitalize the regional ballet movement in this country. Eminent immigrants from other nations have long made significant contributions to dance in America: Pearl Primus, Geoffrey Holder, and Garth Fagan founded their own companies after emigrating from the West Indies, while Peter Martins, successor to Balanchine at City Ballet, came from Denmark. Newcomers, whether from Asia or Africa or South America, are more likely to make their national reputations as performers than as choreographers. Although many ethnic groups tend to stay within their own environs, theatrically speaking, perhaps Ralph Lemon represents the wave of the future. In *Tree,* as well as his earlier piece called *Geography,* presented at the Brooklyn Academy of Music's Next Wave festival, Lemon brings together dancers from the United States with artists he met during his world travels. His performers come from Japan, India, Taiwan, the Ivory Coast, Guinea, and

China—Yunnan in rural China as well as Beijing. He celebrates the differences in their traditions as well as dance training. Anna Kisselgoff, the *New York Times* critic, called the piece "evocative" and praised the choreographer's "poetic gift for evoking a shared humanity."[35]

In *Naked in America* (with text by Jean Dell), South African choreographer Sonjé Mayo presents a tribute to the immigrant experience by one who has recently come through it. In it, she wryly comments on the scene before her, poking fun at her romantic expectations and contrasting them to the sensationalized "reality" cast before her in the press. Mayo's piece explores her feelings about her adopted land—at times satirical, sometimes poignant, overall more reflective than ever before. Back home, where she was a political activist, "It was too dangerous to be introspective, what with the gated communities in which we lived, the barbed wire everywhere, the ubiquitous security guards, my neighbors who were murdered, my friends 'detained' for months by the secret police." Maybe it was better not to acknowledge one's feelings, for people were filled with too much fear. Her latest work, then, represents a letting go of earlier themes concerning political repression and exploitive racism, while she tilts toward the intimate and personal. Slowly, over time, the immigrant voice loses its accent.

At the turn into the twenty-first century, then, many of America's talented dancers and choreographers seem content to remain close to home. However, the exodus of only a decade ago should raise red flags about the future of dance in America. At any time, other countries with a tradition of investment in the arts could reengage and entice our best and brightest away. If many of our greatly talented young artists opt to live in exile, what would this bode for the future of dance in America? How should we better nurture our young artists and encourage them to stay? How does working abroad affect the personal vision of American choreographers? For example, one critic accuses William Forsythe of being derivative of "Euro-trash," and another implies that his work isn't really "American," whatever that means.[36] Already in Europe there exists a "new generation of creative nomads, stateless, self-affirming, bonding with one another through various cultural sensibilities that have little or nothing to do with the official dogma of the countries they currently call home."[37] Will American dancers lose their accent when they join these nomads? Will modern dance become so internationalized as to lose the original flavor from the very land that created it?

At this time, the torch passes to a new generation. The immigrant, the marginal, and the "other" have set a new artistic standard. Theatrical dancers no longer resemble cookie-cutter caricatures of a bulimic ballerina. Nor is dance any longer categorized into radically different genres—rather, an individual-istic, enthusiastic fusion reigns supreme. Disparate techniques from funk to classical ballet to jazz are all joined together in one high energy celebration of the dance, of the dancer. Unlike the "pure dance" exponents of the mid-twentieth century, many choreographers today prefer to look inward and speak to their own experiences, whether as a Korean American choreographer experimenting with Zen dance or as a South African immigrant who explores political repression in her native country. The African American choreographer is free to jettison the false smile of the minstrel mask and speak in his or her authentic voice. Today the American patchwork quilt of diversity in the dance blazons forth in all its glorious colors and shapes.

Through it all, I personally find my own life enriched and touched by what others give. The future for dance in America in the twenty-first century looks joyful, indeed.

NOTES

1. In "John Durang, the First American Dancer" (*Chronicles of American Dance*, ed. Paul Magriel [New York: Henry Holt and Company, 1948]), Lillian Moore touted *La Forêt noire* as "an event of the greatest importance in the history of ballet in America" for she incorrectly believed it to be the "first serious ballet given in this country" (p. 25), even though six other Arnould-Mussot ballets had already been produced here by the Placides. She also erroneously attributed its authorship to the ballerina rather than to Arnould-Mussot.

2. Jean Georges Noverre advocated the primacy of *ballet d'action* (or dramatic ballet) over *divertissement* dances in his *Letters on the Dance and Ballets,* trans. Cyril Beaumont (London: C. W. Beaumont, 1930). Henry Lyonnet's comments appear in *Dictionnaire des comédiens français* (ca. 1910?; reprint, Geneva: Slatkine Reprints, 1969), p. 30. See also John Mason, *Melodrama in France from the Revolution to the Romantic Drama* (Baltimore: J. H. Furst Co., 1912), and my entry for Arnould-Mussot in the *International Encyclopedia of Dance,* ed. Selma Jean Cohen (New York: Oxford University Press, 1998).

3. Bolossy Kiralfy, *Bolossy Kiralfy, Creator of Great Musical Spectacles,* ed. Barbara Barker (Ann Arbor, Mich.: UMI Research Press, 1988).

4. Isadora Duncan, *The Art of the Dance,* ed. Sheldon Cheney (1928; New York: Theatre Arts Books, 1977), p. 63.

5. Ibid., p. 56.

6. Isadora Duncan, "America Makes Me Sick," *Hearst's American Weekly,* Jan., 1923,

reprinted in *Isadora Speaks,* ed. Franklin Rosemont (San Francisco: City Lights Books, 1981), p. 134. See also *Boston Globe,* Nov. 18, 1922.

7. According to data derived from Jane Sherman's book, *The Drama of Denishawn Dance* (Middletown, Conn.: Wesleyan University Press, 1979), Shawn is credited with twenty-nine ballets to St. Denis's sixteen. They also collaborated on three more.

8. Martha Graham, "The American Dance," in *Modern Dance,* comp. Virginia Stewart (New York: A. E. Weyhe, 1935), p. 104.

9. Doris Humphrey, *The Art of Making Dances,* ed. Barbara Pollack (New York: Rinehart & Company, 1959), p. 174.

10. See my biography of Graham in *American National Biography,* ed. John A. Garraty and Mark C. Carnes (New York: Oxford University Press, 1999).

11. Lincoln Kirstein, *The Nation,* Sept. 8, 1938; see my analysis of this piece (Maureen Needham [Costonis], "Martha Graham's *American Document:* A Minstrel Show in Modern Dance Dress," *American Music* 9, no. 3 (Fall, 1991): 297–310).

12. Martha Graham would have been "horrified" to have this piece considered a minstrel show when her intention was just the opposite, according to Ron Protas. In fact, "when Leonard Bernstein wanted to write new music for it as a minstrel show, Martha told him she found that form unacceptable and demeaning to the black experience" (Protas to author, Jan. 13, 2000).

13. Jennifer Dunning, "Alvin Ailey Dancers Follow the Steps of a Trailblazer," *New York Times,* Nov. 22, 1987.

14. Ruth Beckford, *Katherine Dunham* (New York: Marcel Dekker, 1979), p. 72.

15. George Balanchine and Francis Mason, *Balanchine's Complete Stories of the Great Ballets,* rev. ed. (Garden City: Doubleday & Company, 1977), p. 579.

16. Lincoln Kirstein, involved in the conception of the ballet from its origins, acknowledges this motivation in *The New York City Ballet* (New York: Alfred A. Knopf, 1973), p. 152.

17. Doris Hering, "A Review," *Dance Magazine,* Nov., 1958, p. 27. See also A. T. in *Dance Observer,* Mar., 1958, p. 42.

18. Kirstein, *New York City Ballet,* p. 152. See also A. T.'s comments in *Dance Observer,* Mar., 1958, p. 42.

19. The event was reported in the *New York Times* ("Balanchine 'Stars and Stripes' Hails Ex-Hostages," Jan. 26, 1981).

20. Yvonne Rainer, *Work, 1961–73* (Halifax: Press of the Nova Scotia College of Art and Design, 1974), p. 77.

21. Ibid.

22. Anderson Theatre program, Apr. 11, 14, 15, 1968, reproduced in Rainer, *Work,* pp. 70–71.

23. Rainer, *Work,* p. 51.

24. See Renato Poggioli, *The Theory of the Avant-Garde* (Cambridge, Mass.: Belknap Press of Harvard University Press, 1968), for a brilliant analysis of the meaning of the avant-garde.

25. Anna Kisselgoff, "A Titan Passes; Provocations Abound," *New York Times,* Dec. 27, 1998.

26. See Joan Acocella, "Blowup: Bombs Fall on Matthew Bourne's *Cinderella,*" *New Yorker,* May 10, 1999.

27. Linda Small, "Hot Air Balloon," *Village Voice,* July 28, 1987; Susan Reimer-Torn, "Experimentation Is William Forsythe's Forte," *New York Times,* July 5, 1987; Clive Barnes, "Frankfurt's Forsythe Saga," *New York Post,* July 15, 1987; Tobi Tobias, "Review," *New York Magazine,* July 24, 1989.

28. Robert Johnson, "Study Exposes Poverty of U.S. Dancemakers," *Dance Magazine,* Mar., 1994. Johnson cites "Dancemakers," an NEA report, p. 16.

29. John Gruen, "Breaking New Ground," *Dance Magazine,* July, 1995, p. 50.

30. Don Moore, "The Perilous '80s," in *On the Edge: Challenges to American Dance,* proceedings of the 1989 Dance Critics Association, comp. Janice Ross and Stephen Cobbett Steinberg ([New York]: Dance Critics Association, 1990), p. 92.

31. Marika Clark, "Artists as 'Elitists': Deja Vu All Over Again," *Dance Magazine,* Jan., 1998, pp. 47–48.

32. A "dismal picture emerge[d]" when the dance grants were announced in 1998, according to Marika Clark in "Second Year of NEA's New Grand Structure a Battle," *Dance Magazine,* May, 1998, p. 26. Total monies for dance companies dropped 25 percent, while the number of grants awarded increased from thirteen to twenty.

33. After the death of Rudolf Nureyev, *Newsweek* devoted an entire issue to "AIDS and the Arts," featuring a roll call of the fallen (Jan. 18, 1993, pp. 16–32). Tributes to choreographers who died from AIDS complications continued even as the death toll began to decrease; see Paul Ben-Itzak, "Dance Makers Lost to AIDS to Be Remembered in Capital," *Dance Magazine,* Oct., 1996, pp. 29 ff.

34. Bill T. Jones, "Still Here," Bill T. Jones/Arnie Zane Dance Company, Foundation for Dance Promotion, n.d.

35. Anna Kisselgoff, "Playful and Painful Contrasts as China Meets Mississippi in Dance," *New York Times,* Oct. 26, 2000.

36. Tobi Tobias, *New York Magazine,* July 24, 1989. See also Otis Stuart, "Forsythe's Follies," *Ballet Review* 15, no. 3 (Fall, 1987): 41.

37. David R. White, "In the New World of Euro Arts," *New York Times,* Oct. 10, 1999.

CHAPTER 23

The American Heroine (1786)

Jean-François Arnould-Mussot
Translated by Maureen Needham

[In the first part of this three-act pantomime, Jarika, the Indian heroine, falls in love with a shipwrecked English sailor. She hides him from enemies who seek to kill him. He rewards her bravery with treachery: he enslaves
her and sells her to an English ship-captain. The Indians join forces and attack the English sailors, who are forced to flee. Jarika is removed from her fetters by the Indian Chief, who secretly admires her.]

SCENE XIII

The Indians, who have demonstrated mastery of the battlefield, reassemble and
form ranks. An instant later, cannon shots announce the departure of the
English ship-captain's vessel.

An Indian messenger enters to announce that their enemies have fled, and
their boat has set sail.

The Indians urge their Chief to pronounce the death sentence upon Inkle
[the English sailor whom Jarika rescued]. They desire vengeance for the raids
and cruelty caused by the English. He solemnly promises to execute Inkle, and
they all withdraw.

SCENE XIV

Jarika, reduced to despair by her beloved's treachery, takes leave of her wom-
en friends who have attempted to soften his cruelty with their kindness. She
seeks some lonely, secluded spot so that she may give full expression to her
grief.

Jean-François Arnould-Mussot, *L'Héroine américaine* (Paris: Guillot, 1786). Translation of Act III, scenes xiii–xv by Maureen Needham.

A noisy celebration is heard in the distance. It threatens to come closer, so she exits from the stage.

SCENE XV

Procession of Native American men and women. They dance as they enter. The stake is prepared and made ready to bind the prisoner.

Inkle, in chains, is led by four Indians. One carries a tomahawk and the other a huge club.

The usual Indian ceremonies follow as they prepare to kill their prisoner.

He is led to the stake and bound to it. Someone lights the bonfire. The Chief gestures to his aides to begin the tortures that are customary rituals for prisoners to undergo, when the desperate Jarika runs in and restrains his hand. She pleads with great animation and tenderness for the Chief to grant pardon of her perfidious lover. The Chief hesitates, momentarily undecided as to what action to take, but in the end he refuses the request. Seeing that her prayers are in vain, she steps back, draws out a dagger and threatens to kill herself if he does not grant her boon. The Chief, frightened by this action, runs to her side and disarms her. He reproaches her for wasting her love on a traitor who cruelly rejected her tender sentiments and sold her into slavery. In response, Jarika only falls to her knees and redoubles her efforts to persuade him. The Chief listens intently. He is touched by the generosity of the young woman, for whom he harbors a deep love. He weakens and at last grants the favor she begs.

All the other Indians, made unhappy by his clemency, begin to protest. But the Chief, with a single warning glance in their direction, imposes his will upon them and reduces them quickly to silence.

Jarika trembles with joy. She races to her lover, and quickly removes his chains. She pauses for a second, shudders at the sight of the irons when she recalls how they were used to bind her when Inkle sold *her* to the English ship-captain. Terrified with the memory, she throws them far from her.

Inkle is confused and humiliated to discover so much generosity in a woman whom he treated with outrageous cruelty. He falls on his knees at her feet and attempts to embrace her. She shivers visibly at his touch and repulses him with disdain. She indicates the vast distance between his infamous conduct and the noble behavior of her tribe's leader. She *vows an eternal hatred toward him and his nation.* She then offers her hand to the Chief, who receives it with the greatest happiness. At that point he coldly orders Inkle to depart. Inkle begs to remain by Jarika's side, but several Indians advance on him and he is forced to back away. He leaves, but his heart is broken by remorse.

The Indians signify by gestures that they approve of the marriage between the woman and their Chief; they express their joy and prepare to celebrate their union.

The Pantomime ends with a danced divertissement.

CHAPTER 24

America, a Grand Historical Spectacle (1893)

Imre Kiralfy

ACT IV, SCENE 1

Ballet of American Inventions

In which the author has illustrated not only the most important inventions of American genius, but also the costumes of the period during which these inventions were made known to the world, introducing:

Franklin's Lightning-Rod
Whitney's Cotton Gin
Fulton's Steamboat
McCormick's Reaper
Hoe's Printing Press
Morse's Electric Telegraph
Howe's Sewing Machine
Yost's Typewriter
Edison's Telephone
Phonograph
Incandescent Electric Light

Imposing Grand Ballabile

Imre Kiralfy, *America, a Grand Historical Spectacle* (Cincinnati: Strobridge Lithography Co., 1893), Act IV, pp. 31–36. Capitalization and selected matters of style have been modernized for ease of reading.

ACT IV, SCENE 2

In the Far West (1848)

A Rocky Mountain pass at sunset. . . . Progress and Perseverance clad as pioneers.

Perseverance emerges from the hut with an ax on his shoulder, followed by Progress. When about to start, he sees pioneers and travelers approaching, and much pleased, he calls to Progress to look at the newcomers. Now is the time for the development of the great West of America.

An Old Trapper and a Young Adventurer are hospitably welcomed by Progress and Perseverance. The young man beckons the rest of their party to advance. A pioneer mother and her children appear. Progress gives them a hearty welcome, and brings them food. Liberty and Peace, in attire of early pioneers, are leading other travelers to this spot, and all are welcomed by Progress. Perseverance now brings a jar of wine, while the miners enjoy their repast.

Pioneers' Duet and Quintette

> Prospecting is a jolly life,
> That should not bring pain or strife,
> What care we then who stays at home,
> Too faint hearted in wilds to roam.
>
> He who seeks to win must be
> Strong, courageous, bold and free.
> If earnest and of moral worth,
> He'll grasp the gold in mother earth.

Quintette

> So boys/girls, let's drink a measure
> To our lasses/lovers and to pleasure.
> Here's a bumper to their health,
> And to the mine that yields us wealth.

Darkness is gradually approaching and Progress and Perseverance invite the travelers to rest in their hut.

ACT IV, SCENE 3

A Southern Forest by Moonlight (1865)

A night bivouac of Union soldiers with their wounded captain on his camp-bed. One soldier is dressing his wounds while another is looking after his comfort. The Captain is dictating a letter, which is being written by his orderly.

Perseverance (attired as an Union officer), is giving directions for the care of his wounded comrade.

> *Chorus of Union Soldiers:*
> The knapsack is rest for the weary head,
> The cloak a covering, the earth our bed.
> But dreams of happy union after fight
> Beguile the heavy hours of night.

During the chorus the wounded Captain has finished dictating his letter, and with great effort affixes his signature to it, and holds it in his grasp as he falls back on his pillow exhausted.

Lilian, a planter's daughter, now appears, and passing the sleeping soldiers, she is distressed upon seeing the condition of the wounded man she loves. Yet she hesitates because he is a Union soldier and an enemy in arms, but her heart conquers, and with trembling footsteps she draws near to say farewell to her beloved. Seeing the letter held on his breast, she slowly takes it from his hand, and is filled with joy when she reads of the writer's love for her. At this moment, the wounded Captain moves, which startles Lilian, and she quickly hides the letter.

Seeing that her lover is again calm, Lilian stoops and gently kisses the Captain's forehead. He awakens and reaches for water in a small canteen near his cot to quench his burning thirst, but it is beyond his reach, and unseen, Lilian places it within his grasp. He, however, is too feeble to raise it to his lips, but the watchful Lilian, still unseen, supports his hand.

The wounded man now opens his eyes and beholds the fair white hand which has aided him, and drawing it toward him, recognizes Lilian, who blushingly falls into his loving embrace. She now unbinds the bandage on his wound and applies to it some liquid from a vial, and then places a few drops on another liquid into water and gives it to him to drink. At this moment a noise is heard without the camp and Lilian hastily hides behind a tree.

Progress now appears, and while watching over the sleeping hero exclaims:

Behold the heroes of inexorable fate,
Which placed dear brothers in mortal strife.
Though their heart's conscience bids them
To forget and love, to love and forget.
Sleep peacefully, your quiet dreams
Will dawn on victory sublime,
And with it bring redemption to weary slaves.
To enjoy the rights of this great land—
The freest of all nations. Then, tomorrow
Gentle Peace shall smile upon great America.
'Tis the will of Reason, Justice and Humanity,
Made imperishable by the immortal Washington.

Bugle Call—Soldiers arise hurriedly and prepare to join their comrades. The wounded Captain, awakened by the bugle call, is surprised at his returning strength, and although yet weak, he rejoins his soldiers.

In the confusion of the alarm Lilian escapes from her hiding place, but is soon seen by a picket who fires at the moving object. This arouses the soldiers, who rush in the direction of the firing and soon return with Lilian as their prisoner, uninjured, and she is placed under guard.

Drums are heard in the distance, and the Union Army, headed by the General and his staff, military band, and line soldiers march in singing

A Patriotic Chant.

After the troops have halted, a soldier advances and reports to the General that a suspected female spy has been captured, and he commands the prisoner to be brought before him. The Captain is astonished to find that the supposed spy is Lilian. The General orders her to be searched, but the Captain interposes and explains that Lilian is his affianced, and that like a good angel she came to minister to his wounds. In reply to the General's inquiry she blushingly confirms her lover's statements.

At this juncture a mounted orderly hands the General a dispatch announcing that

The War Has Ended.

Upon hearing this the soldiers become enthusiastically jubilant, and indulge in Volleys of Hurrahs! Union and Confederate soldiers now appear in fraternal amity and Exuberant Joy Prevails. Amidst the cheers of the troops President Lincoln appears.

ACT IV, SCENE 4

A Vision of the City of Chicago

A large edifice in course of construction illustrates one of the triumphs of modern engineering. This slowly disappears and reveals to view:

1. Fort Dearborn.

2. The Great Fire, and the Ruins of the City, on the memorable night of October 11, 1871.

This is succeeded by a Vision of the great

3. Phoenix City of America, Chicago of To-Day, the capital of the wealth-producing West.

ACT IV, SCENE 5

The Administration Building of the World's Fair, Chicago,

where all the Nations of the earth congregate. Asia and Africa are here represented by groups of her numerous nationalities.

> *Chorus of Asia:*
> From India and its mountain ranges,
> Whence every creed its birth may trace
> Thy voice in greetings from the Ganges,
> Speaks from the cradle of every race.

Africa is represented by groups of her various peoples.

> *Chorus of Africa:*
> From Afric's vast and arid land,
> We hail thy triumph and renew
> Our hope in thy civilization grand!
> And Freedom's blessings grant us too.

ACT IV, SCENE 6

Triumph of Columbia.
European Representatives in Their National Costumes

> *Chorus of European Groups:*
> Great Europe, mighty nurse of nations,

Who first gave true embrace to thee!
Now bows to thy lofty, fateful station,
And shares the glories of the free.

Groups of Canada and the Republics of South America now appear, fol-
lowed by
Groups representing the
    States and Territories of the American Union.
"America," surrounded by Progress, Liberty, Invention and
    The Genius of Chicago,
approaches and welcomes them all.
    Allegory of the Columbian World's Fair!
Where the representatives from all parts of the globe pay
    Homage to American Genius

End of Play

CHAPTER 25

Isadora Duncan's Vision of America Dancing (1927)

Isadora Duncan

In a moment of prophetic love for America, Walt Whitman said: "I hear America singing," and I can imagine the mighty song that Walt heard, from the surge of the Pacific, over the plains, the voices rising of the vast Choral of children, youths, men and women, singing Democracy.

When I read this poem of Whitman's I, too, had a Vision—the Vision of America dancing a dance that would be the worthy expression of the song Walt heard when he heard America singing. This music would have a rhythm as

Excerpt from Isadora Duncan, *My Life* (Garden City, N.Y.: Garden City Publishing Company, 1927), pp. 339–43. From *My Life* by Isadora Duncan. Copyright 1927 by Horace Liveright, Inc., renewed ©1955 by Liveright Publishing Corporation. Used by permission of Liveright Publishing Corporation.

Isadora Duncan dancing. This original watercolor by Abraham Walkowitz captures the dynamic energy of her dance. Courtesy, Special Collections, Heard Library at Vanderbilt University.

great as the exhilaration, the swing or curves of the Rocky Mountains. It would have nothing to do with the sensual lilt of the jazz rhythm: it would be like the vibration of the American soul striving upward, through labour to harmonious life. Nor had this dance that I visioned any vestige of the Fox Trot or the Charleston—rather was it the living leap of the child springing toward the heights, towards its future accomplishment, towards a new great vision of life that would express America.

It has often made me smile—but somewhat ironically—when people have called my dancing Greek, for I myself count its origin in the stories which my Irish grandmother often told us of crossing the plains with grandfather in '49 in a covered wagon—she eighteen, he twenty-one, and how her child was born in such a wagon during a famous battle with the Redskins, and how, when the Indians were finally defeated, my grandfather put his head in at the door of the wagon, with a smoking gun still in his hand, to greet his newborn child.

When they reached San Francisco, my grandfather built one of the first wooden houses, and I remember visiting this house when I was a little girl, and my grandmother, thinking of Ireland, used often to sing the Irish songs and dance the Irish jigs, only I fancy that into these Irish jigs had crept some of the heroic spirit of the Pioneer and the battle of the Redskins—probably some of the gestures of the Redskins themselves and, again, a bit of Yankee Doodle, when Grandfather Colonel Thomas Gray came marching home from the Civil War. All this grandmother danced in the Irish jig, and I learnt it from her, putting into it my own aspiration of Young America, and, finally, my great spiritual realisation of life from the lines of Walt Whitman. And that is the origin of the so-called Greek Dance with which I have flooded the world. . . .

I often wonder where is the American composer who will hear Walt Whitman's America singing, and who will compose the true music for the American Dance which will contain no Jazz rhythm—no rhythm from the waist down, but from the Solar Plexus, the temporal home of the soul, upwards to the Star-Spangled Banner of the great sky which arches over that stretch of land from the Pacific, over the Plains, over the Sierra Nevadas, over the Rocky Mountains to the Atlantic. I pray you, young American composer, create the music for the dance that shall express the America of Walt Whitman—the America of Abraham Lincoln.

It seems to me monstrous that any one should believe that the Jazz rhythm expresses America. Jazz rhythm expresses the primitive savage. America's music would be something different. It has yet to be written. . . . But some day . . . America will be expressed in some Titanic music that will shape its chaos into harmony, and long-legged shining boys and girls will dance to this music, not the tottering, ape-like convulsions of the Charleston, but a striking, tremendous upward movement, mounting high above the Pyramids of Egypt, beyond the Parthenon of Greece, an expression of beauty and strength such as no civilisation has ever known.

And this dance will have nothing in it of the inane coquetry of the ballet, or the sensual convulsion of the Negro. It will be clean. I see America dancing, standing on one foot poised on the highest point of the Rockies, her two hands stretched out from the Atlantic to the Pacific, her fine head tossed to the sky, her forehead shining with a Crown of a million stars.

How grotesque that they have encouraged in America Schools of, so-called, bodily culture, of Swedish gymnastics, and the ballet. The real American type can never be a ballet dancer. The legs are too long, the body too supple and the spirit too free for this school of affected grace and toe-walking. It is notorious that all great ballet dancers have been very short women with small frames. A tall, finely made woman could never dance the ballet. The type that expresses America at its best could never dance the ballet. By the wildest trick of the imagination you could not picture the Goddess of Liberty dancing the ballet. Then why accept this school in America?

Henry Ford has expressed the wish that all the children in Ford's City should dance. He does not approve of the modern dances, but says, let them dance the old-fashioned Waltz, Mazurka and Minuet. But the old-fashioned Waltz and Mazurka are an expression of sickly sentimentality and romance, which our youth has outgrown, and the Minuet is the expression of the unctuous servility of courtiers of the time of Louis XIV and hooped skirts. What have these movements to do with the free youth of America? Does not Mr. Ford know that movements are as eloquent as words?

Why should our children bend the knee in that fastidious and servile dance, the Minuet, or twirl in the mazes of the false sentimentality of the Waltz? Rather let them come forth with great strides, leaps and bounds, with lifted forehead and far-spread arms, to dance the language of our Pioneers, the Fortitude of our heroes, the Justice, Kindness, Purity of our statesmen, and all the inspired love and tenderness of our Mothers. When the American children dance in this way, it will make of them beautiful beings, worthy of the name of the Greatest Democracy.

That will be America Dancing.

CHAPTER 26

Dancing for Men (1926)

Ted Shawn

In my own case, when I first crystallized upon dancing as my life work, I met, of course, with the usual opposition from nearly everyone. I had the religious opposition from the minister and friends of my church, who, being Methodists, thought that dancing in itself was sinful; I had the opposition of my family who felt that this choice of a career did not promise solid financial standing for my adult years; and particularly I had the opposition of my fraternity brothers in college, who protested that "dancing is effeminate, it is not a *man*'s work, dancing is for women!" . . . [Yet] I have discovered many very illuminating facts, all of which prove conclusively that dancing is and has been essentially and primarily a man's activity. . . .

It would surprise almost every man today, who thinks that he knows a good deal and even thinks that he thinks, to learn in what a high place dancing has been held by every great civilization of the past, and that in all great nations of the past, as well as among savage and primitive peoples, the dancing has been done almost exclusively by men. When the women took part, it was largely as accompaniment, with singing, hand-clapping, or rhythmic movements in one place, not actually joining in the pattern of the dance. . . .

[I]f we can ever call one human quality masculine and another feminine, the essential qualities necessary for success in the dance are masculine qualities. There is no art that requires such a long and arduous preparation, as every real dancer knows. The physical energy which goes into any other sort of art expression is child's play compared to the physical hard work that a dancer does. Physical strength and endurance is considered a masculine quality. Dance technique requires great precision and accuracy of movement and extreme mental control over every part of the body. Precision and accuracy, disciplined by mental control, are generally considered masculine qualities. Therefore instead of considering the man who becomes a dancer effeminate, we should rather, if we are logical, consider the girl who takes up dancing as a

This selection has been abridged from Ted Shawn's "Dancing for Men" in *The American Ballet* (New York: H. Holt and Company, 1926), pp. 87–90, 92–94, 96–98.

career one who loses something of her femininity, inasmuch as she enters upon a work which takes manly qualities to produce a lasting success. . . .

In America the first dance pioneers were women. The prejudice against dancing was the greatest here, through our Puritan traditions, and against men indulging in any form of art. The suppression of the art instinct in men was so strong that in regard to the most despised among the arts it would have been impossible for a man to have presented himself to the public as a dance pioneer twenty years ago. The public in America tolerated women as dancers, and therefore the rising sap of the renaissance of the dance in America, coming through the line of least resistance, burst into first buds in the personalities of two women. . . .

From the standpoint of a career for a man today, there are a great many reasons why he should succeed as a dancer equally as well as does a woman. The physical facts of life are in his favor. In a woman dancer's career there is always the uncertainty of marriage and what it may mean. A man rarely marries unless it is understood in advance that marriage will not interfere with his life work. A woman much more often marries with the equally definite understanding that she becomes her husband's helpmate but has no positive career of her own. Even when in the marriage contract is the agreement that she continues her career, children come with their serious interruption to her work—and in dancing the loss of even a few months of continuous work and practice shows badly in one's execution.

Of course, to offset his physical equipment for success in the dance, the man has the still great prejudice of the general public to fight. This will be one of the most important works of the man dancer's life. The public must be brought back to a realization of the importance of the art of dancing. And when the public in general really appreciates the value of dancing to the advancement of human culture, we will find that they have automatically accepted the fact that the dance is a worthy career for the finest type of men. When we find the public accepting a great man dancer on the same plane as the great in other arts—music, sculpture, painting, literature—even as being of as great a service to humanity as statesmen, scientists and business executives, then we will find that finer types of boys and young men will be drawn into the dance as a life work; now, through family opposition or their own prejudices and misconceptions regarding the subject, they are repelled or discouraged. . . .

Dancing should not, I hardly need say, be limited to the stage. We use the theatre today as almost the only outlet possible, but we are not bound in our scope by the theatre. I would like to see men dancing in gymnasiums and in stadiums; I would like to see the dance reach again the position it held among the Greeks as the most perfect athletic accomplishment, and the finest means of physical training and development. . . .

With the growth of the public thought in relation to the dance as a great and important human activity will inevitably come an acceptance of the idea of dancing as a virile and manly sport and art expression. The dance cannot reach its complete development and fulfillment of expression in this day and age unless it is an equal partnership. It will have to be just as much an art and career for men as for women. There are phases of life and qualities of thought, vital and important, which cannot be expressed through the feminine body no matter how fine or how wonderful the woman is. Just as, of course, there are feminine ideas which a man not only cannot do, but should not attempt to do. If the dance is going to be complete and express the wholeness of life, it must express the great and fine masculinity of movement as well as the delicacy and charm of womanhood.

Our aim in the production of a great American ballet is to have that ballet an expression of the best of American life in the dance. How could woman adequately express the wholeness of America? The history of our country and founding of our nation is the work of both men and women. The achievement of building cities and spanning rivers and putting railroads from sea to sea are man's achievements—the backbone and brawn of America. And if America is going to speak through man as well as woman, we cannot have a great American ballet unless America can produce great men dancers—young men who have high ideals, who are capable of making great lawyers and great merchants and great seafarers, but who see in the dance a wider field of usefulness to humanity.

Fifty percent of the expression of life today is woman's, but I claim that the other fifty per cent can be expressed only by men and that the world must recognize both the fitness and the need for men in the dance, must recognize and respect the career of the creative dance as being not only a permissible career for men but as a calling which, if taken in consecrated devotion, is as high as any of the great professions.

CHAPTER 27

Platform for the American Dance

Martha Graham

A dance reveals the spirit of the country in which it takes root. No sooner does it fail to do this than it loses its integrity and significance.

A dance technique may be learned wherever there are expert dance teachers. But the tendency to leave one's country during the important formative years means making an unnecessary sacrifice. It means leaving a characteristic rhythm which must be made part of the dance of our own country.

Technique is but one integral element necessary to the formation of a dancer. The American dancer may, but need not, go abroad to acquire a dance technique. He must not go to acquire an alien manner and form.

The modern American dance began here. Here it must stay and flourish. Isadora Duncan, the greatest individual stimulus to the dance of modern times, looked to America to develop her dance. Only when the art of her dance had been fully formed did she turn to Europe. The spirit of her dance, its rhythm, vitality, new freedom of the body—all these are of America.

An American dance is not a series of steps. It is infinitely more. It is a characteristic time beat, a different speed, an accent sharp and staccato. Its task is to enrich, illuminate, and intensify the American scene. As we increasingly have something significant to dance, we find more and more persons to dance for.

It is the choreographer, technically trained as a dancer, who creates a dance-form in manner and style typically American. The task is great. It requires that the choreographer sensitize himself to his country, that he know its history, its political and geographic life, and that he direct and correlate his experiences into significant compositions of movement.

No great dance can leave a people unmoved. Sometimes the reaction will take the form of a cold antagonism to the truth of what they are seeing—sometimes a full-hearted response. What is necessary is that the dance be as strong

Martha Graham, undated dance concert program in Vanderbilt's Special Collections, Heard Library, unpaged and no publisher cited. Circa 1930s. Reproduced by permission of Ron Protas, Martha Graham Trust.

as the life that is known in the country, that it be influenced by the prevailing expression of its people, as well as by the geography of the land itself.

To the audience of America, the American dance owes a duty. It must not lull them into complacency by presenting a decorative or imitative dance form as a product of this country. The dance is no easy solution to light entertainment. It is not an effeminate art form.

We look to the dance for affirmation, to make the spectator more keenly aware of the vigor, the human and the variety of life. This is the function of American dance.

CHAPTER 28

Declaration

Doris Humphrey

My dance is an art concerned with human values. It upholds only those which make for harmony and opposes all forces inimical to those values. In part its movement may be used for decoration, entertainment, emotional release or technical display, but primarily it is composed as an expression of American life as I see it today.

This new dance of action comes inevitably from the people who had to subdue a continent, to make a thousand paths through forest and plain, to conquer the mountains and eventually to raise up towers of steel and glass. The American dance is born of this new world, new life and new vigor.

I believe that the dancer belongs to his time and place and that he can only express that which passes through or close to his experience. The one indispensable quality in a work of art is a consistent point of view related to the times, and when this is lost and there is substituted for it an aptitude for putting together bits of this and that drawn from extraneous material and dead methods, there can be no integrity.

Doris Humphrey, undated concert dance program, circa 1930s, in Special Collections, Heard Library, Vanderbilt University. Unpaged with no publisher cited. Reprinted by permission of Charles Woodford, Princeton Publishers.

Doris Humphrey in *Circular Descent* from *Two Ecstatic Themes*. Photographer unknown. Courtesy of Charles Woodford; photograph of his mother from his personal collection.

Since my dance is concerned with immediate human values, my basic technique lies in the natural movements of the body. One cannot express contemporary life without humanizing movement, as distinguished from the dehumanization of the ballet. The modern dancer must come down from the points to the bare foot in order to establish his human relation to gravity and reality.

I wish my dance to reflect some experience of my own in relationship to the outside world; to be based on reality illumined by imagination; to be organic rather than synthetic; to call forth a definite reaction from my audience; and to make its contribution toward the drama of life.

CHAPTER 29

American Document (1938)

Martha Graham

The dance is expression in movement, usually with no word spoken. The dancer translates ideas into line and form, and a dance scenario or libretto is only a statement of the idea and a diagram of the movement through which it is expressed. It can be set down in a program note. Like the silent film, the wordless dance has a purity and an intensity of expression all its own. Yet there are certain things dance can say better when, like the sound film, it is complemented by words and the eloquence of the voice.

In the particular form of theatre dance that Martha Graham has developed in such works as *American Document* and *Letter to the World,* the spoken word is an integral part of the dance. Sometimes the movement evokes the words; sometimes the voice calls forth the patterns of the dance; and sometimes the two play back and forth in dramatic counterpoint. The result is a new kind of dance-play which, without losing any of the unique quality of dance, admits feelings and ideas that are more subtle and more dramatic. One of the inter-

Martha Graham, *American Document with Four Scenes from the Dance* was published in *Theatre Arts* 26, no. 9 (Sept., 1942): 565–74. The premiere of this piece took place in Bennington, Vermont, on August 6, 1938. It is possible that Francis Fergusson, director of theater at Bennington, wrote the preamble to the ballet. Reproduced by permission of Ron Protas, Martha Graham Trust.

Martha Graham in *Herodiade,* 1944, in which she dances facing a large (imaginary) mirror, examining her image with pitiless self-introspection. Photograph by Chris Alexander, courtesy of Ron Protas and the Martha Graham Trust.

esting things about *American Document* in this connection is the way the idea came to Martha Graham. She had been listening to the vicious and terrifying words sent over the air from the Axis countries. It occurred to her that our own country—our democracy—has words, too, with power to hearten men and move them to action. The words she remembered are in this libretto; the dance that came out of these words is one of today's masterworks.

The portions of the spoken script printed in italics were taken from the following: *The Declaration of Independence;* Red Jacket of the Senecas; Jonathan Edwards; *Song of Songs;* Lincoln's *Gettysburg Address, The Emancipation Proclamation, The Second Inaugural Address;* Thomas Paine; John Wise; Francis Fergusson.

AMERICAN DOCUMENT

Martha Graham

*This is a documentary dance. "Our documents are our legends—our poignant-
ly near history—our folk tales."*
The music is by Ray Green.
The choreography is by Martha Graham.
The "form of the piece" is patterned freely after an American Minstrel Show.
The characters are:
  The Actor as Interlocutor.
  The End Figures.
  The Chorus—a dance group and leader.
  Two Principals.

Entrance: Walk Around; Cross-Fire
  The entire company enters and proceeds by definite dance pattern, the *Walk
  Around,* to full-stage assembly facing the audience where a bow is enacted
  in canon, finishing with the Principals. The Interlocutor steps forward and
  speaks.
Ladies and Gentlemen, good evening.
This is a theatre.
The place is here in the United States of America.
The time is now—tonight.
The characters are:
The dance group, led by Sophie [Maslow,]
You, the audience,
The Interlocutor—I am the Interlocutor,
And Erick [Hawkins] and Martha.
  He steps back into place and the music resumes. The company exits as they
  entered, leaving Martha and Erick facing each other from the extreme up-
  stage corners. There follows a *Duet of Greeting* to music but interspersed with
  a drum roll to continue the feeling of the *Walk Around.* As they exit, the
  company re-enters in the *Cross-Fire.* This is a group movement of strong,
  affirmative action using leaps to enter and exit. At its conclusion the Interlocutor speaks.
These are Americans.
Yesterday—and for days before yesterday—
One was Spanish,

One was Russian,
One was German,
One was English,
Today these are Americans.

First Episode: Declaration
An American—
What is an American?
  As he speaks, a girl walks simply across the stage and stops part way across,
  facing the audience as though listening.
1776—
Five men wrote a document.
Its name rings like a bell.
Here it comes:
Declaration!
  To a snare-drum roll the two End Figures run swiftly diagonally across the
  stage three times, finishing downstage right and left corners. They beat the
  foot lightly throughout the next lines.
In CONGRESS, July 4th, 1776, the unanimous declaration of the thirteen Unit-
ed States of America:
We hold these truths to be self-evident: That all men are created equal; that they
are endowed by their Creator with certain unalienable rights; that among these
are life, liberty and the pursuit of happiness; that to secure these rights govern-
ments are instituted among men, deriving their just powers from the consent of
the governed.
  We, therefore, the Representatives of the United States, do solemnly publish and
declare that these united colonies are, and of right ought to be, free and indepen-
dent states. And, for the support of this Declaration, we mutually pledge to each
other, our lives, our fortunes, and our sacred honor.
  During these lines the members of the group enter singly and by a simple
  walk take their places facing the audience. This walking action begins with
  three girls opening the curtains of the backdrop to make three doorways on
  the line, "In Congress," etc. The centre girl begins to walk forward on the
  line, "That they are endowed." The girl on stage left walks forward on "that
  among these." The third girl walks forward on "that to secure." The rest of
  the company flows slowly across the stage. Everyone is still on the line, "And
  for the support," etc., when Sophie and Erick walk forward and take their
  places downstage center for the *Dance of Declaration.* This dance finishes
  with all leaving the stage, Sophie and Erick last.

Second Episode: Occupation
    The Interlocutor crosses from stage right to left, speaking.
America—what is America?
It is a great continent, a new world.
I do not remember,
You do not remember
The flocks of pigeons in the virgin forests
Between the bayous and the Great Lakes:
We do not remember the Indian prairie
Before these states were.
But my blood remembers
My heart remembers
It beats as a drum sometimes, to words—
Listen,
Here they come:
Mississippi, Susquehanna, Allegheny, Monongahela, Pottawatomie . . . [ellipsis
    in original]
    At the first name, Martha enters centre back, walks slowly forward on the
    rest of the names until centre stage is reached. The Interlocutor exits as the
    solo dance of the *Native Figure* begins. It finishes downstage centre with the
    dance kneeling, facing front. The Interlocutor enters at the back.
1811—
The words of Red Jacket of the Senecas—
Lament for the land.
Listen to what we say.
    The group enters one at a time, Martha leaves and they finish entrance by
    kneeling in the final position of her dance. As the Interlocutor speaks, the
    group dances. There are times when he is silent or the dancers are still.
Listen to what we say.
There was a time when our fathers owned this great island.
Their seats extended from the rising to the setting sun.
Listen to what we say.
But an evil day came upon us. Your forefathers crossed the Great Waters,
and landed on this island. They found friends, not enemies. They asked for a small
    seat. We granted their request, and they sat down among us.
Listen to what we say.
Our seats were once large and yours were small. You have now become a great
    people, and we have scarcely a place left to spread our blankets.
Listen to what we say.

They wanted more land . . .
They wanted our country.
Listen to what we say.
You have got our country. [ellipsis in original]

On the final lines the dancers exit as they entered. When the last dancer has disappeared, the Interlocutor leaves in silence.

Six dancers enter immediately with the Interlocutor in the *Walk Around* of the opening dance. They exit, leaving him back centre.

Third Episode: The Puritan
An American—
What is an American?

Martha and Erick enter upstage left.

1620—
A wooden boat grates on the new shore.
Guns in the Indian wilderness.
A stiff-necked generation claims the land.
Claims the Lord,
Denying the tender creature.

1741—
Jonathan Edwards speaks:
Listen:

The Interlocutor walks forward as though delivering a judgment.

We may read in men's foreheads as soon as e'er they are born the sentence of Death.
And we may see by men's lives what hellish hearts they have.

The figures of the man and woman walk hand in hand diagonally across toward the Interlocutor who stands downstage right.

I am my beloved's
And his desire is toward me.

The following speeches from Jonathan Edwards and *Song of Songs* are woven into and around the dance to suggest the conflict that took place in Puritan hearts when faced with the choice of a simple life or an angry life of denial.

Death comes hissing like a fiery dragon with the sting on the mouth of it.
Let him kiss me with the kisses of his mouth,
For thy love is better than wine.
God shall set himself like a consuming, infinite fire against thee, and tread thee
under his feet, who has by sin trod Him and His glory under foot all thy life.
How beautiful are thy feet in sandals,

O Prince's daughter.
Who is she that looketh forth as the morning,
Fair as the moon,
Clear as the sun,
Terrible as an army with banners.
Then shall God surrender thy forsaken soul into the hands of devils, who being
    thy jailers must keep thee till the great day of account.
Set me as a seal upon thine heart,
As a seal upon thine arm.
For love is as strong as Death,
A very flame of the Lord.
Sinners in the hands of an angry God!
I am my beloved's
And his desire is toward me.
> The two dancers leave together, centre back. The Interlocutor exits down-
> stage. Six dancers enter in the *Walk Around* and exit. The Interlocutor en-
> ters alone.

Fourth Episode: Emancipation
The United States of America—what is it?
It is a nation of states.
A state—what is it?
It is a unit in a nation of states.
> Group begins to enter singly.
One state has mountains,
One state has no mountains.
One state has sea,
One state has no sea.
One state has corn,
One state has gold,
One state has cotton.
Once, more than one state had slaves.
> The last dancer takes her place in the three lines that have formed centre
> stage.
Now, no state has slaves.
Now every state has one deep word.
Here it comes:
Emancipation!

Here follows the group in the dance *Emancipation*. Part way through the dance there is a pause. The Interlocutor speaks.

1863—

The government of the people, by the people, and for the people shall not perish from the earth.

The dance resumes. At the end, the group finishes in a semicircle, looking up in an ecstatic gesture, both arms spread to the side. The Interlocutor speaks.

I, Abraham Lincoln, President of the United States, on this first day of January, in the year of our Lord one thousand, eight hundred and sixty-three, do order and declare: that all persons held as slaves shall be then, thenceforward and forever free.

The group exits as Martha and Erick enter upstage opposite each other. There is an ecstatic *Duet*, and they exit centre back. Six dancers enter in the *Walk Around* and exit.

Fifth Episode: Hold Your Hold!

The Interlocutor enters and as he enters, he speaks.

O Ye that love mankind! . . .

Freedom has been hunted round the globe. [ellipsis in original]

Three women enter upstage right in an attitude of sorrow, accompanied by a slow, low drum beat. They dance throughout the following lines.

1942—

Listen to what we say.

We are three women.

We are three million women.

We are the mothers of the hungry dead.

We are the mothers of the hungry living.

We are the mothers of those to be born.

Listen to what we say.

Ours is a lament for the living.

We are three women.

We are three million women.

We are the mothers of the hungry dead.

We are the mothers of the hungry living.

We are the mothers of those to be born.

Listen to what we say.

Ours is a lament for the living.

We are three women.
We are three million women.

>They walk off in silence. Erick enters from opposite side, seeming to be about to follow them off. Instead he turns in centre stage. The Interlocutor speaks.

Brethren, ye have been called unto Liberty.
Therefore, HOLD YOUR HOLD, brethren!

>The drum beat begins faster than for the Three Women. The man dances to this small, dry drum beat and to the words the Interlocutor speaks.

This is one man.
This is one million men.
This man has a faith.
It is you.
This is one man.
This is one million men.
This man has fear.
It is you.
This is one man.
This is one million men.
This man has a need.
It is himself,
And you.

>Erick exits on the last lines. The Interlocutor speaks directly to the audience.

With malice toward none, with charity for all, with firmness in the right as God gives us to see the right, let us strive to finish the work we are in . . . to do all which may achieve and cherish a just and lasting peace among ourselves and all nations.
[ellipsis in original]

>Martha enters for the *Dance of Invocation*. She finishes stage centre where Erick joins her. The group enters to the beat of their own feet without music, and the Interlocutor speaks.

America! Name me the word that is courage.
America! Name me the word that is justice.
America! Name me the word that is power.
America! Name me the word that is freedom.
America! Name me the word that is faith.
Here is that word—
Democracy!

>There follows a dance by the entire company similar to the *Dance of Declaration* at the beginning of the piece. The company exits except for Martha

and Erick, who are in opposite corners of the stage. As they exit, the Interlocutor speaks.

*That government of the people, by the people, and for the people shall not perish
from the earth.*

The entire company enters in the *Walk Around.* They stop in full stage. The
Interlocutor steps two paces forward and speaks.

Ladies and gentlemen, may we wish you goodnight.

The entire company exits as the curtain falls.

CHAPTER 30

Southland (1951)
A Dramatic Ballet in Two Scenes
World Premiere, Santiago de Chile,
January, 1951

Katherine Dunham

PROLOGUE:

The man who truly loves his country is the man who is able to see it in the
bad as well as the good, and seeing the bad, declaim it at the cost of liberty or
life. For countries are no different than men, and all men are made of good
and bad, and must see these things within themselves, and strive toward the
good if there is to be any upward moving.

A dramatic ballet in two scenes with original scenario and choreography by Katherine Dunham and
music by Dino di Stefano. The prologue was narrated by Katherine Dunham for the ballet premiere
at the Opera House, Santiago de Chile, in January of 1951. Published in *Kaiso! Katherine Dunham, An
Anthology of Writings,* ed. VèVè A. Clark and Margaret B. Wilkerson (Berkeley: Institute for the Study
of Social Change, CCEW Women's Center, University of California, 1978), pp. 117–20. Courtesy of
Katherine Dunham and CCEW Women's Center.

Katherine Dunham in *Bal Negre,* 1947. Back cover to 1947 program, "Katherine Dunham presents Bal Negre." Photographer unknown. Courtesy of Katherine Dunham. Author's collection.

North America is a great and wonderful country. I know it and love it from the hills of San Francisco through the prairies of the Middle West to the rugged puritanism of the East sea coast. The people of North America are great and wonderful, too, in their newness and youth and energy. But there is a deep stain, a mark of blood and shame which spreads from under the magnolia trees of the southland area and mingles with the perfume of the flowers.

And though I have not smelled the smell of burning flesh, and have never seen a black body swaying from a southern tree, I have felt these things in spirit, and finally through the creative artist comes the need of the person to show this thing to the world, hoping that by so exposing the ill the conscience of the many will protest and save further destruction and humiliation.

This is not all of America, it is not all of the south, but it is a living, present part. . . .

SCENE I

The first scene is perhaps even too obvious. The Greek chorus of singers who reflect the stage action in song and mime, represent the fundamental simplicity, the earth-dignity of the Negro. At the opening of this ballet, standing before the portals of an ante-bellum southern mansion, they ask with a certain amount of ironic doubt "Is it true what they say about Dixie? Does the sun really shine all the time?" One of them sings a standard concept of a Negro's nostalgia for the Swanee River, another with the same ironic touch sings "Carry me back to old Virginie." Then one steps forward to sing "Steal away" with the ecstatic force of the true Negro spiritual and another unifies the group in the revival hymn "Dry Bones."

The southern mansion gives way to the magnolia tree and at its base the chorus continues its observation on scenes that follow. First a group of field-hands on their way to work. Then plantation square dances and the more African "Juba." Lucille and Richard, lovers, linger behind and after dancing together separate reluctantly.

The pleasant flow of the lazy magnolia-scented afternoon is interrupted by the appearance of Lenwood and Julie, who have been in an embrace behind the magnolia tree. A moment of ridicule, a reaction of resentment and the warm southern atmosphere becomes one of violence, which leaves Julie lying unconscious under the magnolia tree after the attack of her companion. The fieldhands enter again. Despite the mute warnings of the chorus and the flight of his comrades, Richard remains, torn between his natural instincts to help and an awareness of the taboo situation which exists between white and Ne-

gro people in this community. When he touches the girl, she regains consciousness and more terrified than he, cries the hated word "Nigger." Almost immediately, however, she becomes aware of the possibilities of drama and excitement and seizes the opportunity to escape from the sordidness of her own life
by becoming the heroine of a self-created saga of lust and violation. She cries
for help and against a background of the denials of the boy and the chorus,
tells the lie which is the determinating factor in his murder.

The boy is lynched. In her solo dance the "Habanera" the girl epitomizes the
fury of all acts born of hatred and fear and guilt. She is interrupted by the growing flames, the smell of burning flesh which announce the accomplishment of
the crime. The chorus watch her. It is only at the moment when the body of
the lynched boy swings toward her in full view, suspended from the magnolia
tree that she feels the full impact of the crime that she has committed.

Left alone, the sense of power drains from her. But fascinated by what she
sees of herself in the disfigured figure of the man, she approaches the body,
rips a piece of cloth from it as a souvenir of her moment of triumph and in a
deeper sense as a reminder of her guilt. Leaving, she meets the girl Lucille and
for one moment falters in her bravado. The moment passes and she moves on.
Lucille dances in her grief as Rosalie sings of the "strange fruit," which hangs
from the limbs of the sweet-scented magnolia trees in the south. The chorus
becomes the cortege of the mourners which leaves with the broken body of
the lynched boy.

SCENE II

The last scene is "Basin Street" or any other street where because of color, creed
or forced economic inferiority a people are relegated to enjoy in a spirit of
frenzied cynicism what substitutes they may find for the deprivations of their
daily lives, what compensations for its tragedies. A singer stands in a café door-
way. A blind beggar passes and the street activity merges in to a smoky café.
At the height of the tragi-comic diversions of this urban aspect of Negro life,
the passage of the chorus bearing the body of the lynched boy through the café
is purely symbolic. It is inconceivable that the essential tragedy of a people
could escape them, even in the midst of pleasure. The passing of the funeral
cortege is that profound moment of realization of one's own tragic situation
which occurs at some time or another to all of us, intensified certainly in the
lives of those people, in no matter what country, who are denied full freedom
to enter into and partake of every aspect of the community in which they find
themselves. The cards fall from the hands of one boy—a girl weeps—another

boy opens his knife and takes out his chagrin in plunging it into the floor—a couple bury themselves in the sexual embrace of a slow dance movement—another couple dance disjointedly, heedlessly, bumping into the blind beggar.

The blind beggar is the only one who sees the true fact at the moment of the passing of the cortege. Herein for me lies the true human tragedy—the rest feel but cannot define; the blind beggar at that moment has eyes and sees the true fact. He leaves seeking the answer, which all of us who love humanity seek more than ever at this moment.

CHAPTER 31

A Critic Reacts to Balanchine's *Stars and Stripes* (1958)

Lillian Moore

In *Stars and Stripes,* the New York City Ballet has launched its own Intercontinental Ballistic Missile. If Japan and Australia should happen to take it seriously, it might cause as much damage to friendly relations as a genuine ICBM. If they accept its satire, it should repeat over there the smash success it made at its opening performance.

George Balanchine has marshaled a formidable number of ancient, sure-fire dance tricks, including all sorts of kicks, struts, stretches, and spins, which he hurls at the audience until it is breathless. No one but Balanchine would dare to touch such hackneyed material, but he handles it with such keen theatrical craftsmanship and such extraordinary flair that the audience is swept up on a wave of amusement and delight. Hershey Kay's marvelous orchestration of military tunes by John Philip Sousa is, of course, the perfect accompaniment for this carnival.

For each of his three "Campaigns," Balanchine uses the same wedge formation, with a soloist at its apex, and very effective it is. A pert and dashing Al-

"Review" by Lillian Moore, *Dance Magazine,* Mar., 1958, pp. 55–56. Reprinted by permission of *Dance Magazine.*

legra Kent leads the first corps of "Corocoran Cadets" through a series of Rockette-like evolutions spiced with Balanchinian surprises. Robert Barnett heads a group of 13 men who dash through one balletic feat after another, and in two minutes succeed in negating the old accusation that Balanchine cannot choreograph for male dancers. Only slightly less brilliant is the regiment led by Diana Adams, whose lyric style is not quite right for this explosive ballet. . . . Unfortunately, this looks very much like the kind of ballet which will collapse like a pricked balloon once it loses its exhilarating freshness. It is too bad that it cannot have an extended New York run while it is new. By the time the company gets back from overseas it may already have disintegrated.

CHAPTER 32

Flag Dance (1970)

Yvonne Rainer

Early in September of 1970 I was asked by John Hendricks and Jean Toche to participate in a flag show at Judson Church, the purpose of which was to protest recent arrests of people purportedly "desecrating" the American flag. I said I would think about it. In the previous spring—roused by the killings on U.S. campuses and the invasion of Cambodia—I had used *M-Walk* (so-called because it had been inspired by a sequence in Fritz Lang's *Metropolis*) as a protest against these events. Forty people, wearing black armbands, massed in three columns in the middle of Greene Street just below Houston (downtown Manhattan). Swaying in unison from side to side with bowed heads, we snaked our way down Greene, west on Prince where we were stopped momentarily by a policeman and told to get onto the sidewalk; no one spoke or stopped swaying during this interruption), south on Wooster, east on Spring, then north on Greene back to the original starting point. It lasted an hour; by the end most of the participants had dropped away, and only five of us remained.

Yvonne Rainer, *Trio A* at the opening of "The People's Flag Show," Judson Church, Nov. 9, 1970. From *Work, 1961–73* (Halifax: Press of the Nova Scotia College of Art and Design, 1974), pp. 171–72.

Yvonne Rainer in Flag Dance, *Nov. 9, 1970. Photographer unknown. Originally published in Yvonne Rainer's* Work, 1961–73 *(Halifax: Press of the Nova Scotia College of Art and Design, 1974), p. 171. Courtesy of Yvonne Rainer and the Press of the Nova Scotia College of Art and Design.*

During the summer I continued to think about integrating some form of protest against—or at least reference to—the horrors perpetrated by the American government. During a three-week teaching stint at George Washington University in Washington, D.C., I insisted that a huge sign be hung in the gymnasium for that duration. The sign read "Why are we in Vietnam?" On several occasions I conducted classes in the Ellipse opposite the White House. We hung the sign on the fence across the street from a long queue of people waiting to visit the White House. When a guard demanded its removal, we complied. Among other things, I was working with the students on "war games," material that would eventually be incorporated into *WAR*.

Later, the American flag seemed to be an appropriate prop for use in the piece. (I still have memories of heated childhood games of "Capture the Flag.") In *WAR*, proprieties are at all times observed in dealing with the flag in that the performers try not to let it touch the ground and never deliberately step on it. (It can be walked over only if it is sandwiched between two other props: a black overcoat and three-foot square of simulated grass.) The issue of "desecration" did not seem a relevant one in this particular situation. The flag functioned simply as an object that enhanced the subject and imagery of nationalist conflict. For the *Judson Flag Show,* however, I felt a need for a statement with stronger political overtones. I began to think about the other area in theatre that still carries an emotional "load" in its assault on taboos, viz., public nudity. To combine the flag and nudity seemed a double-barreled attack on repression and censorship.

At 6:30 P.M. on November 9th, 1970, Barbara Lloyd, David Gordon, Nancy Green, Steve Paxton, Lincoln Scott, and I gathered in the sanctuary of the Church where a large number of paintings and objects and environments dealing with the flag had already been installed. First tying 3 x 5-foot flags around our necks like bibs, we then undressed totally, dragging non-buttoning upper garments up under our chins, then proceeded to individual spaces to perform *Trio A* twice each.

This particular version was televised by NBC and Global Village. We were not otherwise interfered with, and when we each had completed the task we stopped dancing and put on our clothes. It felt good to do.

CHAPTER 33

Naked in America (1999)

Sonjé Mayo with text by Jean Dell

Naked in America deals with my impressions of America as an immigrant. Whereas words usually complement the dance and facilitate the choreography, I purposely used the narrator's voice to lure the audience into imagining a certain scene and then presented them with the unexpected—the myth versus the reality.

THE ARRIVAL: AMERICA

We've touched down at Kennedy.
Giant eagle,
I have nested in your wings,
Warm, safe;
Screech your triumphant song of welcome. . . .
I have arrived!
My feet touch American soil.
Bastion of democracy,
Land of opportunity,
Land of the free—
I am here, thank God!
Fear and exhilaration vibrate through me in spasms.
"Toes on the yellow line—Next!
Hey listen, this is America,
And we speak English here."

The opening lines are delivered in the dark so that we would get the full attention of the audience. Playing in the background is the "immigrant" song by Pavarotti. At the conclusion of "we speak English here," the lights come up on the dancer. The voice continues . . .

Choreography and concept by Sonjé Mayo; text by Jean Dell.
    Premiere, April of 1998, Nashville, Tennessee, at the Tennessee Performing Arts Center. The text has been shortened and certain episodes omitted.

Saimir Elir Avduli in Sonjé Mayo's *Naked in America*, 1999. Photograph by Martin O'Connor, 1999. Courtesy of Sonjé Mayo and Martin O'Connor.

I know no one
No one knows me.
I have transformed myself into a chameleon
Blending to the point of transparency.
I have become invisible,
No past.
No present.
Escaping into soundless shadows,
Longing for touch.
Loneliness is the spectre.
I am naked in America.

   The lights come up very slowly on the Immigrant, a male dancer lying on a bed. A white sheet is carefully draped across his lower body to conceal his nudity. He is caressing a figure (a plastic blow up doll of human proportions) completely covered by the sheet. . . . The doll deflates, and he continues to twist and turn in helpless insomnia. Lonely and tired, he slides off the bed and withdraws into the fetal position.

BARBIE GETS HER KEN

Innocently seduced
By tales of gallant knights and delicate damsels,
Little girls dream in dimpled innocence,
Damp curls buried in down pillows

Cradling their favorite doll
Crooning wordless lullabies.
Cinderella
got her fella.
Sleeping Beauty
and Snow White.
Found their princes
And they all lived happily ever after
Ever after
Ever after.
All little Barbies
Meet their Ken
And up the aisle they float
Smiling,
Believing,
In happy endings.

Lights come up on a man and woman seated at opposite ends of the bed, their backs to one another. The woman reaches out to find his hand. He withdraws from her touch, then gets up and begins to pace. She reaches out again and slides unassisted across his back and onto the floor. She picks herself up and tries again. He rebuffs her with indifference, his stone-cold rejection inspiring her to cling the more.

Suddenly the mood changes. He pushes her from behind; she falls backwards onto him. He yanks her by the wrist; she hurtles towards his chest, only to land in his arms. The violence escalates in intensity. She participates in this hackneyed game, and the pas de deux becomes increasingly sado-masochistic in nature. He forcefully throws her onto the bed, but withholds himself from further action. They move away from each other, returning to the opening pose on the bed, backs to each other. The lights fade.

PUSH 'EM UP, SUGAR

Push 'em up, sugar,
Push 'em up!
Make like you got lots up there.
Listen darling,
It's all a hype in your Victoria Secret Miracle Bra.
Now—my advice is: don't screw with the lights on, sweetie,
Or he'll find out you're a phoney. . . .

Lights come up to reveal four dark figures posed on a ladder. They are shrouded in black robes with only their eyes visible. Their swaying movements, as they dance accompanied by Middle Eastern music, are severely restricted by the chador. Without warning, the music becomes markedly more rhythmic and sexual in nature. The dancers discard their shrouds to reveal four exquisite "prom queens" with pouffed hairstyles and big smiles. The lonely Immigrant enters, and they line up, undulating and displaying their figures in revealing red velvet evening gowns. He inspects them and chooses the blonde.

THE ELUSIVE ILLUSION

A disposable society
Easy come, easy go
Transient, reversible
Interchangeable.
The elusive illusion.

He removes his trousers and sits on the bed with his lady. He strokes her hair, and her wig slides off to reveal a shaven head. Next the "lady" slides out of her tight dress and reveals himself to be a muscular young boy who flexes his perfectly sculpted muscles. The Immigrant is perplexed by this transformation from prom queen to drag queen, then appalled. An aggressive pas de deux, in all its suggestive ambiguity, follows. The Immigrant becomes increasingly more violent as he repels the young boy's advances but simultaneously is drawn to him. At this point, the young man flashes a police badge and threatens the Immigrant. The lights fade.

I CHOOSE TO STAY

Decisions made
I choose to stay
And plant my seeds of belongingness.
Small roots take hold
Enmeshed with those who have come before me;
I am repeating the pattern of all immigrants.
The thread of my life
Begins to form its own shape/song
In the vast tapestry of this great land.
My spirit surges—

Unresisting, ecstatic,
And the bald headed eagle circles overhead
Screeching my song of triumph.

Once again, we see the Immigrant lying on his bed. His rapid, energetic movements indicate a new determination. He buttons his vest, grabs the sheet and maneuvers it about like a matador's cape. He walks briskly to the ladder in center stage and mounts it. Each rung indicates his progress on the corporate ladder of Success, American style. The piece ends with our Immigrant perched on top of the ladder, a self-satisfied expression on his face as he surveys the audience below.

The American Dream is alive and well.

CHAPTER 34

Last Supper at Uncle Tom's Cabin/ The Promised Land (1990)

Bill T. Jones with Peggy Gillespie

PART ONE: THE CABIN

A gingham drape runs around the entire proscenium of the theatre, and behind that drape is another one, a jagged two-dimensional drape with stylized magnolias and hanging moss. Behind that stands the naive representation of a log cabin.

Text abridged from Bill T. Jones with Peggy Gillespie, *Last Night on Earth* (New York: Pantheon Books, 1995), pp. 209–16, 218–23. Performers' names have been changed, in most instances, to those of the characters they were playing, in order to prevent reader confusion. For the same reason, the five Elizas are designated as Eliza I, Eliza II, Eliza III, etc. *Last Supper at Uncle Tom's Cabin/The Promised Land* premiered at the Next Wave Festival, Brooklyn Academy of Music, Brooklyn, New York, in 1990. Music was created by Julius Hemphill, and the text taken from words of R. Justice Allen, Ann T. Greene, Bill T. Jones, Estella Jones, Heidi Latsky, Sojourner Truth, as cited on p. 284 of *Last Night on Earth*. By permission of the publisher and by permisson of Bill T. Jones.

To the raucous, rasping saxophones of the Julius Hemphill Sextet, the curtain opens and we're introduced to R. Justice Allen as the narrator and to Sage Cowles as Harriet Beecher Stowe. They stand apart from the proceedings.

The story starts slowly, introducing the fidelity of Uncle Tom, the purity of Little Eva, the tragic reluctance of the liberal master Mr. St. Clare, and the twisted values of the evil slave trader Simon Legree. All performers . . . are masked. The novel is told in a ludicrously blunted, stylized fashion, with some performers playing several parts. . . . Heidi Latsky, fragile, small, wearing a white frock and angelic mask with built-in locks of gold, wafts about as the saintly child, Little Eva. Justice Allen doubles as the evil Simon Legree, who ravishes the beautiful octoroon, played by Maya Saffrin, and whips "our Tom" to death.

It's at this point in the narrative that we send the entire proceedings into retrograde. In a "coup de théâtre" we are back at the point where Legree is about to whip Tom. I [Bill T. Jones] then take the liberty of inserting a "correct" ending—the one we would like to have seen, in which Tom, instead of dying at the hands of his aggressor, stands up with all the other slaves and resists Simon Legree.

The entr'acte drape is lowered.

Julius Hemphill's plaintive march, which has accompanied Legree's orgy of violence, is now transformed into an upbeat burlesque that ushers . . . [in] twin lines of male dancers wearing black T-shirts, jock straps, combat boots and muzzles. These are the eight "dogs" [who] . . . perform an unnerving routine of arm gestures that resemble both military drill and football practice. To the heavy staccato thud of their combat boots, in groups of two they dash from the stage and run out through the auditorium.

PART TWO: ELIZA ON THE ICE

The entr'acte curtain rises upon a world inhabited by four personifications of Eliza. The four silhouetted women crisscross the stage performing signature movements, then exit, leaving Eliza I. . . . [The narrator] begins to recite Sojourner Truth's celebrated address as Eliza dances: ". . . I could work as much and eat as much as a man—when I could get it—and bear the lash as well. And ain't I a woman?" . . . In a series of lyrical, loping movements that originated in the pelvis, coursed up the back, and resulted in the languorous coiling and uncoiling of the arms, [the dancer] abstracted the movement impulses that I have witnessed or invented through my mother, grandmother, and any number of women I have been privileged to know.

From stage right, the nearly forgotten corps of "dogs" comes sprinting across in pursuit of Eliza I, who exits, leaving Harriet Beecher Stowe to welcome the small, fragile Eliza II. . . . Her movements are convoluted, turned in, interrupted with the sharp slicing of the air by her arms and feet. She appears deeply troubled, if not demented. From the pit a clarinet laments. . . .

[The dancer speaks of her anger]

My father,
My father told me to turn the other cheek.
My mother,
My mother told me not to expect much.
They both told me be honest, have faith, be good.
I believed them. . . .

[She] stomped about, slammed a small chair, lunged, then slapped the floor, signaling the appearance, once again, of the ludicrous dogs. [She] exited just ahead of them.

The third Eliza enters with the dogs. . . . She is the Eliza who commands men—part Joan of Arc, part dominatrix, and part martial arts master. Her movements were designed to show the length of her extension, the range of motion in her supple hips, and the glorious flexibility of her back. She strikes the floor with the staff she wields and the dogs appear to leap through hoops like circus lions. And yet there is tension implicit in the fact that she can never turn her back on them. These dogs may be silly, but they are also dangerous. Suddenly, she throws down her staff and bolts. . . . [T]he pack of hounds rushes off in pursuit.

[Eliza I], the historical Eliza, reappears with the exotically pretty . . . Eliza number four, who is dressed as a coquette from a turn-of-the-century French postcard.

Choosing to exploit [her] beauty, I exaggerated something voluptuous and desirable about her. Other than the simple hopscotch she performs with [the first Eliza], who is chased away by the dogs, her movement is not her own. She barely, if ever, touches the floor. Instead, she is passed, pulled, and stretched by the coarse dogs, to whom she is simultaneously a football and a rape victim. Here is an Ann-Margaret nightclub act combined with *The Perils of Pauline*.

The dogs abandon her. She is then gathered up by the three other Elizas. And the four together perform a resolution of sorts before leaving to the historical Eliza's proud, rolling gait.

The dogs return and, in counterpoint with their opening routine, burlesque a line-dance—"The Electric Slide." Harriet Beecher Stowe seems to grow weak. She crawls off, reciting Sojourner Truth's address in retrograde. The dog's exit reveals one more Eliza—in this instance, [a six-foot-two-inch man], who wears a white miniskirt and struggles for balance in high-heeled pumps. He executes an incantation of grasping arms, jabbing fingers, wobbling knees, and extended tongue before coolly gathering himself to exit with the rolling gait of the historical Eliza who preceded him. . . .

ENTR'ACTE: THE PRAYER

During this interlude, [the singer] moves on stage on my arm. She is swaying, humming, incanting quietly to herself, dabbing the profusion of sweat that has already broken on her brow or using her handkerchief as a fan. . . . She swings into her version of "I Shall Not Be Removed." . . . I dance beside her as she prays. Moved by the rhythm and the meaning of her words, my solo is based on a shudder and a shout that originates somewhere in my hips and like two claps of thunder moves down my thighs and up my back. When she has completed her benediction, I take her arm and whisper my thanks as I lead her off the stage. . . .

PART THREE: THE SUPPER

The entr'acte curtain rises.

The entire company has gathered on the stage. They assume the poses of those gathered at Leonardo da Vinci's *Last Supper* table. This section is an orgy of inchoate imagery: there is a frantic sequence of what appears to be a classroom or a religious observance. [Two dancers] play an undisclosed game, [two] move like spirits through the frenetic proceedings. Like metronomes, the dancers rock in unison on . . . fetishistic chairs.

Suddenly all is still.

Justice bounces an invisible basketball, and in seamless and breathtaking slow motion, deftly dribbles, then with the concentration of a Zen archer, takes aim at an imaginary basket somewhere above the blue-white of [the narrator's] head, who stands in Christ's place in the *Last Supper* painting. He then takes his place, matter-of-factly, in the position reserved for Judas.

I meant for this section to be a kind of religious Dada—propelled by the hyperactivity of the dancers but grounded in a friezelike religious tableau.

Towards the end, Justice moves downstage right and . . . swings into his rap, "Something to think about."

The section ends to his shouting, "They call me Justice, Justice, Justice," at which time all the dancers who had been standing on their chairs jump to the floor as the curtain falls.

ENTR'ACTE: FAITH

When the curtain rises again, the *Last Supper* table is still in full view but now the space around it is empty. A minister, a rabbi, or a priest, invited from the community, sits at its right end. I, flanked by [two others], am seated at its middle. My back is to the audience.

The person of faith relates the story of Job. To this recitation . . . I rise to enact in dance the story of the Man of Perfect Faith, who is tested again and again by God in his wager with Satan. [Two sentinels perform] large, stylized gestures that frame me. . . . [One] produces a large kitchen knife and proceeds to shred the shirt off my back in oblique reference to the tragedies and sicknesses that befall Job. Later, when Job is vindicated by his faith and God gives back all, I am given a new shirt and my jacket is returned. . . .

I dance Job's ecstasy. When done, I sit at a right angle to the religious man or woman and begin to ask questions—simple, almost childlike questions: *What is faith? Is Christianity a slave religion? What is evil? Does God punish us? Does hell exist? Is homosexuality a sin? Is AIDS punishment from God?* . . .

SECTION FOUR: THE PROMISED LAND

The curtain opens, for the final time, on an organized group of some sixty or so local people [selected from the most demographically diverse group possible]. In the half-light they listen intently as [two dancers] begin a whispered conversation that is in fact the retrograded "I Have a Dream" speech.

The whispered conversation grows into a heated argument and then an all-out brawl: *.true become must this ,nation great a be to is America if and*—"*ring freedom let ,side mountain every from ;pride pilgrim's the of land ,died fathers my where land ;sing I thee of ;liberty of land sweet ;thee of 'tis country My.*

Then a series of arena-inspired sequences occurs in which the . . . company performers, divided into two groups, attack one another as the spectators all around them shout raucous encouragement. This noisy, violent episode is interrupted by the lanky prancing of [a dancer] performing what I called

"Warming Up in Dixie." [His] movements are inspired by the image of silhouetted "Darkies" dancing around the campfire on the cover of some sheet music
from the early part of the century. . . . [He] finishes with a one-two-three-
shuffle-grin flourish and then the on-stage pandemonium resumes. When it
seems that everyone would keel over from exhaustion, the stage picture reverts
back to its original orderliness.

Justice (as Clay) and Sage (as Lula) step atop the table, face each other from
opposite ends, and begin to enact excerpts from LeRoi Jones' Dutchman. . . .
[They] do not touch until the last tense moments of the scene, when Sage's
Lula, in a lovely white evening dress, shouts, "Uncle Tom-Big-Lip," which pro-
vokes Justice's Clay to slap her as thirty dancers strike the floor with their open
palms. The scene becomes calm as Clay/Justice positions himself, back turned
to the audience, in front of Lula/Sage, saying "I'm sorry Baby, I don't think
we're going to make it." Lula/Sage in a stylized gesture, part dance, part pantomime, suggests a small knife that she plunges into his chest, saying, "Sorry
is right. Sorry is the rightest thing you've said." She stands like a vengeful fury
over [his] prone body as it rests in the arms of a large group of dancers.

John, Sage's bespectacled husband, dressed in a black suit and looking at
once like one of Grant Wood's American Gothic figures and the chairman of
the board that he had in fact been, stands at the middle of the table. He has
looked on as his wife, in the role of a young Jezebel, has seduced and then killed
the young man, Clay, who is also Justice, the ex-convict. John's impassive presence on the stage serves as a witness to the replay of the time-honored ritual
of sex, power and race.

The work develops in an ever more abstract direction. Long lines of dancers travel across the stage performing thirteen gestures culled from religious
iconography as varied as a Tiepolo fresco in Venice, a bit of kitsch pottery from
Little Italy, or an ancient painting from a church in remotest New Mexico.
These lines coming and going sometimes break into clusters of individuals
partnering, handling each other gently. Sometimes the arena madness returns,
as it does in the "Revival Meeting" sequence, wherein one person in each of
twelve trios behaves as if possessed and is either assisted or restrained by the
two others. This frenetic field of activity coalesces into a statuary through
which the fully clothed John Cowles and a naked young woman whom we call
"The Innocent" enact a touching, oddly unsettling duet that is part seduction,
part confession. Sage stands nearby reciting simple instructions: "He will take
you by the hand, and take you to another place. If you fall he will reach out
for you . . . [ellipsis in original]."

Over the course of this half-hour segment of *Last Supper at Uncle Tom's Cabin/The Promised Land* participants could choose to remove articles of clothing until they were completely naked. In the final moments of the piece, the ever-present drive of Julius Hemphill's score mellows to a single saxophone line performing a lulling counterpoint to a stage covered with the fat, skinny, rich, poor, old, young, male, female, Asian, Spanish, gay, straight, black, Native American, and European, naked, singing together. Robert Wierzel's evocation of nineteenth-century stage lighting, which had illuminated "The Cabin" section, is now warm, golden, flattering, supportive as the cast ambles forward and back, sounding nonsense syllables in childlike harmony.

The Promised Land, with its hordes of naked flesh coming wave after wave into the footlights, pubic patches, pert breasts, sagging breasts, wrinkled knees, blissful eyes, furtive expressions of shame, is a visual manifestation of my profound sense of belonging. This is my portrait of us. All of us. And this is who I am too. One of us. It was my battle to disavow any identity as a dying outcast and to affirm our commonality. In it, some one thousand people from thirty cities stood naked, took a bow, and said, "We are not afraid."

Uncle Tom's Cabin was three and one half hours long, and it toured for almost two years. It was denounced by the Vatican. It was deemed sprawling and full of platitudes, applauded for its reliance on community, the process by which it was created, its humanity, and its scope. It was the largest work I ever made and a work that came out of my desire to sum up everything I believed. It was impossible for it to succeed, but it did not fail.

SUGGESTED BOOKS AND FILMS

Acocella, Joan. *Mark Morris.* New York: Noonday Press, 1995.

Ailey, Alvin, with Peter Bailey. *Revelations: The Autobiography of Alvin Ailey.* Secaucus, N.J.: Carol Publishing Company, 1995.

Amberg, George. *Ballet in America, the Emergence of an American Art.* New York: Duell, Sloan, and Pearce, [1949].

Anderson, Jack. *The American Dance Festival.* Durham, N.C.: Duke University Press, 1987.

Aschenbrenner, Joyce. *Katherine Dunham: Reflections on the Social and Political Contexts of Afro-American Dance.* Dance Research Annual, no. 12. New York: Congress on Research in Dance, 1981.

Baker, Josephine, and Jo Bouillon. *Josephine.* Trans. Mariana Fitzpatrick. New York: Harper & Row, 1977.

Banes, Sally. *Terpsichore in Sneakers: Post-Modern Dance.* Middletown, Conn.: Wesleyan University Press, 1987.

Blair, Fredrika. *Isadora: Portrait of the Artist as a Woman.* New York: McGraw-Hill, 1986.

Brown, Jean Morrison, ed. *The Vision of Modern Dance.* 2d ed. Princeton, N.J.: Princeton Book Company, 1998.

Buckle, Richard, with John Taras. *George Balanchine, Ballet Master.* New York: Random House, 1988.

Clark, VèVè A., and Margaret B. Wilkerson. *Kaiso! Katherine Dunham, an Anthology of Writings.* Berkeley: Institute for Study of Social Change, CCEW Women's Center, University of California, 1978.

Cohen, Selma Jeanne, ed. *The Modern Dance: Seven Statements of Belief.* Middletown, Conn.: Wesleyan University Press, 1965.

Daly, Ann. *Done into Dance: Isadora Duncan in America.* Bloomington: Indiana University Press, 1993.

de Mille, Agnes. *America Dances.* New York: Macmillan Publishing Company, 1980.

———. *Martha: The Life and Works of Martha Graham.* New York: Random House, 1991.

Dodge, Roger Pryor. *Hot Jazz and Jazz Dance: Roger Pryor Dodge Collected Writings, 1929–1964.* Selected and edited by Pryor Dodge. New York: Oxford University Press, 1995.

Duncan, Dorre, Carol Pratl, and Cynthia Splatt. *Life into Art: Isadora Duncan and Her World*. Foreword by Agnes de Mille; text by Cynthia Splatt. New York: W. W. Norton & Company, 1993.

Duncan, Irma. *Duncan Dancer*. Middletown, Conn.: Wesleyan University Press, 1966.

Duncan, Isadora. *The Art of the Dance*. Ed. Sheldon Cheney. Rev. ed. 1928; New York: Theatre Arts Books, 1977.

———. *My Life*. Garden City: Garden City Publishing Company, 1927.

Dunham, Katherine. *Island Possessed*. Chicago: University of Chicago Press, 1994.

———. *A Touch of Innocence*. 1959; reprint, New York: Books for Libraries, 1980.

Dunning, Jennifer. *But First a School: The First Fifty Years of the School of American Ballet*. New York: Viking Press, 1985.

Emory, Lynne Fauley. Foreword by Katherine Dunham. *Black Dance from 1619 to Today*. 2d rev. ed. with addition by Brenda Dixon-Stowell. Princeton, N.J.: Dance Horizons Book, 1988.

Frank, Rusty E. *Tap!* Foreword by Gregory Hines. Rev. ed. New York: Da Capo Press, 1994.

Garis, Robert. *Following Balanchine*. New Haven, Conn.: Yale University Press, 1995.

Genthe, Arnold. *Isadora Duncan: 24 Studies*. New York: M. Kennerly, 1929.

Giordano, Gus. *Anthology of American Jazz Dance*. Evanston, Ill.: Orion, 1975.

Graham, Martha. *Blood Memories*. New York: Doubleday, 1991.

———. *The Notebooks of Martha Graham*. Introduction by Nancy Ross. New York: Harcourt Brace Jovanovich, 1973.

Halprin, Anna. *Moving Towards Life: Five Decades of Transformational Dance*. Edited by Rachel Kaplan. Hanover, N.H.: Wesleyan University Press, 1995.

Haskell, Barbara. *Blam! The Explosion of Pop, Minimalism, and Performance 1958–1964*. New York: Whitney Museum of American Art with W. W. Norton & Company, 1984.

Hawkins, Erick. *The Body Is a Clear Place and Other Statements on Dance*. Princeton: Dance Horizons, 1992.

Humphrey, Doris. *Doris Humphrey: An Artist First*. Ed. Selma Jeanne Cohen. Middletown, Conn.: Wesleyan University Press, 1972.

———. *The Art of Making Dances*. Edited by Barbara Pollack. New York: Rinehart & Company, 1959.

Jamison, Judith, with Howard Kaplan. *Dancing Spirit: An Autobiography*. New York: Doubleday, 1993.

Jones, Bill T., with Peggy Gillespie. *Last Night on Earth*. New York: Pantheon Books, 1995.

Jowitt, Deborah. *Time and the Dancing Image*. Berkeley: University of California Press, 1989.

Kendall, Elizabeth. *Dancing: A Ford Foundation Report.* New York: Ford Foundation, 1983.

———. *Where She Danced.* New York: Alfred A. Knopf, 1979.

King, Eleanor. *Transformations: The Humphrey-Weidman Era, a Memoir.* Brooklyn: Dance Horizons, 1978.

Kiralfy, Bolossy. *Bolossy Kiralfy, Creator of Great Musical Spectacles: An Autobiography.* Edited by Barbara Barker. Ann Arbor, Mich.: UMI Research Press, 1988.

Kirstein, Lincoln. *The New York City Ballet.* New York: Alfred A. Knopf, 1973.

———. *Three Pamphlets Collected: Blast at Ballet, 1937; Ballet Alphabet, 1939; What Ballet Is All About, 1959.* Brooklyn: Dance Horizons, 1967.

Klosty, James, ed. *Merce Cunningham.* New York: Saturday Review Press, 1975.

Kriegsman, Sali Ann. *Modern Dance in America: The Bennington Years.* Boston: G. K. Hall and Company, 1981.

Long, Richard A. *The Black Tradition in American Dance.* New York: Rizzoli International Publications, 1989.

Magriel, Paul, ed. *Chronicles of American Dance.* New York: Henry Holt and Company, 1948.

Martin, John. *The Modern Dance.* New York: A. S. Barnes and Company, 1933.

McDonagh, Don. *George Balanchine.* Boston: Twayne Publishers, 1983.

Morgan, Barbara. *Martha Graham: Sixteen Dances in Photographs.* 1st rev. ed. Dobbs Ferry, N.Y.: Morgan & Morgan, 1980.

Murphy, Jacqueline. "Unrest and Uncle Tom: Bill T. Jones/Arnie Zane Dance Company's Last Supper at Uncle Tom's Cabin/Promised Land." In *Bodies of the Text: Dance as Theory, Literature as Dance,* ed. Ellen Goellner and Jacqueline Murphy. New Brunswick, N.J.: Rutgers University Press, 1995.

Oxenham, Andrew. *Dance Today in Canada.* Toronto: n.p., 1977.

Rainer, Yvonne. *Work, 1961–73.* Halifax: Press of the Nova Scotia College of Art and Design, 1974.

Rose, Phyllis. *Jazz Cleopatra: Josephine Baker in Her Own Time.* New York: Doubleday, 1989.

Ruyter, Nancy Lee Chalfa. *Reformers and Visionaries: The Americanization of the Art of Dance.* Brooklyn: Dance Horizons, 1979.

Shawn, Ted. *Every Little Movement.* Reprint. Brooklyn: Dance Horizons, 1968.

Shawn, Ted, with Gray Poole. *One Thousand and One Night Stands.* Garden City: Doubleday & Company, 1960.

Shelton, Suzanne. *Divine Dancer: A Biography of Ruth St. Denis.* Garden City: Doubleday & Company, 1981.

Sherman, Jane. *The Drama of Denishawn Dance.* Middletown, Conn.: Wesleyan University Press, 1979.

Siegel, Marcia. *Days on Earth: The Dance of Doris Humphrey.* New Haven, Conn.: Yale University Press, 1987.

Sontag, Susan. *Cage—Cunningham—Johns: Dancers on a Plane: In Memory of Their Feelings.* New York: Alfred A. Knopf, 1990.

Sorell, Walter. *Hanya Holm: The Biography of an Artist.* Middletown, Conn.: Wesleyan University Press, 1969.

Steegmuller, Francis, ed. *Your Isadora: The Love Story of Isadora Duncan and Gordon Craig.* New York: Random House and the New York Public Library, 1974.

Stewart, Virginia, comp. *Modern Dance.* New York: A. E. Weyhe, 1935.

Stodelle, Ernestine. *Deep Song: The Dance Story of Martha Graham.* New York: Schirmer, 1984.

Tamiris, Helen. "Tamiris in Her Own Voice: Draft of an Autobiography," ed. Daniel Nagrin, and "Tamiris: A Chronicle of Her Dance Career 1927–1955," ed. Christena L. Schlundt. *Studies in Dance History* 1, no. 1 (1989).

Taylor, Paul. *Private Domain.* New York: Alfred A. Knopf, 1987.

Thorpe, Edward. *Black Dance.* Woodstock, N.Y.: Overlook Press, 1990.

Zimmer, Elizabeth, and Susan Quasha, eds. *BODY against BODY: The Dance and Other Collaborations of Bill T. Jones and Arnie Zane.* New York: Station Hill Press, 1989.

Many sources distribute movies on the subject of American theatrical dance, so consulting the Dance Films Association's *Dance Film and Video Guide* for other suggestions, as well as places to rent or purchase films and videos, is recommended (see Selected General Readings and References on Theatrical Dance). Videos and films may be obtained from a variety of sources, such as local distributors, universities and state or public libraries. Some of the best films on dance were produced by PBS for the Dance in America series; a number of these are in the process of being rereleased in video format.

Ailey Dances. 90 minutes, color. Kultur, 1982. Judith Jamison introduces the works of Alvin Ailey, including the masterpiece *Revelations.* Also performed by the Alvin Ailey American Dance Theatre are *Cry, Night Creatures,* and *The Lark Ascending.* (Also see bibliography for part 2).

Anna Sokolow. 20 minutes, color. Dance Horizons. Film clips and interview with the modern dance choreographer who worked with Martha Graham and then established her own company.

Anthony Tudor. 60 minutes, color. Dance Horizons Video. Unlike his contemporary Balanchine, this ballet choreographer preferred dramatic pieces to abstract. Contains interviews of dancers and choreographers from American Ballet Theater with whom he worked; also includes selections from *Undertow, Jardin aux Lilas, Dark Elegies,* and *Pillar of Fire.*

The Balanchine Celebration, part 1. 86 minutes, color. PBS, 1993. Selections from *Apol-*

lo, Vienna Waltzes, Union Jack, Theme and Variations, Scherzo à la Russe, Square Dance, and *Walpurgisnacht Ballet.* Part 2. 86 minutes, color. *Agon, Western Symphony, Stars and Stripes, Who Cares?* A selection of excerpts from some of his earliest works as well as some of his ballets from the '60s on.

Balanchine: Prodigal Son/Chaconne. 57 minutes, color. PBS. Baryshnikov stars in one of Balanchine's earliest and most dramatic works, while Susanne Farrell and Peter Martins dance together in *Chaconne.*

Balanchine: Four Temperaments/Andante from Divertimento no. 15/ Tzigane. 54 minutes, color. PBS. Excerpts danced by New York City Ballet, including the haunting *Four Temperaments* by Hindemith.

Balanchine: Selections. 56 minutes, color. PBS. Selections from *Jewels* (*Diamonds* and *Emeralds*), plus *Stravinsky Violin Concerto,* two of his most famous ballets produced for the New York City Ballet.

Bill T. Jones: Dancing to the Promised Land. 60 minutes, color. PBS. Discussion of his own works and partnership with Arnie Zane, rehearsal shots and performance by the leading modern dance artist Bill T. Jones. Some nudity.

Cage/Cunningham. 95 minutes, color. Interviews with these critical avant-garde artists, known for their collaboration. Excerpts from *Summerspace, Rainforest, Walkaroundtime.*

Charles Weidman: On His Own. 60 minutes, color. Dance Horizons Video. One of the great modern dance pioneers performing and talking about his own work. Historical performance footage with Doris Humphrey and contemporary performances of *Lynchtown* with excerpts of *Flickers, On My Mother's Side,* among others.

Dance Black America. 87 minutes, color. Dance Horizons Video. An exuberant dance festival captured on film; features Mama Lu Park's Jazz Dancers, Alvin Ailey American Dance Theatre, Garth Fagan's Bucket Dance Theatre, plus historical footage of cakewalk, etc. Performance of Katherine Dunham's *Shango.*

Dance Theatre of Harlem. 120 minutes, color. Features the Harlem-based ballet troupe in de Mille's *Fall River Legend,* North's satire *Troy Game,* Horton's *The Beloved,* and Mitchell's *John Henry.*

Dance Works of Doris Humphrey: With My Red Fires and New Dance. 60 minutes, color. Dance Horizons Video. Two of Humphrey's most ambitious group works, the first dealing with the conflict between romantic and possessive love, the other envisioning a democratic society that works together with a harmonious vision.

Dancing. Set of 8 1–hour videos, PBS. Divided into topics: Dance at Court, Dance Centerstage, Dancing in One World, The Individual and Tradition, Lord of the Dance, New Worlds/New Forms, The Power of Dance, Sex and Social Dance. A lavish and rather unfocused tour of the infinitely varied worlds of dance.

Davidsbündlertänze. 43 minutes, color. Home Vision. New York City Ballet performs one of George Balanchine's later creations, set to the music of Robert Schumann's piano pieces. Four couples perform eighteen impressionist vignettes portraying different kinds of romantic relationships, with some episodes inspired by the turmoil of Clara and Robert Schumann's love life.

Denishawn: The Birth of Modern Dance. 40 minutes, color. Kultur, 1988. Historical footage of St. Denis and Shawn, plus several danced reconstructions of their works and a dramatized dialogue. Jane Sherman has reconstructed Denishawn dances.

Doris Humphrey Technique. 45 minutes, color. Dance Horizons Video. Discussion of Humphrey dance technique with film of Humphrey and her group performing *Air for the G String* as introduced by a member of that company, Ernestine Stodelle. Also performances of *Quasi-Valse, Two Ecstatic Themes,* and *Etude Patètico.*

The Enduring Essence: The Technique and Choreography of Isadora Duncan, Remembered and Reconstructed by Gemze De Lappe. 60 minutes, color. Images. De Lappe discusses her own training in the Duncan technique and demonstrates applications of it in the classroom setting.

Erick Hawkins' America. 58 minutes, color. Dance Horizons Video. A documentary of modern dance choreographer Erick Hawkins with many works based on American characters, including his *Plains Daybreak,* inspired by Native American spiritual themes.

Griot New York. 87 minutes, color. PBS. The innovative Garth Fagan collaborates with Wynton Marsalis to create this jazzy statement from this dancing "griot," who blends African, Caribbean, and American traditions in his dance and is best known for his choreography for the Broadway version of *The Lion King.*

Hanya, Portrait of a Pioneer. 60 minutes, color. Dance Horizons. Traces Hanya Holm's career from Europe to Broadway and beyond. Interviews her and those influenced by her work, such as Nikolais. Prize-winning film at Cannes film festival.

The Hard Nut. 87 minutes, color. PBS. A laugh riot of a *Nutcracker* ballet, complete with gender shifts before your eyes and postmodern sensibility, as choreographed by Mark Morris.

Isadora Duncan Dance. 60 minutes, color. Dance Horizons Video. Demonstration of Duncan dance and performances by the artist-scholar Andre Seidel. Excerpts from *Southern Roses;* waltzes by Strauss, Schubert, and Chopin; dances from the Gluck operas, and the Russian studies *Varshivianka* and *Dubinushka.*

Martha Graham: An American Original in Performance. 93 minutes, black and white. Kultur. A collection of three films made when Graham was still dancing in her own works. Includes *A Dancer's World,* which Graham narrates as her company goes through its paces during a class, and two of her great masterpieces, *Night Journey* and *Appalachian Spring.* Originally released in 1957.

Martha Graham Dance Company. 90 minutes, color. Nonesuch. Graham reminisces about her dance company. Includes *Diversion of Angels, Lamentations, Frontier, Adorations, Cave of the Heart,* and a pale version of *Appalachian Spring* (see above for a superior performance).

Martha Graham: The Dancer Revealed. 60 minutes, color. PBS. Traces the life and ca-
    reer of Martha Graham, whose imprint on twentieth-century dance is incalcula-
    ble. Film clips of Graham in interviews as well as in performance. Excerpts from
    *Heretic, Lamentation, Frontier, Every Soul Is a Circus, American Document, Primi-
    tive Mysteries,* and *Night Journey.*

Martha Graham: Three Contemporary Dances. 85 minutes, color. Dance Horizons Video.
    Graham discusses her works and her company performs two of her famous
    "Greek" pieces, *Errand into the Maze* and *Cave of the Heart,* as well as *Acts of Light.*

Men Who Danced: The Story of Ted Shawn's Male Dancers, 1933–1940. 30 minutes, col-
    or. Dance Horizons Video. Performances of Ted Shawn's choreography designed
    for an all-male company of dancers. Historical footage from the '30s; interviews.
    Includes excerpts from *Labor Symphony* and *Polonaise.*

Stormy Weather. 78 minutes, black and white. Key Video, 1943. The plot is dated, but
    the talent is not—a young and beautiful Katherine Dunham dances with her
    troupe, Bill Robinson and the Nicholas Brothers tap-dance up a storm, and Lena
    Horne sings.

Sylvie Guillem at Work. 53 minutes, color. Home Vision. Despite the ludicrous (and
    highly sexist) narration that purports to describe a working day in the life of a Paris
    Opéra dancer, the film has value as it is the only available footage of William For-
    sythe in rehearsal with *In the Middle, Somewhat Elevated.*

APPENDIX

Chronology of Selected Dance Styles and Genres as Performed in North America

Pre–Cultural Contact	Native American dance
Pre-Missionary	Native Hawaiian dance
Sixteenth Century	Ballet
Seventeenth Century	English country dance
Eighteenth Century	Harlequinades
	Minuet
	Bolero and fandango
	Sailor's Hornpipe
	Ballet en action or dramatic ballet
	Opera-Ballet
	Contradanse
Nineteenth Century	Waltz
	Quadrilles or square dance
	Minstrel shows
	Polka
	Musical theater
	Cachucha
	Cakewalk
	Skirt dance
	Tap
	Ghost Dance
Twentieth Century	Ragtime
	Tango
	Castle walk/foxtrot
	"Greek" or interpretive dance

Jazz
Charleston
Modern dance
Lindy/jitterbug/swing
Rumba/samba
Disco
Performance art
Break dancing/hip hop
Salsa
Post-modern dance

SELECTED GENERAL READINGS AND
REFERENCES ON THEATRICAL DANCE

Adamczyk, Alice J. *Black Dance: An Annotated Bibliography.* New York: Garland Publishing Company, 1986.

Amberg, George. *Ballet in America.* New York: Duell, Sloan & Pearce, 1949.

Anderson, Jack. *Ballet and Modern Dance: A Concise History.* Princeton, N.J.: Princeton Book Company, 1986.

Balanchine, George, and Francis Mason. *Balanchine's Complete Stories of the Great Ballets.* Rev. ed. Garden City: Doubleday & Company, 1977.

Bopp, Mary. *Research in Dance: A Guide to Resources.* New York: G. K. Hall, 1994.

Coe, Robert. *Dance in America.* New York: E. P. Dutton, 1985.

Dance Films Association. *Dance Film and Video Guide.* Compiled by Deirdre Towers. Princeton, N.J.: Dance Horizons/Princeton Book Company, 1991.

Dance Magazine, 1928– . Recent issues available on the Internet.

de Mille, Agnes. *America Dances.* New York: Macmillan Publishing Company, 1980.

Emery, Lynne Fauley. *Black Dance from 1619 to Today.* 2d rev. ed. Foreword by Katherine Dunham, with new chapter by Brenda Dixon-Stowell. Princeton, N.J.: Princeton Book Company, 1988.

Foster, Susan Leigh. *Reading Dancing.* Berkeley: University of California Press, 1986.

———, ed. *Choreographing Movement.* Bloomington: Indiana University Press, 1995.

Getz, Leslie. *Dancers and Choreographers: A Selected Bibliography.* Wakefield, R.I.: Asphodel Press, 1995.

Gottschild, Brenda Dixon. *Digging the Africanist Presence in American Performance: Dance and Other Contexts.* Westport, Conn.: Greenwood Press, 1996.

International Encyclopedia of Dance. Edited by Selma Jeanne Cohen. New York: Oxford University Press, 1998.

Kendall, Elizabeth. *Where She Danced.* New York: Alfred A. Knopf, 1979.

Kirstein, Lincoln. *Movement and Metaphor;* reissued as *Four Centuries of Ballet: Fifty Masterworks.* New York: Dover Publications, 1984.

Koegler, Horst. *The Concise Oxford Dictionary of Ballet.* 2d ed., rev. Oxford: Oxford University Press, 1987.

Krokova, Rosalyn. *The New Borzoi Book of Ballets.* New York: Alfred A. Knopf, 1956.

Lloyd, Margaret. *The Borzoi Book of Modern Dance.* New York: Alfred A. Knopf, 1949.

Long, Richard A. *Black Tradition in American Dance.* New York: Rizzoli International Publications, 1989.

McDonagh, Don. *The Complete Guide to Modern Dance.* Garden City, N.Y.: Doubleday & Company, 1976.

Magriel, Paul, ed. *Chronicles of American Dance.* New York: Henry Holt and Company, 1948.

Martin, John. *Introduction to the Dance.* New York: W. W. Norton, 1939.

Mazo, Joseph. *Prime Movers.* New York: William Morrow and Company, 1977.

Moore, Lillian. *Echoes of American Ballet.* Edited by Ivor Guest. New York: Dance Horizons, 1976.

New York Public Library. *Dictionary-Catalogue of the Dance Collection.* Boston: New York Public Library, Astor, Lennox, and Tilden foundations & G. K. Hall & Company, 1974, and annual supplements thereafter.

Overby, Lynnette Y., and James H. Humphrey. *Dance: Current Selected Research.* New York: AMS Press, 1990.

Prevots, Naima. *Dancing in the Sun: Hollywood Choreographers, 1915–1937.* Ann Arbor, Mich.: UMI Research Press, 1987.

Sorell, Walter. *Dance in Its Time.* Garden City, N.Y.: Anchor Press/Doubleday, 1981.

————. *The Dance through the Ages.* New York: Grosset & Dunlap, 1967.

Stearns, Marshall, and Jean Stearns. *Jazz Dance: The Story of American Vernacular Dance.* 1968; reprint, New York: Da Capo Press, 1994.

Stewart, Virginia. *Modern Dance.* New York: A. E. Weyhe, 1935.

Swift, Mary Grace. *Belles and Beaux on Their Toes: Dancing Stars of Young America.* Washington, D.C.: University Press of America, 1980.

Thorpe, Edward. *Black Dance.* London: Chatto & Windus, 1989.

Washabaugh, William. *The Passion of Music and Dance: Body, Gender and Sexuality.* New York: Oxford University Press, 1998.

Editor's Note: The Internet has changed the nature of research references. It expands daily, and therefore no useful purpose can be served by listing addresses. At this point the New York Public Library has a page to direct the user to various categories of references with direct ties to the addresses, including sources for videos, books, information on the Oral History Project and AIDS Initiative, etc. Listing services provide on-line access to such periodicals as *Dance Magazine.* The Library of Congress provides on-line nineteenth-century sources on the dance, called the American Heritage Project. The possibilities seem endless.

INDEX

MAUREEN NEEDHAM has been an associate professor of dance history at Vanderbilt University since 1985. She teaches courses in the history of American theatrical dance, African American dance, and ballet, as well as Broadway musical theater. She received her bachelor's degree from Harvard University, where she choreographed an all-male kickline for Hasty Pudding's 111th annual theatricals, and her Ph.D. in dance history from New York University. She is the recipient of an award from the National Endowment for the Humanities to research the origins of the first ballerina in seventeenth-century Paris, as well as grants from Vanderbilt University's provost, the Lifeworks Foundation, and the Tennessee Council for the Humanities. Her publications include *Therapy in Motion* (University of Illinois Press, 1978) and numerous entries for *Grove's New Dictionary of Opera; Encyclopedia of Dance; American National Biography, Dictionary of Ballet, Latin America and the Caribbean: A Critical Guide to Resources,* and other encyclopedias. Her scholarly writings focus on seventeenth- and eighteenth-century French ballet, the origins of American ballet, and the rise of modern dance. She also critiques dance and Broadway productions for the *Nashville Scene* and is currently at work on a book that traces the history of American musical theater.

Composed in 10.5/13 Minion
with Minion display
by Jim Proefrock
at the University of Illinois Press
Designed by Dennis Roberts
Manufactured by Thomson-Shore, Inc.

University of Illinois Press
1325 South Oak Street
Champaign, IL 61820-6903
www.press.uillinois.edu